OUR COUNTRY
And Its REGIONS

Grade 4

Mc
Graw
Hill
Education

PROGRAM AUTHORS

James A. Banks, Ph.D.
Kerry and Linda Killinger
  Professor of Diversity Studies
  and Director, Center for
  Multicultural Education
University of Washington
Seattle, Washington

Kevin P. Colleary, Ed.D.
Curriculum and Teaching
  Department
Graduate School of Education
Fordham University
New York, New York

Linda Greenow, Ph.D.
Associate Professor and Chair
Department of Geography
State University of New York at
  New Paltz
New Paltz, New York

Walter C. Parker, Ph.D.
Professor of Social Studies
  Education, Adjunct Professor
  of Political Science
University of Washington
Seattle, Washington

Emily M. Schell, Ed.D.
Visiting Professor, Teacher
  Education
San Diego State University
San Diego, California

Dinah Zike
Educational Consultant
Dinah-Mite Activities, Inc.
San Antonio, Texas

CONTRIBUTORS

Raymond C. Jones, Ph.D.
Director of Secondary Social
  Studies Education
Wake Forest University
Winston-Salem, North Carolina

Irma M. Olmedo
Associate professor
University of Illinois-Chicago
College of Education
Chicago, Illinois

HISTORIANS/SCHOLARS

Ned Blackhawk
Associate Professor of History
  and American Indian Studies
University of Wisconsin
Madison, Wisconsin

Sheilah F. Clarke-Ekong, Ph.D.
Professor of Anthropology
University of Missouri-St. Louis
St. Louis, Missouri

Larry Dale, Ph.D.
Director, Center for Economic
  Education
Arkansas State University
Jonesboro, Arkansas

mheducation.com/prek-12

Send all inquiries to:
McGraw-Hill Education
8787 Orion Place
Columbus, OH 43240

ISBN: 978-0-07-675963-7
MHID: 0-07-675963-6

Printed in the United States of America.

3 4 5 6 7 QVS 20 19 18 17 16

ii

Our Country and Its Regions

CONTENTS, Volume 1

| **Unit 1** Our National Story | **1** |

The Big Idea What are some events that shaped our nation?

PEOPLE, PLACES, AND EVENTS	2
Why Study History?	4
Chart and Graph Skills: Read a Time Line	6
Lesson 1: The First Americans	8
Lesson 2: Three Worlds Meet	16
Lesson 3: A Nation Is Born	24
Lesson 4: The Nation Grows	32
Lesson 5: War and Changes	40
Lesson 6: A Changing World	48
Lesson 7: A Modern World	56
Review and Assess/Test Preparation	62
The Big Idea Activities	64

(bl) MediaImages/StockTrek Images/Getty Images/Craig Tuttle

Unit 2   The United States: Its Land and People   65

Big Idea   How do people meet their needs?

PEOPLE, PLACES, AND EVENTS   66

Lesson 1: From Sea to Sea   70

   Map and Globe Skills: Use Elevation Maps   77

Lesson 2: Our Country's Regions   78

Lesson 3: Our Country's Climate   84

Lesson 4: Our Economy   92

   Chart and Graph Skills: Read Line Graphs   99

Lesson 5: State and Local Governments   100

   Map and Globe Skills: Latitude and Longitude   106

Lesson 6: Our Nation's Government   108

   Global Connection: The United Nations   112

Lesson 7: Our Democratic Values   114

Review and Assess/Test Preparation   120

The Big Idea Activities   122

Unit 3 The Northeast 123

What causes a region to change?

PEOPLE, PLACES, AND EVENTS	124
Lesson 1: The Geography of the Northeast	128
Map and Globe Skills: Compare Maps at Different Scales	135
Lesson 2: The Economy of the Northeast	136
Lesson 3: The People of the Northeast	144
Global Connection: New York City's Caribbean Festival	149
Review and Assess/Test Preparation	152
The Big Idea Activities	154

(bkgd)M Swiet Productions/Getty Images

Unit 4 The Southeast 155

How do people affect the environment?

PEOPLE, PLACES, AND EVENTS 156

Lesson 1: The Geography of the Southeast 160

   Chart and Graph Skills: Read Circle Graphs 167

Lesson 2: The Economy of the Southeast 168

Lesson 3: The People of the Southeast 176

Review and Assess/Test Preparation 184

The Big Idea Activities 186

Unit 5 The Midwest 187

How do natural resources affect a region's growth?

PEOPLE, PLACES, AND EVENTS 188

Lesson 1: The Geography of the Midwest 192

   Chart and Graph Skills: Compare Bar and Line Graphs 199

Lesson 2: The Economy of the Midwest 200

   Global Connection: Kansas Wheat 205

Lesson 3: The People of the Midwest 208

Review and Assess/Test Preparation 216

The Big Idea Activities 218

Unit 6   The Southwest   219

How do people adapt to their environments?

PEOPLE, PLACES, AND EVENTS   220

Lesson 1: The Geography of the Southwest   224

  Map and Globe Skills: Use Special Purpose Maps   232

Lesson 2: The Economy of the Southwest   234

Lesson 3: The People of the Southwest   240

Review and Assess/Test Preparation   248

The Big Idea Activities   250

Unit 7   The West   251

How does technology change people's lives?

PEOPLE, PLACES, AND EVENTS   252

Lesson 1: The Geography of the West   256

  Map and Globe Skills: Use Road Maps   264

Lesson 2: The Economy of the West   266

  Global Connection: International Trade   272

Lesson 3: The People of the West   274

Review and Assess/Test Preparation   280

The Big Idea Activities   282

(b)Michael Busselle/Digital Vision/SuperStock

Reference Section

Reading Skills   R2   Glossary   REF1
Geography Handbook   GH1   Index   REF9
Atlas   GH12   Credits   REF16

Skills and Features

Reading Skills   New York City's Caribbean Festival 149
Sequence Events   R2   Kansas Wheat   205
Compare and Contrast   R4   International Trade   272
Main Idea and Details   R6   **DataGraphic**
Summarize   R8   United States: Average January
Draw Conclusions   R10   Temperatures   89
Cause and Effect   R12   Jobs in the Southeast   173
Make Generalizations   R14   Population Growth   245
Map and Globe Skills   **Citizenship**
Use Elevation Maps   77   Volunteering   117
Understand Latitude and Longitude 106   Working for the Common Good   150
Compare Maps at Different Scales 135   Being Informed   181
Use Special Purpose Maps   232   Express Your Opinion   213
Use Road Maps   264   Be Informed   230
Chart and Graph Skills   Volunteering   271
Read a Time Line   6   **Primary Sources**
Read Line Graphs   99   Lucy Larcom   139
Read Circle Graphs   167   John T. Edge   179
Compare Line and Bar Graphs   199   Alvin McDonald   196
Global Connections   Cabeza de Vaca   243
The United Nations   112   Isaac Staat   277

Skills and Features

Charts, Graphs, and Diagrams

Amazing Geographic Facts 71

Lake Effect 88

Annual Precipitation, inches: 2005 89

Business Resources 95

Circular Flow 98

Duties of Government 101

Three Jobs, Three Branches 102

How a Bill Becomes Law 103

Executive Branch 110

Legislative Branch, Judicial Branch 111

United States Cultural Groups, 2005 118

Population of Tennessee, 1960-2000 120

Plants and Animals of the Northeast 129

Hydro Electric Power Plant 133

Lowell Mills 138

Service Workers in the Northeast 140

Plants and Animals of the Southeast 161

Islands in the Southeast 163

Air Movement in Sea and
    Land Breezes 164

Leading U.S. States in the
    Production of Grapefruit 167

Strip Mining 171

Employment in the Southeast 173

Service Jobs in the Southeast 173

Plants and Animals of the Midwest 193

Open-pit Mine 202

How an Elevator Works 203

Assembly Line 206

Population of the
    Great Lakes States, 2005 216

Plants and Animals of the Southwest 225

Population Growth in the Southwest 245

Plants and Animals of the West 257

Section of North American Plate 260

Maps

Union and Confederacy 42

Landforms of the United States 73

United States: Elevation 77

Regions of the United States 81

Elevation Map: Mount Hood 85

United States: Average
    January Temperatures 89

Lines of Latitude 106

Lines of Longitude 106

Global Grid 107

Illinois: Latitude and Longitude 107

The Northeast 126

Maine 135

Acadia National Park, Maine 135

Products of the Northeast 137

Northeast Population 142

The Southeast 158

Farm Products in the Southeast 169

The Midwest 190

Flowing Rivers 194

Resources of the Midwest 201

Celebrations of the Midwest 212

The Southwest 222

Population Density of
    Arizona and New Mexico 233

Population Distribution
    of Arizona and New Mexico 233

Products of the Southwest 235

Phoenix, Arizona 245

The West 254

Montana Highways 265

Products of the West 268

Utah Road Map 280

The United States: Physical GH6

Northern Ohio GH9

The Hemispheres GH10

The World GH11

United States Political GH12

United States Physical GH14

World Political GH16

North America:
    Political/Physical GH18

x Aaron Roeth Photography

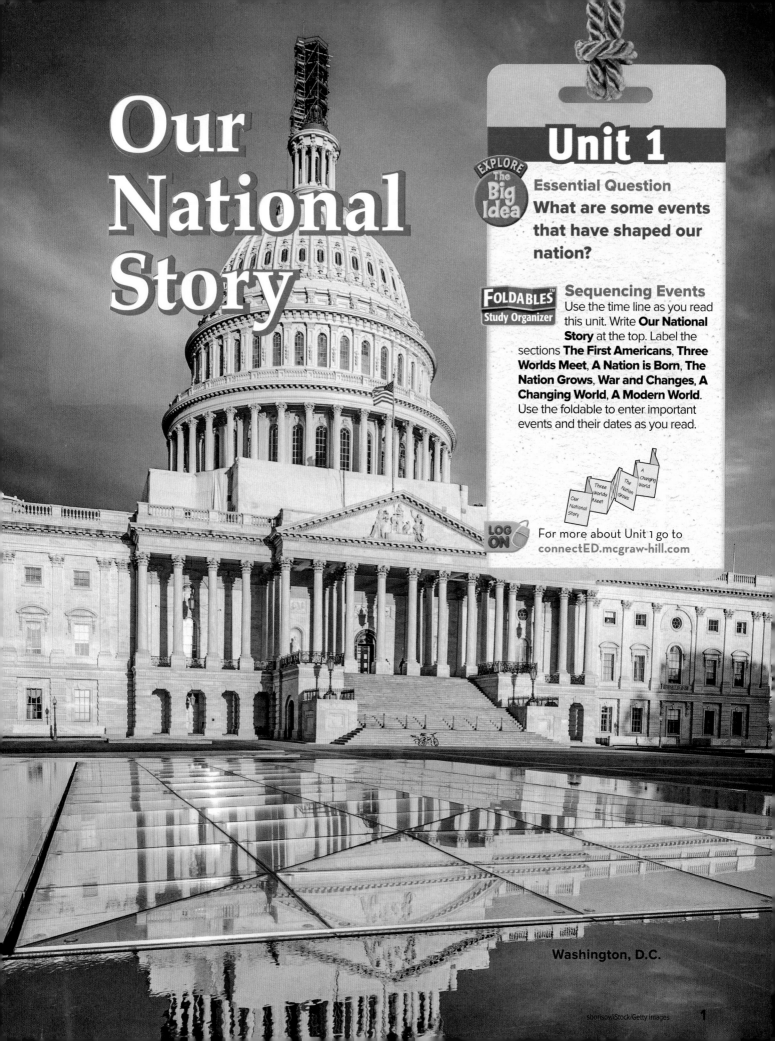

Our National Story

Unit 1

EXPLORE The Big Idea

Essential Question
What are some events that have shaped our nation?

FOLDABLES™ Study Organizer

Sequencing Events
Use the time line as you read this unit. Write **Our National Story** at the top. Label the sections **The First Americans**, **Three Worlds Meet**, **A Nation is Born**, **The Nation Grows**, **War and Changes**, **A Changing World**, **A Modern World**. Use the foldable to enter important events and their dates as you read.

LOG ON
For more about Unit 1 go to connectED.mcgraw-hill.com

Washington, D.C.

1

PEOPLE, PLACES, and EVENTS

The Founders

Independence Hall

The Founders gathered at **Independence Hall** on May 25, 1787, to create the government of the United States.

Today you can visit Independence Hall in Philadelphia, Pennsylvania.

Dr. Martin Luther King, Jr.

March on Washington

On August 28, 1963, more than 250,000 people listened to **Dr. Martin Luther King, Jr.,** give a speech about civil rights during the **March on Washington**.

Today you can learn more about Dr. Martin Luther King, Jr., at The King Center in Atlanta, Georgia.

(tl)Architect of the Capitol, (tr)Photographs in the Carol M. Highsmith Archive, Library of Congress, Prints and Photographs Division [LC-DIG-highsm-12311], (bl)NPS Photo, (br)Library of Congress Prints and Photographs Division [LC-DIG-ppmsca-03128]

Gettysburg

Drummer Boy

The Civil War is the only war to have been fought between Americans in America. Over 3 million people battled in the 4-year-long war. Young boys joined the war as **drummer boys**.

Today you can visit the Civil War battlefield at **Gettysburg, Pennsylvania**.

US Space and Rocket Center

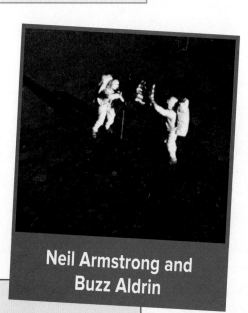

Neil Armstrong and Buzz Aldrin

On July 16, 1969, the United States sent its first manned spacecraft to the moon. **Neil Armstrong and Buzz Aldrin** became the first Americans on the moon.

Today you can learn more about the space program at the **US Space and Rocket Center** in Huntsville, Alabama.

Why Study History?

Why do you watch movies or read novels? Could it be because they're fun and you like a good story? Reading about history is nearly the same thing. The one big difference is that history really happened.

Learning about the past is not only fun, it also helps you understand the world you live in today. For example, do you know why we celebrate Thanksgiving every year? No? Well, keep reading to find out. The more history you know, the better you'll understand how the world around you was put together. That can make every day a little more interesting.

Family photographs are part of history.

(bkgd)Harrell Fletcher

Sources of the Past

You can learn about and create history in different ways. When you write something in a diary, take a photograph, or draw a picture, you're making history. This is also how we learn about the past. Have you ever found an old coin or looked at an old photograph? Why are these things so interesting? Because they are clues to the past.

Just as you are making history by leaving clues for people many years from now, you can learn about the past from people who have left clues for you. To learn about their experiences, you can read their words in diaries, letters, old newspapers, and look at their photographs.

Old photographs are part of history.

History All Around Us

One of the most amazing things is that history is something that all Americans share. Whether your family came to this country yesterday or long ago; whether they are African American, white, Native American, Hispanic, or Asian, the history of the United States is their history, too.

New photographs are part of history.

Americans of all backgrounds share a history.

Chart and Graph Skills

Read a Time Line

To understand history, it is important to know when events happened. Sometimes it is not easy to remember what happened first, next, and last. A time line can help sequence events. A time line is a diagram that shows the order of events in history. It also shows the amount of time that passed between events. This helps to give a sense of order to history.

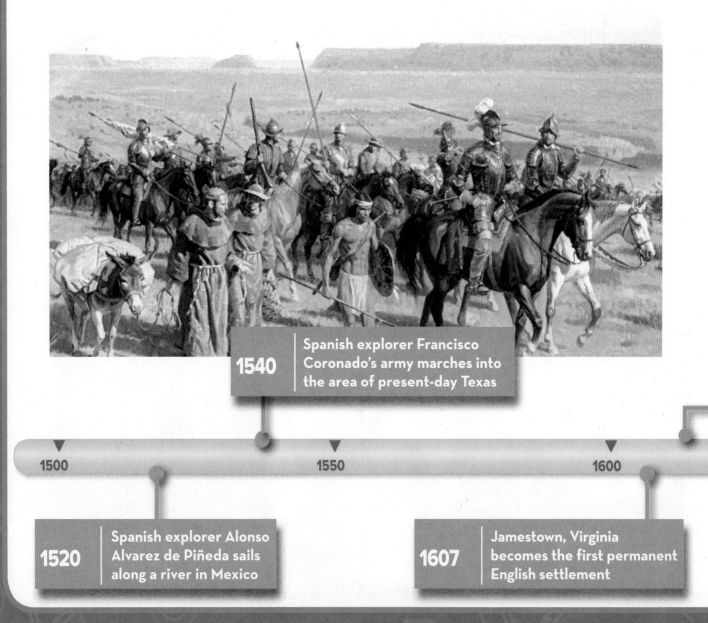

1540 Spanish explorer Francisco Coronado's army marches into the area of present-day Texas

1500   1550   1600

1520 Spanish explorer Alonso Alvarez de Piñeda sails along a river in Mexico

1607 Jamestown, Virginia becomes the first permanent English settlement

Tom Lovell

Learn It

- Time lines are divided into parts. Each part represents a certain number of years. The time line on this page is divided into parts 50 years long. It tells of the first explorers, settlements, and colonies over a period of 200 years.

- Read the captions from left to right. You can see that the earliest event happened to the left and the latest event happened on the right. On this time line, the first explorer came to Mexico in 1520. When was the last settlement in this time period founded?

Try It

Look at the time line to answer the questions.

- Did French explorers or Spanish explorers reach the Southwest first?

- Did Coronado's army march into Texas before or after de La Salle built a colony on the Texas coast?

Apply It

Use the time line on this page to answer the question below.

- Find important dates of your life by talking with family members.

- Find an important event for each year. Try to draw a picture or place a photograph for each event. Make a time line of your life.

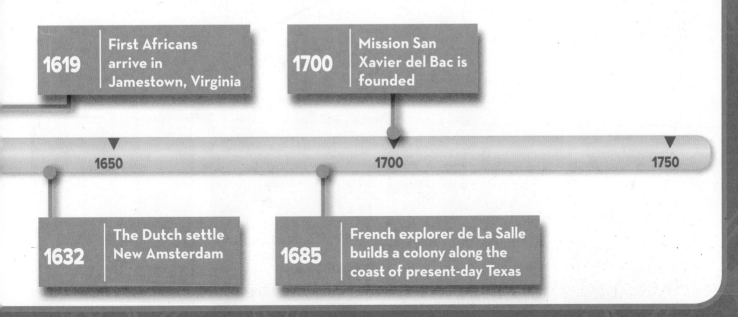

| 1619 | First Africans arrive in Jamestown, Virginia |
| 1700 | Mission San Xavier del Bac is founded |

1650   1700   1750

| 1632 | The Dutch settle New Amsterdam |
| 1685 | French explorer de La Salle builds a colony along the coast of present-day Texas |

The First Americans

VOCABULARY

prehistory

artifact

resource

hunter-gatherer

technology

READING SKILL

Sequence Events

Copy the chart. As you read, fill it in with events from the lesson.

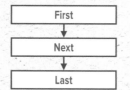

First

↓

Next

↓

Last

STANDARDS FOCUS

SOCIAL STUDIES — People, Places, and Environments

GEOGRAPHY — The Uses of Geography

Cahokia was one of the first cities in North America.

Visual Preview

How did the first Americans use resources to survive?

A Early Americans built a city called Cahokia.

B The Eastern Woodlands people formed a union.

C The Pueblo and Lakota lived in the Southwest.

D Native Americans adapted to their environment.

Ⓐ EARLY AMERICANS

How did the first Americans get here? They probably walked for thousands of miles from Asia. Others may have come in small boats from Europe. They came long ago during the last Ice Age, a time called **prehistory**, *before written history.*

To find out about our prehistory scientists called archaeologists use artifacts. Almost anything that people used long ago can be an artifact—tools, weapons, clothes, even jewelry. These earliest Americans used stone tools and weapons, hunted wild animals, and picked wild plants for food.

Cahokia

About the year 700, a group known as the Mississippians built a city near the Mississippi River, across from where St. Louis, Missouri, is now. The city, Cahokia, was one of the very first cities in North America. About 20,000 people lived there. How could so many people have enough to eat?

Unlike the earlier people who hunted and gathered their food, the Mississippians were farmers. They had learned to grow corn, and were able to grow enough to feed a large population. Since they were located at the center of trade routes that crisscrossed most of North America, they also became traders. Cahokia became a center for arts and crafts. Sometime around 1300, Cahokia was abandoned.

PEOPLE

MOUND BUILDERS

For about 3,000 years, the Adena, Hopewell, and Mississippian cultures lived in the Ohio and Mississippi River valleys. We call them mound builders because they built huge mounds of earth in their towns and cities. Some mounds were used as burial sites, while others had temples and homes built on top.

QUICK CHECK

Sequence **When was Cahokia built?**

EASTERN WOODLANDS

PEOPLE

HIAWATHA

Hiawatha is known today for being one of the founders of the Iroquois League. He was a great peacemaker who was respected by each of the League peoples. His powerful speeches helped convince the Iroquois to band together.

Many years ago, the eastern half of North America was covered with forests. These forests were a good material, or **resource,** for the Native Americans that lived there.

Hunting and Farming

The people of the Eastern Woodlands got their food from the forest. They hunted deer and other animals. They also

An Iroquois Longhouse

smoke hole

storage platform

elm tree bark

cooking

sleeping platform

preparing animal skins

gathered fruits, nuts, and grains. People who get most of their food by hunting wild animals and gathering wild plants are known as **hunter-gatherers**.

Some people of the Eastern Woodlands, such as the Lenape, also grew their own food. Their most important crops were maize, beans, and squash.

A United People

Over time, some Native American groups decided to join forces with other groups. One of these united groups was the Iroquois.

The Iroquois people formed a union with five different Native American groups that set up a government called the Iroquois League. Each member had a say in how the government was run. Later, a sixth group joined.

The Iroquois League was very successful. It was so successful that some believe it influenced the founders of our own government.

QUICK CHECK

Summarize **What was the Iroquois League?**

gathering berries

collecting firewood

Diagram Skill

What jobs do you see people doing?

11

The Great Plains are a grassy, flat area in the middle of the United States. Near the Great Plains is a dry landscape known as the Southwest region. Native Americans in this region used the resources available to them.

The Lakota and Comanche

The Lakota lived in the northern part of the Great Plains. They were always moving, because the Lakota followed the buffalo. They used the buffalo for everything, including food, clothing, shelter, and tools.

The Comanche lived further south. It was warmer than the north, so grains and nuts were easier to find. Like the Lakota, the Comanche depended on the buffalo, but the Comanche also traded clothing and tools for fresh food with nearby farming peoples.

People of the Southwest

Long ago, a people known as the Ancestral Pueblo moved to the Southwest. They built towns high up in shallow caves along cliff walls. They left these communities around 1300. Their descendents, the Pueblo people, built similar towns, and still live in the area today.

The Ancestral Pueblo built this community in the side of a cliff. It had 150 rooms and 23 kivas. A kiva is a common area used for ceremonies.

EVENT

TRAVELING WITH TEEPEES

The Plains people moved around a lot following the buffalo. They needed a home they could put up and take down easily. Teepees could do that. Teepees were made of wooden poles with buffalo hides stretched over them. Some had painted patterns on them that described hunts and battles or that told of the family's origins.

The Spanish, the first Europeans to meet them, called these Native Americans Pueblo. Pueblo is the Spanish word for town or village.

The Pueblo and other Native Americans in the Southwest learned to farm in a hot, dry land. Their technology, or skills and tools, allowed them to grow corn and squash in the sandy soil. Others, such as the Apache, moved across the region, following buffalo and other large animals.

QUICK CHECK

Summarize Why did the Lakota live in teepees?

Hidden under animal skins, hunters could creep close to a buffalo.

13

D THE WEST

PLACES

OZETTE

Ozette is an ancient Makah village in Washington state. It was buried by a mudslide around the year 1500. Since 1970, archaeologists have dug up more than 55,000 artifacts, including toys, baskets, hats, and tools from the site. Today, fishing hats are very similar to the fishing hats worn by Makah hundreds of years ago.

The western United States is a very large region. Today, eleven states are in the western region. Many different Native American groups lived in the West.

Native Americans of the West, like all people, learned to adapt to their surroundings. Each group's economy was influenced by the environment. This was true whether they lived in the mountains, along the coast, or in the desert.

The Northwest coast, from Oregon to Alaska, was a place rich in resources. People such as the Makah didn't have to farm. There were plenty of berries, roots, and other wild plants to gather. Sometimes they hunted beaver, bear, deer, and elk in the forest, but most of their food came from the sea. They fished and gathered seaweeds and shellfish.

Ozette was a busy Makah village in the 1400s.

Milliram Publishing

A Region of Plenty

Like the Makah, the Tlingit went to the sea for food. They developed technology to build dams and traps for catching salmon. They also made large canoes that could travel long distances. They traded their surplus resources with neighboring people. This made the Tlingit wealthy.

Native Americans who lived in the mountains hunted and gathered food from the forests. Some, such as the Nez Perce, also fished in the mountain streams.

The West has a vast, dry region known as the Great Basin. People such as the Shoshone had to use the resources of the Great Basin carefully. These hunter-gatherers had to keep moving to find food.

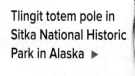

Tlingit totem pole in Sitka National Historic Park in Alaska ▶

QUICK CHECK

Make Inferences How do the Makah use resources today?

Check Understanding

1. **VOCABULARY** Summarize this lesson using these vocabulary words.

   resource   technology

2. **READING SKILL** Sequence Events Use the chart to tell about Cahokia.

First
↓
Next
↓
Last

3. **Write About It** Why is it important to learn about the history of Native Americans?

VOCABULARY

mission

Northwest Passage

colony

READING SKILL

Sequence Events

Copy the chart. As you read, fill it in with events from the lesson.

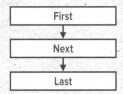

First

↓

Next

↓

Last

STANDARDS FOCUS

SOCIAL STUDIES — Global Connections

GEOGRAPHY — Places and Regions

Three Worlds Meet

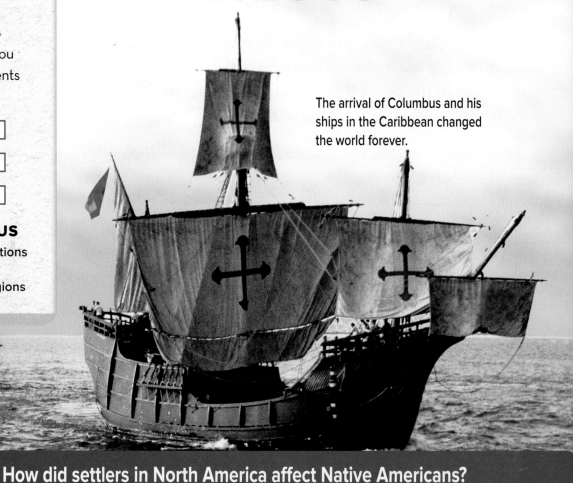

The arrival of Columbus and his ships in the Caribbean changed the world forever.

Visual Preview

How did settlers in North America affect Native Americans?

A Columbus met Native Americans on a Caribbean Island.

B Spanish and French explorers settle in North America.

C English and Dutch settlers make colonies.

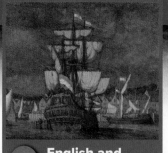

D The French and British fight over Native American lands.

A THE FIRST EUROPEANS

In the middle 1400s, many Europeans read a book that told of jewels, delicious spices, and other wonders of China. Europeans wanted to get some of these amazing things.

At the time, the journey from Europe to Asia took a long time. A man named Christopher Columbus wanted to try a faster route. In 1492 he set out with three ships for Asia. Instead of sailing east, he sailed west. When he finally landed, he wasn't in Asia. He was on an island in the Caribbean Sea.

This was the beginning of an exchange that would forever change the lives of Europeans, Native Americans, and Africans. The Spanish introduced horses and oranges to Native Americans, while Europeans learned about chocolate, tomatoes, and popcorn.

The meeting wasn't always good. In time, Europeans took over the land. Native Americans had no immunity against European diseases, and huge numbers of Native Americans died. Many Africans were brought to the Americas against their wills.

EVENT

THE COLUMBIAN EXCHANGE

Suppose you had never eaten chocolate, potatoes, or corn! American foods were unknown in Europe until returning sailors brought them back. These foods eventually became a part of the European diet.

Native Americans await the arrival of European ships.

QUICK CHECK

Summarize **How did the encounter between Europeans, Native Americans, and Africans change their lives forever?**

THE SPANISH AND FRENCH IN NORTH AMERICA

PLACES

SANTA FE

One of the earliest Spanish settlements was Santa Fe, now the capital of New Mexico. San Miguel Chapel in Santa Fe, built around 1610, is one of the oldest churches in the United States.

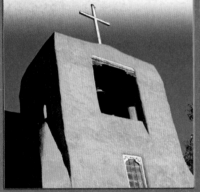

The first Europeans to explore North America were from Spain. A few were accompanied by African explorers. They thought they would find gold and other riches. Explorers such as Francisco Coronado traveled throughout the Southwest.

Priests also came to North America to talk about Christianity and settle the area. They set up **missions**, or settlements, throughout the West and Southwest. By the late 1600s, Spain controlled Mexico, much of South America, and most of what is now the southwestern United States and Florida.

Coronado traveled throughout the Southwest with a large expedition between 1540 and 1542.

French Traders

The French also explored North America. They hoped to find a route that would lead from the Great Lakes to Asia. They called it the **Northwest Passage**. As it turned out, no such route existed, but the French explorers claimed these lands for France.

The French explorers were looking for gold and fur. At that time, hats and coats made of beaver fur were very fashionable in France. French trappers came and offered Native Americans weapons and metal tools in exchange for the plentiful beaver furs.

Soon, France claimed a huge piece of North America for itself and made it a **colony**—a land ruled by another country. They called it New France. Like the Spanish, the French also sent priests to teach Native Americans about Christianity.

PEOPLE

RENÉ-ROBERT CAVELIER, SIEUR DE LA SALLE

Robert de la Salle explored the Great Lakes region and the Mississippi River. In 1682 he traveled from present-day St. Louis to the Mississippi's mouth at the Gulf of Mexico. He named the area Louisiana in honor of the French king, Louis the Fourteenth.

QUICK CHECK

Summarize **Why did the French explore North America?**

C THE DUTCH AND ENGLISH IN NORTH AMERICA

The French and the Spanish weren't the only nations in Europe that wanted settlements in North America. The English and the Dutch also wanted colonies in North America. They wanted to find riches for their countries.

The English Colonies

In 1607, after a few failed attempts at settling in North America, a new group of English settlers set up a colony in what is now Virginia. They called the settlement Jamestown in honor of King James of England. The first Africans arrived in Jamestown in 1619. It became the first permanent English colony in North America and helped set a pattern for later colonists to follow.

New Amsterdam as it was in 1640

EVENT

THANKSGIVING

In 1620 people called Pilgrims left England in search of religious freedom. They landed in what is now part of New England and named their colony Plymouth. The Pilgrims survived with help from Native Americans. Pilgrims and Native Americans celebrated their friendship by having a great feast in the autumn of 1621. This feast has been called our country's first Thanksgiving.

New Netherland

The Dutch, like the French, came to North America to make money, particularly in the fur trade. They came from the Netherlands. In 1624 they settled along the Hudson River and named their colony New Netherland.

Two years later, the Dutch governor, Peter Minuit, bought Manhattan Island from Native Americans living there and called it New Amsterdam.

The English colonies began to spread out, and in 1664 they took control of New Amsterdam from the Dutch. New Amsterdam soon changed its name to New York. The English also began colonizing other lands near the Atlantic coast. By 1732 England had thirteen colonies stretching from New Hampshire to Georgia.

QUICK CHECK

Sequence Events **What happened in New Netherland after the Dutch settled there?**

Land was what everyone wanted in the 1700s. The English, French, Dutch, and the Spanish kept coming to North America. This was hard for the Native Americans who had been living there because all these new colonists wanted more land.

The French and Indian War

The French and the English, who had been enemies in Europe, started fighting in North America, too. When the English colonies began filling up, English settlers started to head west into the Great Lakes region and the Ohio River valley. These lands had already been claimed by France. Before long, the English and the French were at war over the question of who owned the land.

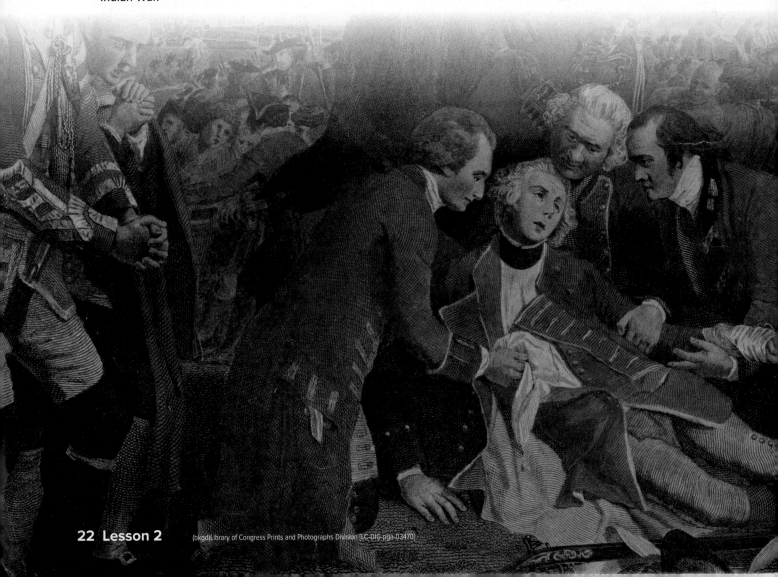

The siege of Quebec during the French and Indian War.

(bkgd)Library of Congress Prints and Photographs Division [LC-DIG-pga-03470]

Many Native Americans in the region fought alongside the French in this war. They hoped that the French could help them drive the English out of North America altogether. For this reason, the war was called the French and Indian War.

British Victory

Even though the French had help from Native Americans, the English won the war in 1763. The English seized the Ohio River valley. Great Britain now claimed almost all of the present-day United States east of the Mississippi River. To the surprise of the Native Americans, they chose to keep English settlers out of the Ohio River valley and leave the land to the Native Americans.

QUICK CHECK

Summarize What sparked the French and Indian War?

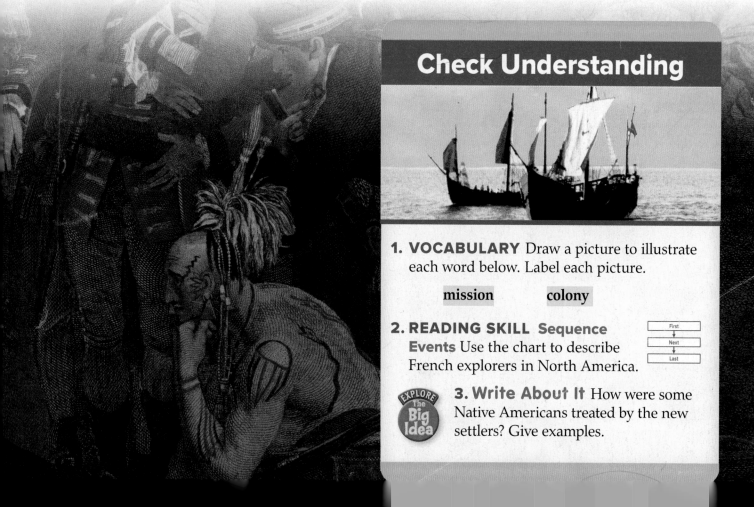

Check Understanding

1. **VOCABULARY** Draw a picture to illustrate each word below. Label each picture.

   mission   colony

2. **READING SKILL** Sequence Events Use the chart to describe French explorers in North America.

   First
   ↓
   Next
   ↓
   Last

3. **Write About It** How were some Native Americans treated by the new settlers? Give examples.

EXPLORE The Big Idea

Lesson 3

VOCABULARY

tax

revolution

Declaration of Independence

independent

READING SKILL

Sequence Events

Copy the chart. Fill it in with events from the lesson.

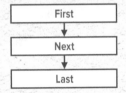

First
↓
Next
↓
Last

STANDARDS FOCUS

SOCIAL STUDIES   Civic Ideals and Practices

GEOGRAPHY   Human Systems

A Nation Is Born

Boston Tea Party, December 16, 1773

Visual Preview

Why was independence important to the colonists?

A   Great Britain taxed colonists. The colonists protested.

B   The colonists prepared for war and independence.

C   Great Britain and Patriot soldiers went to war.

D   The colonies became an independent nation.

A TAXES AND PROTESTS

*The French and Indian War was expensive.
Great Britain needed a way to pay for it.
They decided to make the colonists pay
new **taxes**. Taxes are money paid to a
government for its support.*

Many of the colonists were already angry because Great Britain had said they couldn't settle west of the Appalachian Mountains. Settlers wanted those lands. When Great Britain's lawmakers (called Parliament) made them pay taxes, they got even angrier. They said Great Britain was being unfair. The colonists were also upset that they didn't have any representatives in Parliament to vote. The people in Great Britain did. Some colonists thought about having a **revolution** to break from the government, but most colonists didn't want that at the time. All they wanted was the same rights as people in Great Britain.

When the government passed a tax on tea, the colonists were angrier than ever. First, they refused to buy the tea. Then, they decided to show Great Britain exactly what they thought of the tax. One night, a group of men sneaked on board three British ships in Boston Harbor and dumped a load of expensive tea overboard. The event, known as the Boston Tea Party, made the British government furious.

EVENT

THE STAMP ACT

The first tax the British passed was called the Stamp Act. It was a tax on all paper sold in the colonies. Government officials placed a special mark, or stamp, on items once the tax had been paid.

QUICK CHECK

Sequence Events **Which came first, the Stamp Act or the tax on tea?**

INDEPENDENCE HALL

In 1776, representatives from the 13 colonies met in this Philadelphia building to sign the Declaration of Independence. Later they would meet here to approve the United States Constitution. "Independence Hall" is now a museum.

Great Britain wanted to punish the colonists for dumping the tea. It forbade the colonists to hold town meetings and closed the harbor until the colonists paid for the tea they had dumped. Colonists couldn't pay for the tea if the harbor was closed—that's where half of the people in Boston worked. This made the colonists angrier. People began to worry that they might starve. By the spring of 1775, things were very tense in Boston. The colonists finally felt the situation had gone on long enough. They were going to do something about their problem. More people began talking about independence.

The British government sent soldiers to Boston and said that it was to "protect" the colonists, but Britain wanted to show the colonists that it had control.

Battle of Lexington, 1775

The First Shots

In April 1775, British spies learned that colonists were storing weapons in nearby Concord. Soldiers started to march from Boston to Concord to seize the weapons. A colonist named Paul Revere heard about their plan and rode toward Concord to warn the town. "The British are coming!" he called out all along the way.

The next morning, volunteer soldiers were waiting when the British troops reached Lexington. Fighting broke out in Lexington and again at Concord. The American Revolution had begun.

Declaring Freedom

In the summer of 1776, a group of colonists met and chose Thomas Jefferson to write the **Declaration of Independence**. It told the world why the colonies wanted independence. Signing this document took courage. It also meant war.

QUICK CHECK

Main Idea and Details **How did the British respond to the Boston Tea Party?**

PEOPLE

DEBORAH SAMPSON

Deborah Sampson was a Massachusetts woman. She so strongly believed in the Patriot cause that she disguised herself as a man and joined the army. At that time, women were not allowed to fight in wars. She served for nearly a year before she was struck by a fever and her secret was discovered.

Strengths and Weaknesses

At the beginning of the war, all of Europe, and a good many Americans, didn't think the colonists stood a chance against Great Britain. The British navy was the best in the world. Its army had huge supplies of guns and ammunition. Many Patriot soldiers didn't have uniforms. Guns and food were in short supply. The Patriots had some advantages. They were defending their homes and knew the land well.

Since Great Britain was very far away, it was expensive to send supplies and troops across the Atlantic to fight in North America. People in Great Britain began to wonder whether the war was worth the trouble.

Patriot Soldiers

Native Americans and African Americans

At first, Native Americans refused to take sides. Later, the British convinced some of the Iroquois Confederacy to help them. The Iroquois were angry that the settlers had taken their lands. They believed that if Great Britain won, the colonies would not expand into their homelands. About 5,000 African Americans served as soldiers in the Continental Army. Others piloted boats and worked as shipyard carpenters in the Patriot Navy.

QUICK CHECK

Summarize What advantages and disadvantages did the Patriots have in the war with England?

PLACES

VALLEY FORGE

George Washington and his army spent the winter of 1777–1778 in Valley Forge, Pennsylvania. About 2,500 patriots died of hunger, cold, and disease during the long, cold winter. Today you can visit the Valley Forge National Historic Park.

British Soldiers

The British defeated the Patriots at the Battle of Bunker Hill, but suffered significant casualties in doing so.

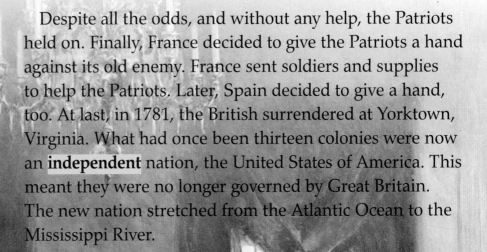

Despite all the odds, and without any help, the Patriots held on. Finally, France decided to give the Patriots a hand against its old enemy. France sent soldiers and supplies to help the Patriots. Later, Spain decided to give a hand, too. At last, in 1781, the British surrendered at Yorktown, Virginia. What had once been thirteen colonies were now an **independent** nation, the United States of America. This meant they were no longer governed by Great Britain. The new nation stretched from the Atlantic Ocean to the Mississippi River.

PEOPLE

JAMES MADISON

We can thank James Madison for our Constitution. It was Madison who planned it, wrote it, and fought for its approval. He is known today as "the father of the Constitution."

Constitutional Convention, Philadelphia

A Plan for Government

The next task was to plan a new government. The country struggled for ten years, but it was soon clear that the plan the patriots had for a new government did not work. In 1787 leaders came together and agreed on a different plan of government—a new constitution. The United States Constitution divided power between the states and the national government. The Constitution was approved by the states in 1788. Three years later, the Bill of Rights was added. The Constitution is still the law of our country today.

QUICK CHECK

Summarize How did the French and Spanish help the Patriots to become an independent nation?

Check Understanding

1. **VOCABULARY** Write a paragraph about the colonies using these words.

   tax   revolution   independent

2. **READING SKILL** Sequence Events Use the chart to tell what led to war.

First
Next
Last

3. **Write About It** How did the patriots form their own nation?

Lesson 4

VOCABULARY

territory

Louisiana
Purchase

expedition

canal

frontier

READING SKILL

Sequence Events

Copy the chart. As
you read, fill it in with
information about the
growth of our nation.

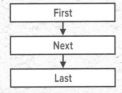

| First |
| Next |
| Last |

STANDARDS FOCUS

SOCIAL STUDIES Time, Continuity, and
Change

GEOGRAPHY Environment and
Society

THE NATION GROWS

Visual Preview

What were the effects of growth on the new nation?

A The Northwest
Territory caused
conflict.

B Lewis and Clark
explored lands of
the Louisiana Purchase.

C Canals and
railroads made
travel faster.

D Texas freedom
and gold helped
the country grow.

A OVER THE MOUNTAINS

Great Britain had closed the land west of the Appalachians to settlers.
Now that the country was independent, some settlers began moving west.
They were looking for inexpensive land and good soil.

The new United States government passed two laws to oversee the vast new territory west of the mountains. The first law called for the land to be measured. The second law officially named the area north of the Ohio River as the Northwest **Territory**. A territory is land owned by a country. The law also stated that once enough settlers lived there, the territory could become a state. Slavery was not allowed in the territory or states.

Growth and Conflict

Congress thought Native Americans would be willing to sell their land. Many were angry that the treaties they had signed with the British meant little to the settlers. Several Native American nations attacked the settlers. After they lost the Battle of Fallen Timbers in Ohio, many Native American leaders had to sign a treaty giving up their lands.

In 1800 part of the Northwest Territory had enough people to become the territory of Ohio. A year later, the western part of the Northwest Territory became the territory of Indiana.

PEOPLE

TECUMSEH

Tecumseh was a Shawnee chief. He traveled great distances visiting Native American villages. He tried to get them to unite to protect their lands. Despite his leadership, Native Americans were forced to give up most of their land in the Northwest Territory.

QUICK CHECK

Sequence What happened after Native Americans refused to sell their land?

MOVING WEST

By 1803, the United States controlled most of the land east of the Mississippi River. Still, many Americans were eager to push past the Mississippi River into Louisiana Territory. At the time, Louisiana belonged to France.

France needed money for a war it was fighting in Europe against Great Britain. The French offered to sell all of Louisiana to President Thomas Jefferson. Jefferson agreed and bought the entire territory for about $15 million. The new territory, known as the **Louisiana Purchase**, was huge. It stretched from the Mississippi River to the Rocky Mountains. Americans knew little about this area.

Lewis and Clark

Jefferson wanted to know everything about the land he had just bought. He organized an **expedition**, or a journey of exploration. He hired Meriwether Lewis and William Clark to lead it. He asked them to make maps as they traveled and to record what they found.

PEOPLE

SACAGAWEA

Sacagawea helped Lewis and Clark speak with the Native Americans they met. She also showed them which plants were safe to eat. Sacagawea's brother, a Shoshone chief, provided the group with horses to continue the journey over the mountains.

Lewis and Clark traveled by river for much of their journey.

Lewis and Clark hired a French trader named Charbonneau and his Shoshone wife, Sacagawea, as guides. For two years, they led more than 40 men across the West. They climbed high mountains in terrible weather.

The expedition reached the Pacific Ocean in 1805. By 1806, they had returned to Missouri. They brought back exciting information about America's new territory.

QUICK CHECK

Cause and Effect **Why did Jefferson send Lewis and Clark into Louisiana?**

Lewis and Clark explore the West. ▶

As the country grew larger, distances between cities were long and traveling was slow. In the early 1800s, the fastest way to travel on land was by horseback. The only way to ship goods across land was by wagon.

Building a Waterway

In 1825 the New York state government finished building a waterway called the Erie **Canal**. The Erie Canal connected the Hudson River to the Great Lakes. Canal boats were pulled by horses or mules that walked along paths at the canal's edge. Now merchants could ship products from New York City to the Great Lakes and back. Many settlers bought these goods. The success of the Erie Canal inspired other states to build canals. Soon canals were being built all over the country.

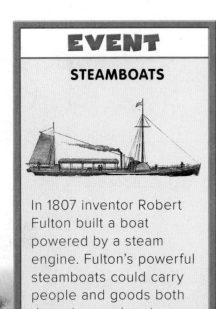

EVENT

STEAMBOATS

In 1807 inventor Robert Fulton built a boat powered by a steam engine. Fulton's powerful steamboats could carry people and goods both downriver and upriver.

Toledo, Ohio, as it appeared in 1876. Notice the many different types of transportation.

Railroads

Railroads were the next big improvement. At first, railroad cars were pulled by horses over iron rails. Then, a British inventor figured out how to get a steam engine to pull the railroad cars.

By the early 1830s, work crews were laying railroad tracks in the United States. It wasn't long before railroads crisscrossed the eastern states.

▲ Steam engines pulled railroad cars faster and more cheaply than did horses.

QUICK CHECK

Main Idea and Details **What changes were made in transportation in the early 1800s?**

As more and more people came, the **frontier**, or the edge of the settled area, kept moving west. Some Americans began to feel that the United States had a right to all of the land out west—that it was the country's destiny to extend from the Atlantic to the Pacific.

Texas and the Mexican War

Mexico won its independence from Spain in 1821. Americans began settling in northern Mexico in the 1820s in an area named Texas. They soon outnumbered the Mexicans living there. Then, in 1835, some of the Americans started a revolution. Americans living in Texas wanted to be independent from Mexico. In April 1836, they defeated the Mexican Army and won their independence. The government of the new nation asked to join the United States. In 1845 the United States government agreed, and Texas became the 28th state.

PLACES

THE ALAMO

The Alamo was a mission in San Antonio, Texas, that later became a fort. In 1836 it was the site of a bloody battle between Texas settlers and the Mexican army. Among the settlers who defended the Alamo were Sam Houston and Davy Crockett. Today, the Alamo is a museum.

Settlers in wagon trains traveled across the country.

(t)McGraw-Hill Education, (bkgd)Yale University Art Gallery

Mexico and the United States disagreed about where the border of Texas should be. The United States and Mexico went to war over this in 1846. The United States won. In the peace treaty of 1848, Mexico gave up half its territory, including California. In return, the United States paid Mexico $15 million.

The California Gold Rush

In 1848 a California settler discovered gold. The news spread rapidly across the country. Thousands of people traveled to California. They hoped to become rich. Two years after gold was first discovered, California had enough people for statehood.

▲ Thousands of people looked for gold in California.

QUICK CHECK

Cause and Effect **How did the United States expand westward?**

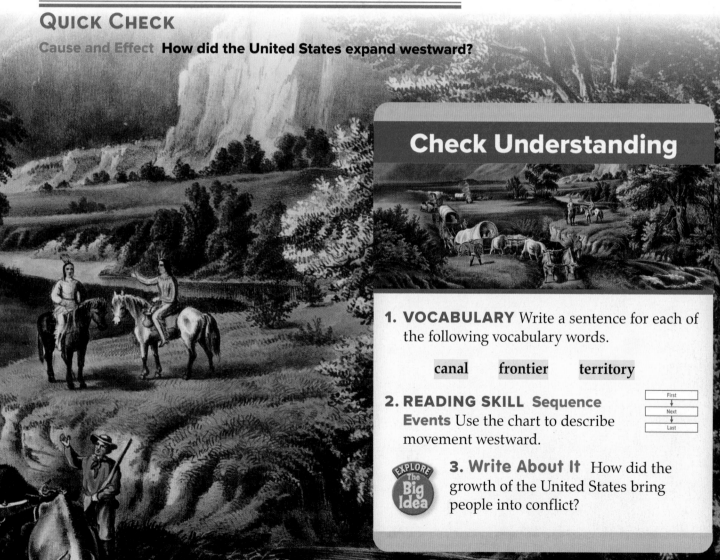

Check Understanding

1. **VOCABULARY** Write a sentence for each of the following vocabulary words.

   canal   frontier   territory

2. **READING SKILL Sequence Events** Use the chart to describe movement westward.

   First
   ↓
   Next
   ↓
   Last

3. **Write About It** How did the growth of the United States bring people into conflict?

Lesson 5

VOCABULARY

Civil War

Emancipation Proclamation

Reconstruction

immigrant

invention

READING SKILL

Sequence Events
Copy the chart. As you read, fill it in with information about the Civil War.

First
↓
Next
↓
Last

STANDARDS FOCUS

SOCIAL STUDIES Individuals, Groups, and Institutions

GEOGRAPHY Places and Regions

WAR AND CHANGES

African American soldiers in the Civil War.

Visual Preview

How did the Civil War change the nation?

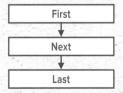

A The North has industry. The Civil War begins.

B Lincoln issues the Emancipation Proclamation.

C Reconstruction begins and the nation is rebuilt.

D Immigrants move to the plains and ideas bring progress.

A NORTH AND SOUTH

By 1850, differences between the North and the South were threatening to split the country. As each new territory became a state, people in the North and South argued about whether slavery would be allowed there.

In the South, a way of life had come to depend on slave labor. In the North, slavery had been abolished, or made illegal, by this time. Many Northerners worked in factories and were paid wages. They saw slavery as a threat to wage labor. Others saw it as a terrible moral wrong. Some people in the North began to oppose slavery.

The Nation Divides

Then came the election of 1860. Abraham Lincoln, who was against the spread of slavery, was elected President. Many Southerners were afraid that Lincoln wanted to end slavery altogether. One by one, in the early months of 1861, Southern states broke away from the United States. They formed the Confederate States of America, with Jefferson Davis as their President.

In April 1861, Confederate forces opened fire on Fort Sumter. The **Civil War**, or the war between the Union and the Confederacy, had begun.

PEOPLE

HARRIET BEECHER STOWE

In 1852 Harriet Beecher Stowe published *Uncle Tom's Cabin*, a novel about enslaved men and women. Stowe's book described the evils of slavery. More and more people wanted to end slavery because of this book.

In the North, people worked in factories making goods such as cloth. ▼

QUICK CHECK

Sequence What did Southern states do after Lincoln was elected in 1860?

STRENGTHS AND WEAKNESSES

Both sides had strengths and weaknesses. The South's greatest strength was its army. Men in the South knew how to ride horses and hunt, which were good skills for soldiers. The South also had many well-trained officers. Robert E. Lee, one of these officers, became the commander of the Confederate army. However, one of the South's weaknesses was that the farms there grew mostly cotton, not food.

EVENT

THE *MONITOR* AND THE *VIRGINIA*

During the 1860s, most warships were made of wood. The Union ship *Monitor* and the Confederate ship *Virginia*, however, were ironclads. Their iron sides protected them from cannonballs and made them hard to sink. In an 1862 battle, neither ship could sink the other.

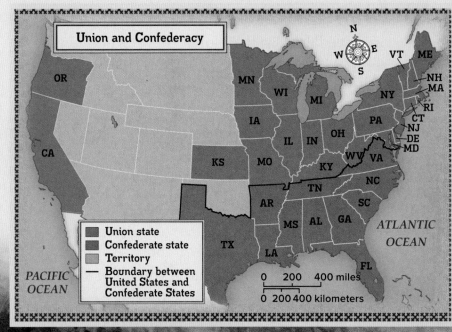

Union and Confederacy

- Union state
- Confederate state
- Territory
- Boundary between United States and Confederate States

PACIFIC OCEAN

ATLANTIC OCEAN

0   200   400 miles
0 200 400 kilometers

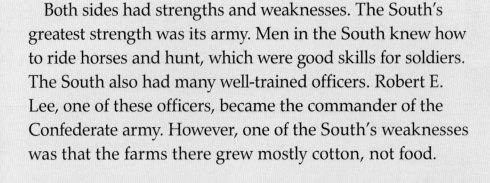

The North had a much larger population than the Confederacy, but the people did not have many fighting skills. The North had supplies for a larger army because most of the country's factories were there. The factories made weapons and uniforms. The North also grew most of the country's food. Plus, the North had most of the railroads that could move troops and supplies.

Lincoln Ends Slavery

At first, Lincoln wanted to keep the Union together. Soon, the goal of the war included ending slavery. On January 1, 1863, Lincoln issued the **Emancipation Proclamation**. This document said that all enslaved people in the Confederacy "shall be . . . forever free."

More than 600,000 men from the Union and the Confederacy died during the war. Finally, on April 9, 1865, after four years of fighting, the Confederacy surrendered. Northerners celebrated at first, but joy quickly turned to sadness. On April 14, 1865, President Lincoln was shot and killed as he watched a play in Washington, D.C.

PEOPLE

ABRAHAM LINCOLN

In 1865, near the end of the War, Lincoln spoke about healing the nation. His wish was to bring the country together "with malice towards none, with charity for all."

QUICK CHECK

Summary **What were the strengths and weaknesses of the two sides that fought in the Civil War?**

In 1863 the Union army won a major victory at Gettysburg, Pennsylvania. ▼

ⓒ REBUILDING THE NATION

Now came the job of putting the nation back together again. This period became known as **Reconstruction**. President Johnson's plan for rebuilding the country was to have the Southern states pledge their loyalty to the Union and abolish slavery. By the fall of 1865, every state but Texas had rejoined the Union.

Important Changes

Congress also amended, or changed, the Constitution. The changes were written in the 13th, 14th, and 15th amendments to the Constitution. They made slavery illegal, said that all people born in the United States were citizens, gave all male citizens the right to vote, and protected the rights of all citizens.

Violence and Jim Crow Laws

Most white Southerners did not want African Americans to be treated as their equals. The new parts of the Constitution were often not enforced, and African Americans were denied their rights. Laws called Jim Crow laws were passed to make the separation of African Americans and whites legal. People who tried to object were threatened and sometimes killed.

After emancipation, thousands of African Americans tried to find their families. Many were reunited, but others were not. Some former slaves moved out of the South, hoping to find a better life. Many stayed where they were.

QUICK CHECK

Main Idea and Details **What changes did Congress make to the Constitution after the Civil War?**

Grant.

PUBLISHED & PRINTED BY

1 Reading Emancipation Proclam.
2 Life Liberty and Independence
3 We Unite the Bonds of Fellowsh
4 Our Charter of Rights the Holy S

(bkgd)Library of Congress, Prints and Photographs Division [LC-USZC4-2399]

THE FIFTEENTH AMENDMENT

Education will prove the Equality the Races.
Liberty Protects the Mariage Alter.
Celebration of Fifteenth Amendment May 19th 1870
The Ballot Box is open to us.
9 Our representive Sits in the National Legislature
10 The Holy Ordinances of Religion are free
11 Freedom unites the Family Circle.
12 We will protect our Country as it defends our Rights.
13 We till our own Fields.
14 The Right of Citizens of the U.S. to vote shall not be denied or abridged by the U.S. or any State on account of Race Color or Condition of Servitude 15th Amendment

▲ This poster shows people and events related to the passing of the 15th Amendment to the Constitution, which gave the right to vote to all male citizens.

PEOPLE

THOMAS EDISON

Edison invented many things we now take for granted. In 1879 he perfected the first practical light bulb. A few years later, he developed a system that made it possible to provide electricity to an entire city.

After the Civil War, pioneers began moving westward to claim cheap land on the Great Plains. Many of the **immigrants**, who came to the United States from places as far away as Germany, Norway, and Russia, also headed west. An immigrant is a person who comes to a new country to live. The population of the United States grew.

The Plains Wars

What about the Native Americans that already lived on the Great Plains? They were losing more and more land to settlers. In addition, white hunters were wiping out the buffalo, destroying the Native Americans' way of life.

The Lakota, Cheyenne, and Arapaho joined together to protect their lands. They fought United States soldiers at battles such as Little Bighorn, but in the end, they lost. By 1877, the last Native Americans of the Great Plains were moved to reservations.

As trains made travel easier, people began to build small towns where they stopped.

(t)Patrick Guenette/Alamy; (bkgd)Yale University Art Gallery

Technology Changes Lives

Meanwhile, dozens of **inventions**, or new products, were changing American lives. Farmers had new machinery that made work easier. The telephone was invented in 1876 by Alexander Graham Bell. Telephones made it easier for Americans to communicate. Electric lights made it easier and safer for people to work indoors and at night. A cheaper way was found to make steel, and soon, steel was used to build skyscrapers and improve railroad tracks.

With machinery to do the work, farms needed fewer workers. Many people found jobs in factories that were built to meet the demand for new goods. Immigrants continued to travel to "the land of opportunity." Many settled in the growing cities.

QUICK CHECK

Draw Conclusions How did telephones change life in America?

Check Understanding

1. **VOCABULARY** Write a paragraph about the end of the war using these words.

   Reconstruction   **immigrant**

2. **READING SKILL** Sequence Events Use the chart to tell about slavery ending.

First
Next
Last

3. **Write About It** What events helped to shape the nation in the late 1800s?

A Changing World

Lesson 6

VOCABULARY

suffrage

dictator

Allies

Axis

READING SKILL

Sequence Events

Copy the chart. As you read, fill it in with information about World War I, the Great Depression, and World War II.

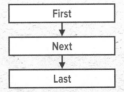

First

↓

Next

↓

Last

STANDARDS FOCUS

SOCIAL STUDIES: Time, Continuity, and Change

GEOGRAPHY: Human Systems

This home in San Simeon, California, stood in sharp contrast to the homes of those who lived in poverty.

Visual Preview

How did economic and political changes affect the nation?

A There was a sharp contrast between the wealthy and poor.

B Changes came about with World War I and women's suffrage.

C The Great Depression took place at the end of the 1920s.

D The New Deal helped America after World War II.

A TIME OF CONTRASTS

In the early part of the 20th century, there were some big differences in the way people lived in our country. People such as Cornelius Vanderbilt, John D. Rockefeller, and Andrew Carnegie were millionaires. At the same time, many people lived in terrible poverty, especially in the cities.

Although there were some millionaires in the United States, most people worked ten hours or more a day, sometimes as many as 80 hours a week. They worked in factories that were hot, crowded, and often dangerous. Even children as young as five or six worked in mines and factories. If workers complained, they were fired.

Working for Change

Wealthy people such as Carnegie and Rockefeller gave money to help people. Others also tried to improve life for the poor. Jane Addams opened a house in Chicago where poor people could get an education and advice.

Workers began to join together to form labor unions. Unions are groups of workers who organize to make agreements with employers about better wages and safer working conditions.

PLACES

THE STATUE OF LIBERTY

The Statue of Liberty stands on an island in New York Harbor. France gave the statue to the United States as a gift in 1886. To many immigrants, the statue symbolized justice and freedom.

QUICK CHECK

Sequence **What did workers do to get safer working conditions?**

In cities, children often worked in factories. ▶

In 1914 a struggle for power in Europe led to war. England, France, Japan, Italy, and Russia were the Allied Powers. They were fighting Germany, Austria-Hungary, and Turkey, or the Central Powers. So many countries were involved in this struggle that people called it the "Great War." Later, it became known as World War I.

At first, the United States tried to stay out of the war. After all, the battles were happening in Europe. Finally, in 1917, the United States joined the side of the Allied Powers. The United States helped win the war against the Central Powers.

As the United States entered World War I, posters such as this one encouraged citizens to join the armed forces. ▼

(bl)Library of Congress Prints & Photographs Division [LC-USZC4-8136], (bkgd)Library of Congress, Prints and Photographs Division [LC-DIG-ggbain-12924]

Changes for Women

Did you know that when the Constitution was written, only men could vote? As far back as the 1840s, some people were working for women's **suffrage**, or right to vote. In 1920 Congress finally amended the Constitution to give women the right to vote.

QUICK CHECK

Summarize **What were some of the events of the early 1900s?**

▼ These young girls hold signs to show that they want to vote when they are women.

After World War I ended, people wanted to forget their troubles. For many, the 1920s were good times. Many Americans had jobs and money to spend. Now that Henry Ford had found a cheaper way to build cars, it seemed almost everyone in America could buy one. Americans played phonograph records, listened to the radio, and went to the new moving picture shows.

Stocks

In the 1920s, many people bought stocks, or shares of businesses. People buy and sell their stock on the stock market. Buyers were hoping the stocks would go up in value and make them rich.

Prices had been going up and up, but then they started to fall. On October 29, 1929, stock owners panicked and rushed to sell their stocks all at once. The prices fell very quickly, or "crashed." The stock market crash put an end to the good times of the 1920s. Banks ran out of money and closed. Many businesses closed. Many people lost all their savings, and suddenly millions were out of work.

EVENT

THE OKIES

In the 1930s, many farmers fled the Dust Bowl. They came from many states, but most came from Oklahoma. Eventually, all of the migrants, no matter where they were from, became known as "Okies."

The Bad Times

The stock market crash began a period of economic hard times known as the Great Depression. People all over the country were out of work. People stood in bread and soup lines to get food. Some people sold apples or pencils on street corners.

Farmers had an especially hard time. Many farmers had borrowed money from banks to buy equipment. When the farmers could not pay back the loans, they lost their farms.

To make matters worse, many states were hit by a drought. The drought lasted for so long, the soil turned to dust and was blown around in dust storms. Texas, Oklahoma, and Kansas were the hardest-hit states. These areas became known as the Dust Bowl. Many Dust Bowl farmers moved to California, hoping for a better life.

▲ John Steinbeck's novel, *The Grapes of Wrath*, which was later turned into a movie (shown above), tells the story of Dust Bowl farmers who left their homes for a chance at a better life in California.

QUICK CHECK

Cause and Effect **What happened after stock prices crashed on October 29, 1929?**

During the Great Depression, people stood in long lines to get food.

RECOVERY AND WAR

In 1932 Franklin Roosevelt was elected President. In his first speech he declared,

"**The only thing we have to fear is fear itself.**"

People were taking all their money out of banks because they were worried that the banks would close and their money would be gone. To stop people from doing this, Roosevelt declared a bank holiday and closed the banks.

A New Deal

The New Deal was a plan to help Americans recover from the Great Depression. Social Security was established to provide income to retired Americans. Other programs paid for building new roads and bringing electricity to rural areas. These projects created jobs and improved the quality of life for many people.

Franklin Roosevelt sitting at his desk. ▼

In the surprise attack on Pearl Harbor, Japanese bombs sank five huge battleships. Over 2,400 Americans were killed.

Another World War

Problems from World War I were still brewing in Europe. Adolf Hitler came to power in Germany in 1933. He was a **dictator**, or a person who rules a country without sharing power. In 1939 another world war began. The **Allies** were countries that fought against the **Axis** in World War II.

The Allies were England, France, and the Soviet Union. The Axis were Germany, Italy, and Japan. In 1941 Japan bombed the American naval base at Pearl Harbor, Hawaii, in a surprise attack. The United States joined the war on the side of the Allies.

Suddenly, the Great Depression was over. The war created new jobs and work for many Americans. Women worked in factories building tanks and airplanes. African Americans from the South moved north to work in cities. The Allies won World War II in 1945.

PEOPLE

WOMEN IN WWII

During World War II, so many men were away from home fighting the war that women were able to get jobs they had never had before. By the end of 1943, more than 300,000 women worked in the aircraft industry alone. Women also worked in the military in noncombat roles.

QUICK CHECK

Main Idea and Details **What ended the Great Depression?**

Check Understanding

1. **VOCABULARY** Create a poster about World War II using these words.

   dictator   Axis   Allies

2. **READING SKILL** Sequence Events Use the chart to describe the events in the 1920s.

First
Next
Last

3. **Write About It** How did the Great Depression affect the nation?

Lesson 7

VOCABULARY

communism

discrimination

civil rights

terrorism

READING SKILL

Sequence Events

Copy the chart. As you read, fill it in with information about the modern United States.

```
┌─────────────┐
│    First    │
└─────────────┘
       │
       ▼
┌─────────────┐
│    Next     │
└─────────────┘
       │
       ▼
┌─────────────┐
│    Last     │
└─────────────┘
```

STANDARDS FOCUS

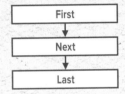

SOCIAL STUDIES — Individual Development and Identity

GEOGRAPHY — Environment and Society

A Modern World

The NASA mission control computer room in 1962.

Visual Preview

How did modern conflicts shape the country?

A The Cold War led to a space race.

B The civil rights movement worked for equal rights.

C America faces challenges and energy concerns.

Ⓐ   A COLD WAR

In the late 20th century, we sent people to the moon and entered the computer age. It was a time of conflict, but also one of accomplishments and changes. Americans entered the 21st century ready to face the challenges ahead.

The Soviet Union, a group of nations controlled by Russia, fought on the same side as the Allies in World War II. The Soviet Union had a communist government—this meant that the government owned and controlled everything. After World War II, the United States began to worry that **communism** would spread. The two nations became enemies in the Cold War. The war was not fought with guns and armies, but instead with ideas and money.

The two nations were involved in an arms race. Each nation worked to build more atomic weapons than the other. Each side thought these powerful weapons would keep the other side from attacking.

A War in Korea

The Korean peninsula had been divided into two countries, North Korea and South Korea. North Korea had a communist government. In June 1950, North Korea attacked South Korea. The United States rushed troops to help South Korea. In 1953 a settlement was reached that ended the conflict between the two nations.

PEOPLE

HARRY S. TRUMAN
Harry S. Truman became President after the death of President Roosevelt. Truman's decision to use atomic bombs against Japan helped end World War II. Truman was also President during the Korean War.

QUICK CHECK

Sequence Events When did the United States enter into a Cold War with the Soviet Union?

B STRUGGLES AT HOME AND OVERSEAS

You might have thought that the Civil War improved the lives of African Americans. People of color were still not treated equally in many ways. In both the North and South, there was still **discrimination**, or an unfair difference in the way people are treated.

During World War II, African American soldiers and sailors had risked their lives just as other soldiers had. Now, they and others began demanding equal rights at home.

People joined together to take action. They began a **civil rights** movement. Civil rights are the rights of all citizens to be treated equally under the law. Leaders such as Martin Luther King, Jr., organized marches and protests to gather

In August 1963, thousands of people came to see Martin Luther King, Jr., speak about civil rights on the Mall in Washington, D.C.

(bkgd)National Archives and Records Administration (542068)

support. In 1964 the first of several laws, called the Civil Rights Acts, were passed. Finally, discrimination was illegal.

Another War in Asia

Starting in 1961, the United States became involved in a war in Vietnam, a country in Southeast Asia. Americans were bitterly divided about the Vietnam War. Finally, in 1975, the United States brought its soldiers home.

QUICK CHECK

Sequence Events **What happened before the Civil Rights Acts were passed?**

On September 11, 2001, something happened that most Americans will never forget. Terrorists took over American airplanes and used them to attack the United States. Thousands of people died. President George W. Bush declared a war on **terrorism**. Terrorism, or using fear and violence to achieve political goals, has been a growing problem in the world.

President Bush created a new department called the Department of Homeland Security. One of the actions this department has taken is to increase the security at our airports. American troops were also sent to fight in Afghanistan and in Iraq, two countries in Asia whose leaders were believed to help terrorists.

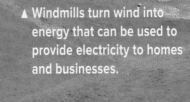

▲ Windmills turn wind into energy that can be used to provide electricity to homes and businesses.

▲ Rescue workers begin to clear the rubble of the World Trade Center after the terrorist attacks of September 11, 2001.

New Kinds of Energy

Another huge challenge our nation faces is finding enough energy sources. Think about how our lives would be different if we ran out of gasoline for our cars or couldn't use electricity in our homes.

You know that gasoline is made from oil. The United States produces some oil, but not enough for everyone. We buy oil from other countries, including countries in the Middle East.

In August 2005, Hurricane Katrina hit the Gulf Coast of the United States. Our oil production in that region was completely shut down for a time. This event showed us how important it is to conserve energy and to find other types of fuel.

QUICK CHECK

Summarize What are some of the challenges facing the United States today?

EVENT

EARTH DAY

Burning gasoline produces carbon dioxide that can pollute the air. Since trees use carbon dioxide for food, one way people celebrate Earth Day is by planting trees to reduce air pollution. People also reduce how much energy and water they use.

Check Understanding

1. **VOCABULARY** Write a sentence for each vocabulary word.

   discrimination   terrorism   civil rights

2. **READING SKILL** Sequence Events Use the chart on page 56 to talk about the Cold War.

First
Next
Last

3. **Write About It** How did the civil rights movement shape our nation?

Unit 1   Review and Assess

Vocabulary Review

Copy the sentences below. Use the list of vocabulary words to fill in the blanks.

artifact   **Louisiana Purchase**

Civil War   **terrorism**

1. A(n) ___ can tell us about people of the past.

2. The territory that President Thomas Jefferson bought from the French was the ___.

3. The Union and Confederate armies fought in the ___ .

4. On September 11, 2001, an act of ___ occurred.

Comprehension and Critical Thinking

5. Why did colonists object to taxes passed by the British government?

6. Why was the transcontinental railroad important?

7. **Reading Skill** What events led to Sacagawea helping the Lewis and Clark expedition?

8. **Critical Thinking** What do you think was the most important invention of the 1800s?

Skill

Use Time Lines

Use the time line to answer each question.

9. Was gold discovered in California before or after Columbus's first visit to America?

10. How many years after Cahokia was built was gold discovered in California?

700	1492	1848
Cahokia is built	**Columbus's first visit to America**	**Gold is discovered in California**

500   1000   1500   2000

Test Preparation

Read the passage. Then answer the questions.

> The Huron were a Native American group that lived in what is now Michigan. The Huron way of life was built on family relationships. Among the Huron, children were members of their mother's clan, not their father's. When a man married, he became part of his wife's clan and went to live in her family's house.
>
> The Huron were loving parents. They believed that children learned from example, not from punishment. Huron children knew their parents would be disappointed if they misbehaved. The children did not want to let their families down, so they learned to do the right thing.

1. What is the main idea of this passage?

   A. The Huron lived in Michigan.

   B. Family relationships were important to the Huron.

   C. The Huron punished their children.

   D. The Huron had small families.

2. What inferences can be made from this passage?

   A. Parents did not care for their children.

   B. Huron children lived with their mothers only.

   C. The children pleased their parents.

   D. The Huron believed in discipline.

3. Which statement is an opinion?

   A. The Huron were a Native American group.

   B. Huron children did not want to let their families down.

   C. Huron homes were very comfortable.

   D. When a Huron man married he became a part of his wife's clan.

4. How might the Huron have come to the conclusion that children learn best by example?

What are some events that have shaped our nation?

Write About the Big Idea

Narrative Essay

In Unit 1 you read about some of the events that have shaped our nation. Review your notes in the completed foldable. Write an essay describing some of the events that have shaped our nation. Begin with an introductory paragraph, stating how past events influence the present. Your final paragraph should summarize the main ideas of your essay and give ideas about how the events discussed have shaped our nation.

FOLDABLES™
Study Organizer

Our National Story
Three Worlds Meet
The Nation Grows
A Changing World

Build a Model

Work with a partner to make a model. Follow these steps to make your model:

1. Choose a time you read about in Unit 1.

2. Research what the buildings and clothing looked like and what jobs people did.

3. Use materials to build a model of a building and people at work in the time period.

4. Using your research, write a description of the building and what the people are doing.

5. Present your model to the class.

EXPLORE The Big Idea

Essential Question
How do people meet their needs?

FOLDABLES™ Study Organizer

Compare and Contrast
Use a layered book foldable to take notes as you read Unit 2. Write **The United States** on the cover. Label the three tabs **Geography**, **Economy**, and **Government**. Use the foldable to organize information.

Government
Economy
Geography
The United States

LOG ON
For more about Unit 2 go to
connectED.mcgraw-hill.com

The United States:
Its Land and People

PEOPLE, PLACES, AND EVENTS

John D. Rockefeller

Rockefeller Center

John D. Rockefeller was an American businessman and philanthropist. Dominating the oil industry, he became the world's richest man, and the first American billionaire.

Today you can visit Rockefeller Center, a complex of 19 commercial buildings located in New York City.

Donna House

Smithsonian Folklife Festival

The Smithsonian Institution is the world's largest museum complex. The grounds of its newest museum, the National Museum of the American Indian, were designed by **Donna House**.

Today visit the museums and attend festivals such as the **Smithsonian Folklife Festival** in Washington, D.C.

Americans Vote

Soldiers Vote

Americans vote in national, state, and local elections. Voting is an important part of being a good citizen. Even **soldiers vote** in special stations set up just for overseas military people.

Today visit the National Museum of American History in Washington, D.C., to learn more about voting's history.

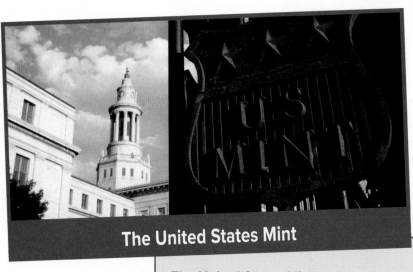

The United States Mint

Printing Money

The **United States Mint** makes coins used in the United States. **Mint workers** inspect all the coins before the money goes into circulation.

Today you can tour the mint in Denver, Colorado, or Philadelphia, Pennsylvania, and see how money is made.

THE UNITED STATES

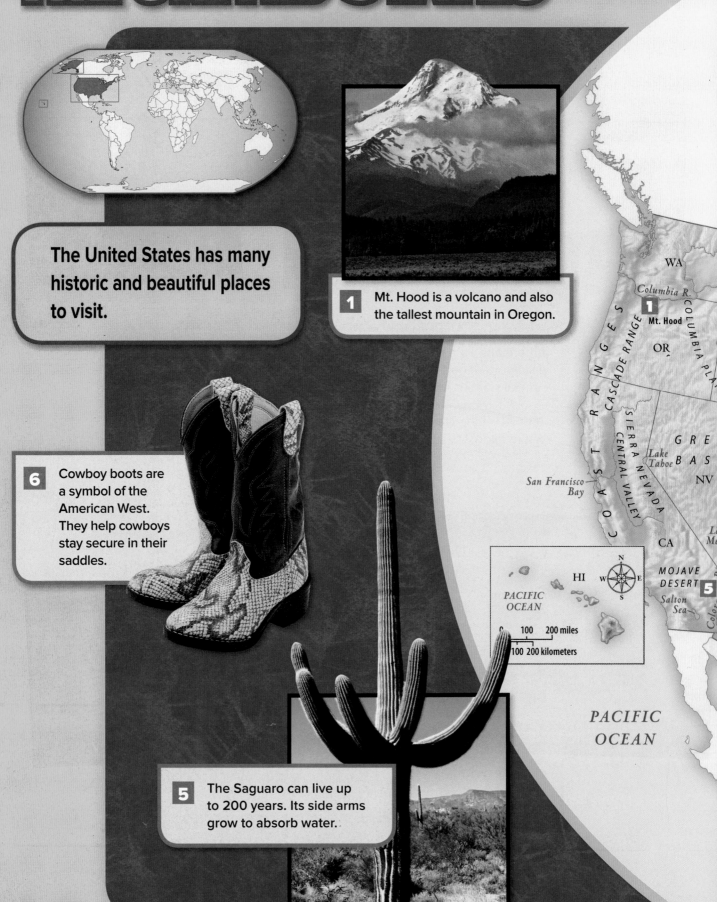

The United States has many historic and beautiful places to visit.

1 Mt. Hood is a volcano and also the tallest mountain in Oregon.

6 Cowboy boots are a symbol of the American West. They help cowboys stay secure in their saddles.

5 The Saguaro can live up to 200 years. Its side arms grow to absorb water.

WA
Columbia R.
COAST RANGES
CASCADE RANGE
Mt. Hood
1
OR
COLUMBIA PLATE
SIERRA NEVADA
CENTRAL VALLEY
Lake Tahoe
GREA BASI
NV
San Francisco Bay
CA
La Mea
MOJAVE DESERT
5
Salton Sea
Colorado River

HI
PACIFIC OCEAN
N W E S
0 100 200 miles
100 200 kilometers

PACIFIC OCEAN

(tr)Alan Sealls/WeatherVideoHD.TV, (c)Iconotec/Glow Images, (br)Amanda Clement/Photodisc/Getty

ARCTIC OCEAN

RUSSIA

BROOKS RANGE

AK

CANADA

Yukon River

ALASKA RANGE

Gulf of Alaska

Aleutian Islands

0   400 miles

0   400 kilometers

2 The Gateway Arch in St. Louis, Missouri, marks the city as the "Gateway to the West."

3 The Capitol Building is in Washington, D.C.

CANADA

Missouri River

MT

6

ND

GREAT

MESABI RANGE

Lake Superior

GREAT LAKES

St. Lawrence

ME

MN

Mississippi River

WI

Lake Huron

Lake Ontario

ADIRONDACK MOUNTAINS

VT

NH

NY

MA

CT RI

SD

BLACK HILLS

WY

Lake Michigan

MI

Lake Erie

PA

NJ

IA

CENTRAL PLAINS

River

OH

APPALACHIAN MOUNTAINS

MD

DE

Great Salt Lake

NE

Platte River

Missouri River

IL

IN

Ohio River

WV

3 Washington, D.C.

EAT LAKE ERT

CO

KS

Arkansas River

MO

2 St. Louis

Wabash River

KY

VA

PIEDMONT

Chesapeake Bay

UT

OLORADO

ATEAU

OZARK PLATEAU

TN

Tennessee River

NC

ATLANTIC COASTAL PLAIN

NM

Pecos River

Red River

OK

AR

OUACHITA MOUNTAINS

Mississippi River

Savannah River

SC

ATLANTIC OCEAN

River

Brazos River

TX

Colorado River

MS

AL

Alabama River

GA

Chattahoochee River

ORAN ERT

Rio Grande

EDWARDS PLATEAU

GULF COASTAL PLAIN

LA

Mobile Bay

4

FL

N

W E

S

Galveston Bay

MEXICO

Gulf of Mexico

4 The American Alligator is only found in the Southeast. They can grow up to 19 feet long!

0   200   400 miles

0   200   400 kilometers

From Sea to Sea

VOCABULARY

mineral

erosion

tributary

plateau

basin

READING SKILL

Compare and Contrast
Copy the chart. As you read, fill it in with information about the eastern and western parts of the United States.

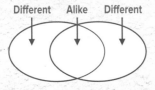

Different   Alike   Different

STANDARDS FOCUS

SOCIAL STUDIES   People, Places, and Environments

GEOGRAPHY   Physical Systems

The United States has many kinds of landforms.

Visual Preview

How have people in the United States adapted to geography?

A The United States has a wide variety of landforms.

B In the East are coastal plains, the Appalachian Mountains, and interior plains.

C The West has the Rocky Mountains, plateaus, and dry deserts.

D There are many different habitats and environments in our country.

Ⓐ A VARIED LAND

*If you could soar like an eagle across the United States, you'd fly
over snowcapped mountains and across sunbaked deserts.
You'd spot mighty rivers and lakes that stretch farther than an
eagle's eye can see. You'd see forests, hills, plains, and more.*

Our country is big! It's almost 3,000 miles from coast to coast. There are all sorts of landforms—the shapes that make up Earth's surface—including mountains, hills, valleys, and flatlands, or plains.

There is water, too. The Atlantic Ocean is on our east coast and the Pacific Ocean is on our west coast. Large cities have grown up along the coasts at harbors where ships can be protected. Besides the oceans, there are thousands of rivers, streams, and lakes throughout the countryside.

Our country has many resources— rich farmlands, forests of tall trees, coal and oil, and **minerals** such as iron, silver, copper, and gold. A mineral is a resource found in nature. In each part of our country, people have learned to use these resources to supply the things they need to live.

Let's fly over the country and take a look at our water, landforms, and natural resources.

QUICK CHECK
Compare and Contrast How are Denali and Death Valley different?

Amazing Geographic Facts

TALLEST	LOWEST	COLDEST	HOTTEST	DEEPEST

Denali (Mount McKinley), Alaska	Death Valley, California	Prospect Creek, Alaska	Death Valley, California	Crater Lake, Oregon
20,320 ft.	**282 ft. below sea level**	**-80.0 °F**	**134.7 °F**	**1,932 feet**

Let's start the flight at the Atlantic coast. What will you see in the East? Use the map as you read to follow along.

Along the Coast

In most places, the land along the coast is low and flat. This is the coastal plain. As you fly, you see many beaches of golden sand, but there are places where the waves crash against rocky shores.

When settlers first came here from Europe, they settled on this coastal plain. The plains were covered with forests then, but little by little the settlers cut down the forests to make farms and to build towns. Today most of the forests are gone.

The Appalachian Mountains

As you move inland away from the coastal plain, you come to the Appalachian Mountains. These are very old mountains. Once they had high, sharp peaks. Over the years, they've been worn down by **erosion**. Erosion is the wearing away of Earth's surface. Millions of years of wind, water, and ice have made the mountains rounded and lower.

Farming is not easy here, but these mountains are rich in coal. Many people came to the mountains of Pennsylvania and West Virginia to make a living mining coal.

The Blue Ridge Mountains are part of the Appalachian Mountains.

(bkgd)daveallenphoto/123RF

Across the Plains

West of the Appalachians, the land is flat again. This is the interior plain. The rich soil here makes it one of the best places in the United States for farming. You look down on colorful fields, like a patchwork quilt of wheat, corn, soybeans, and other crops.

Great Lakes and Long Rivers

From up above, the Great Lakes look like giant puddles. This area was once covered by thick sheets of ice. When the ice melted, it formed the Great Lakes.

The lakes are important routes for transportation and shipping. That's why cities such as Chicago, Cleveland, and Detroit were built along their shores.

Next you'll cross over the Mississippi River, our country's longest river. Many **tributaries**, or smaller rivers, flow into the Mississippi. People have used the Mississippi River for transportation for thousands of years.

QUICK CHECK

Cause and Effect **How were the Great Lakes formed?**

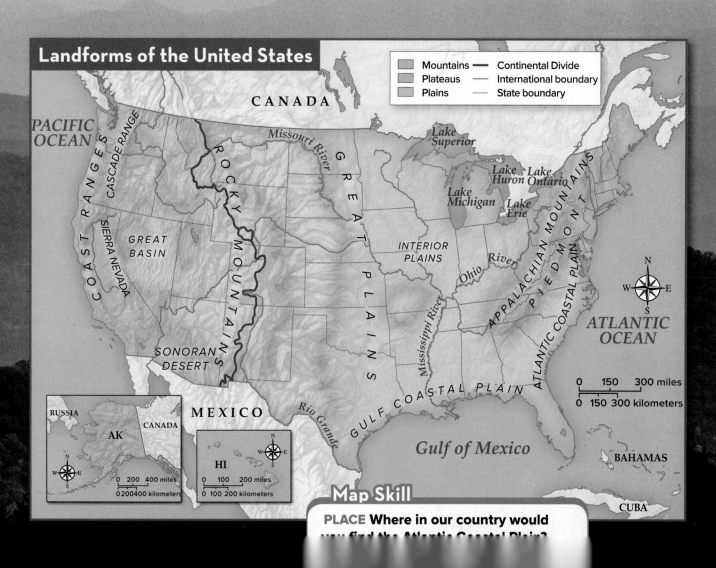

Landforms of the United States

Mountains — Continental Divide
Plateaus — International boundary
Plains --- State boundary

CANADA

PACIFIC OCEAN

CASCADE RANGE

COAST RANGES

SIERRA NEVADA

GREAT BASIN

ROCKY MOUNTAINS

SONORAN DESERT

Missouri River

GREAT PLAINS

Lake Superior

Lake Huron
Lake Ontario

Lake Michigan
Lake Erie

INTERIOR PLAINS

Ohio River

APPALACHIAN MOUNTAINS

PIEDMONT

ATLANTIC COASTAL PLAIN

ATLANTIC OCEAN

Mississippi River

GULF COASTAL PLAIN

Rio Grande

MEXICO

Gulf of Mexico

BAHAMAS

CUBA

0   150   300 miles
0   150 300 kilometers

RUSSIA   CANADA
AK
0 200 400 miles
0 200 400 kilometers

HI
0   100   200 miles
0 100 200 kilometers

Map Skill

PLACE Where in our country would
~~you find the Atlantic Coastal Plain?~~

As you travel west of the Mississippi River, the land rises. Now you are on the Great Plains. It is drier, and there are few trees. These vast plains are good places to raise cattle or grow wheat and corn.

The plains seem endless, but then you see the Rocky Mountains. The Rockies stretch from Alaska to New Mexico. They are higher, sharper, and they formed thousands of years after the Appalachians. From their topmost ridge, rivers and streams flow either east into the Atlantic Ocean or west into the Pacific Ocean. This dividing ridge is called the Continental Divide.

Highlands and Lowlands

Beyond the Rockies, there are several large plateaus. A **plateau** is a high, flat area that rises steeply from the land around it. The huge Great Basin covers parts of Nevada and several other states. A **basin** is a low landform—the opposite of a plateau. It is shaped like a bowl and surrounded by higher land. The Great Basin gets very little rain, so it's a desert. People who live there have learned to use water wisely.

Saguaro cactuses grow in the deserts of the Southwest.

▲ Many wildflowers grow in the Rocky Mountains.

(bl)John Foxx/Getty Images, (cr)Sodapix AG, Switzerland/Glow Images, (bkgd) Alexey Stiop/Alamy

Next, you come to even more mountain ranges—the Cascades in the north, and the Sierra Nevada in California. When you reach the Pacific Ocean your journey across the United States is almost over.

Alaska and Hawaii

To find Alaska, you fly northward along the coast through Canada until you see the snow-covered Alaska Range. Here, you find the country's tallest mountain, Denali (Mount McKinley). As you near the Arctic Ocean, the land becomes low and flat again.

To reach Hawaii, you mustfly out over the Pacific Ocean. Hawaii is a chain of islands that were formed by volcanoes on the ocean floor. Once, Hawaii was an independent nation. Its last ruler was Queen Liliuokalani. Many people visit Hawaii to enjoy its warm weather and beautiful beaches.

QUICK CHECK

Compare and Contrast **What is the difference between a basin and a plateau?**

Hawaii has beautiful beaches.

PEOPLE

Queen Liliuokalani was the last ruler of the Hawaiian Islands. She was forced to give up her throne before Hawaii became part of the United States in 1898.

Queen Liliuokalani

Palm trees grow where it is warm.

MANY ENVIRONMENTS

Because our country is so large, land and weather can vary from place to place. There are also many different kinds of ecosystems. An ecosystem is all of the things, living and nonliving, in a certain area. It is like a nature neighborhood. The air, the water, and the soil in each place are all part of the ecosystem.

Each member of the ecosystem depends on the other members. Each has adapted in order to survive in its environment. For instance, deer and raccoons live in the rainy woodlands of the Appalachian Mountains. Lizards and jackrabbits live among cacti in the Great Basin.

People are also part of an ecosystem. As people move and settle in new places in our country, they learn to use the plant, animal, and mineral resources they find. They learn to use different farming methods, or to grow different crops. Like the animals and plants, they learn to adapt to meet their needs in their environment.

QUICK CHECK

Cause and Effect **Why are animals different in each ecosystem?**

This moose lives in the woodlands of the East.

Check Understanding

1. **VOCABULARY** Draw a picture to illustrate each word below. Label each picture.

   tributary   plateau   basin

2. **READING SKILL** **Compare and Contrast** Use your chart to write about the eastern and western parts of our country.

    3. **Write About It** Write about ways people use the different landforms of the United States to meet their needs.

Map and Globe Skills

Use Elevation Maps

VOCABULARY

elevation

sea level

How would you know which state has the highest mountains? For this kind of information, you need an **elevation** map. Elevation is the height of land above **sea level**, or the level of the surface at the sea. Elevation at sea level is zero feet.

Learn It

- Elevation maps use colors to show the height, or elevation, of land. Not all maps show the same elevation levels.

- The map key tells what each color on the map stands for, in both feet and meters.

Try It

- Which state has a higher elevation, Illinois or New Mexico?

- What states have elevations above 5,000 feet?

Apply It

- Compare the elevations of the states along the Atlantic Coast with the states along the Pacific Coast.

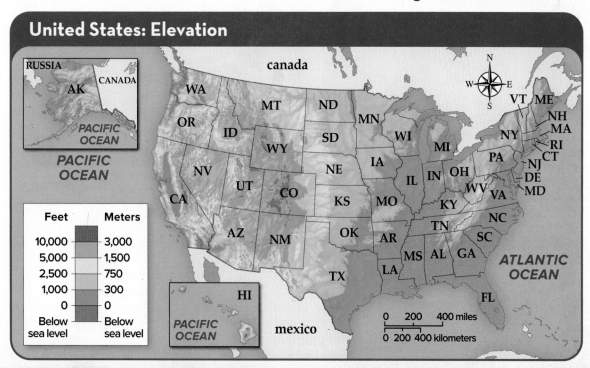

United States: Elevation

Feet	Meters
10,000	3,000
5,000	1,500
2,500	750
1,000	300
0	0
Below sea level	Below sea level

0   200   400 miles
0 200 400 kilometers

Our Country's Regions

VOCABULARY

region

economy

agriculture

interdependent

READING SKILL

Compare and Contrast
Copy the chart. Fill it in with facts about our country's regions.

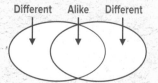

Different   Alike   Different

STANDARDS FOCUS

| SOCIAL STUDIES | People, Places, and Environments |
| GEOGRAPHY | Places and Regions |

The building styles in the Southwest show the region's Spanish history.

Visual Preview

How are regions affected by natural resources?

A Regions can be described by geography or culture.

B Regions of the United States share natural and economic resources.

C States in a region work together to protect their resources.

A WHAT IS A REGION?

Our country is so varied that it's hard to describe. It has highlands and lowlands, cold winters and warm winters. It all depends on what part of the country you are talking about.

The United States is a large country, so it makes sense that one place in our country can be very different from another. To help us understand our country more easily, we divide it into **regions**, or groups of states with common features.

Kinds of Regions

One kind of region is a geographic region. A geographic region shares similar landforms and climates. There are mountain regions, plains regions, and desert regions.

Other kinds of regions are cultural regions. This means they are based on human features, such as history or language. For instance, the states of the Southwest share a history. They were once part of Mexico.

If you visit the Southeast, you might eat southern fried chicken or hear gospel music on the radio. You might notice that people there speak a little differently than people in the North or in the West. All these things—food, music, language, even holidays and customs—are part of culture, the way of life that a people share. A common culture can make an area a region, too.

QUICK CHECK

Compare and Contrast How are geographic regions and cultural regions different?

The people of the Southwest share many customs. ▶

Look at the five regions of the United States on the map. These regions are based on geographic features such as landforms and climate. They're based on human features such as history and culture. Each region's geography, economy, and people are unique.

Shared Resources

Natural resources, such as forests or rivers, don't usually stop at state borders. States in a region share many of the same resources. Since the resources are important, states work together to protect them. Suppose a river runs through several states. If one state passes laws to stop pollution, but the other states don't pass similar laws, it won't help the river.

The Mississippi River is home to many kinds of wildlife, including this Great Blue Heron.

The Mississippi River is an important resource for many states. Ron Kind is a government leader in Wisconsin. He is concerned about taking care of the river.

"We could work together . . . to draw attention to the resources that are needed along the Mississippi River."

Clean air is important, too. In the Northeast, for example, states are working together to pass laws to fight air pollution that affects all of them.

QUICK CHECK

Summarize Besides landforms, what are some other things that states in a region may share?

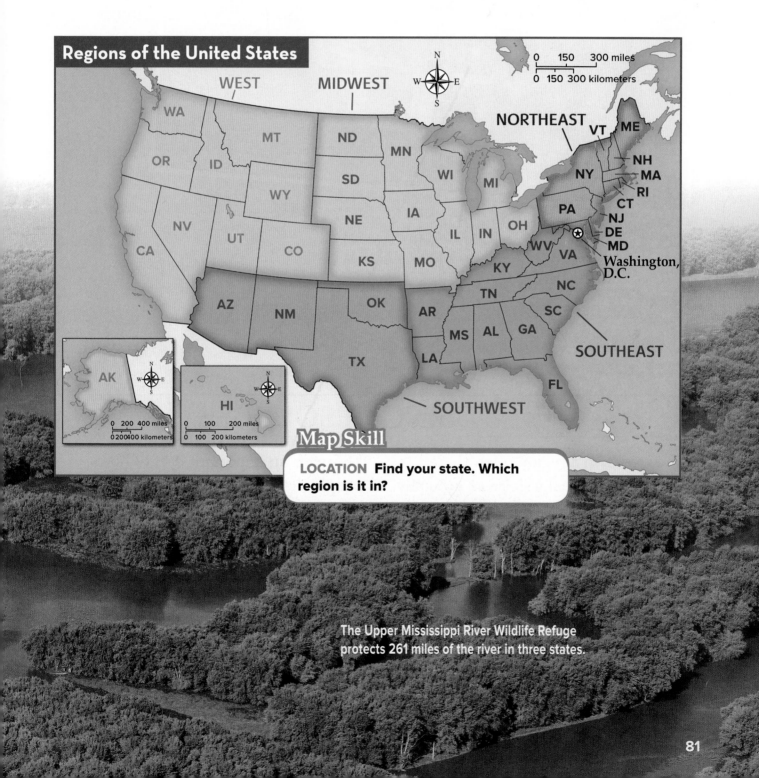

Regions of the United States

WEST

MIDWEST

NORTHEAST

SOUTHEAST

SOUTHWEST

0 150 300 miles
0 150 300 kilometers

WA
MT
OR
ID
NV
UT
WY
CA
CO
AZ
NM
ND
SD
NE
KS
OK
TX
MN
IA
MO
AR
LA
WI
MI
IL
IN
OH
KY
TN
MS
AL
GA
WV
VA
NC
SC
FL
PA
NY
VT
ME
NH
MA
RI
CT
NJ
DE
MD
Washington, D.C.

AK
0 200 400 miles
0 200 400 kilometers

HI
0 100 200 miles
0 100 200 kilometers

Map Skill

LOCATION Find your state. Which region is it in?

The Upper Mississippi River Wildlife Refuge protects 261 miles of the river in three states.

▲ Mining coal is important to the economy of the Southeast, but other parts of the country also depend on the Southeast's coal.

ⓒ USING RESOURCES

Since states in a region often share resources, they usually share an **economy**. This makes sense when you think that the economy is the way a region uses its resources to provide the things that people need. For example, **agriculture**, or farming, is very important in almost every state of the Midwest.

Another example is the coal-mining in the states of the Appalachian Mountains.

Mining is an important part of how people there make a living. So the people in this region share the same concerns. Since the states in this region share an economy, the people in those states are linked together.

Resources Link Regions

Today, states and regions are **interdependent**, or dependent on each other. We might live in Illinois but buy

(inset)abutyrin/Shutterstock.com, (bkgd)Creatas/SuperStock

▲ In many places, like in this mine in Montana, there is coal just underneath the surface.

oranges from Florida and grapes from California. The coal mined in Kentucky provides energy for people in other regions. Mining links the people of the Southeast to each other and to the rest of the country.

QUICK CHECK

Summarize **How does sharing resources in a region make states interdependent?**

Check Understanding

1. **VOCABULARY** Create a poster about your region. Be sure to illustrate each of the vocabulary words in your poster.

   region   economy   agriculture

2. **READING SKILL** **Compare and Contrast** Use the diagram to write about how geogrw aphic regions and cultural regions are alike and different.

   Different   Alike   Different

3. **Write About It** Write a paragraph about how people use a region's resources.

   EXPLORE The Big Idea

83

Our Country's Climate

The climate near Mount Hood in Oregon is good for growing pears and apples.

VOCABULARY

precipitation

rain shadow

lake effect

tornado

hurricane

READING SKILL

Compare and Contrast
Copy the diagram. Use it to compare and contrast the climate of places in the lesson.

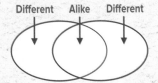

Different   Alike   Different

STANDARDS FOCUS

SOCIAL STUDIES   People, Places, and Environments

GEOGRAPHY   Physical Systems

Visual Preview

How does climate affect people in the United States?

A Distance from the equator and elevation affect climate.

B Mountains affect where rain falls.

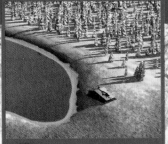

C The climate in an area is based on temperature and precipitation.

D Some places get extreme weather.

WEATHER AND CLIMATE

It's 10 degrees Fahrenheit outside on a typical winter day in Wisconsin. Meanwhile, it's 75 degrees in Florida! It's hard to believe both places are in the same country.

How's the weather today? Is it hot or cold? Is it raining? Weather describes the air and the temperature at a certain time and place. Climate is a little different. Climate is the pattern of weather over time—the kind of weather a place *usually* has.

On a spring day in Portland you might be comfortable outdoors wearing just a T-shirt. On the same day, only a few miles away at the top of Mt. Hood (11,234 feet high), you'd need a warm coat and mittens!

Temperature

The temperature is cold at the North and South Poles and hot at the equator. As you move away from the poles and closer to the equator, temperatures get warmer. The southern part of our country is closer to the equator, so temperatures there are usually warmer than in the North.

Elevation also affects temperature. The higher up a mountain you go, the colder it gets. Places at high elevations are usually colder than places at low elevations.

QUICK CHECK

Compare and Contrast How do temperatures at the North Pole and the equator differ?

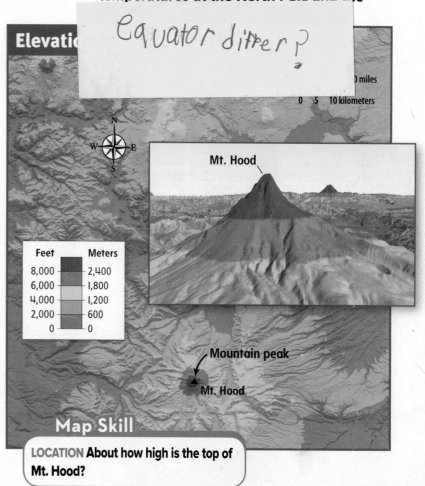

Elevation

Feet	Meters
8,000	2,400
6,000	1,800
4,000	1,200
2,000	600
0	0

Mt. Hood

Mountain peak

Mt. Hood

Map Skill

LOCATION **About how high is the top of Mt. Hood?**

Rain, rain, go away! Did you learn this rhyme when you were little? If you live in an area with very little **precipitation**, you might want the rain to fall. Precipitation is the moisture that falls to the ground as rain, sleet, snow, or hail.

Mountains and Rainfall

2 Clouds form.

3 When air reaches the mountains, it rises and cools.

1 The winds blowing in from the ocean usually carry a lot of moisture.

4 As the air cools, the moisture in the clouds turns into rain or snow. The side of the mountain that faces the ocean gets a lot of rain or snow.

Monkey Business Images/Shutterstock.com

Mountains and Rainfall

How do mountains affect rainfall? We say the side of the mountain that faces away from the ocean is in the **rain shadow**. The western slopes of Oregon's Cascade Mountains can get 200 inches of precipitation a year. Only a few dozen miles to the east, the other side of the mountains gets less than 8 inches of precipitation a year.

QUICK CHECK

Cause and Effect Why does the eastern side of the mountains in Oregon get very little rain or snow?

5 The side of the mountain away from the ocean might get very little rain or snow. By the time the winds cross over the mountain, almost all the moisture has fallen.

If you like snow, you might want to move to Houghton, Michigan, on Lake Superior. It gets an average of 177 inches of snow per year! Another snowy city is Rochester, New York, on Lake Ontario.

The reason these two cities get so much snow is something called **lake effect**. Large bodies of water such as big lakes or the ocean affect the climate of the land near them. How does this happen?

Lake Effect

WINTER ❶ In winter, winds blow from west to east across the Great Lakes. ❷ They pick up moisture from the lakes below. ❸ During the winter, the air over the land is usually colder than the air over the lakes. When the clouds blow over the cooler land, the moisture in the clouds is cooled, and snow falls.

SUMMER In summer, the land is warmer than the lake water. Winds blowing off the lakes bring cool air and help keep the temperatures on land from getting too high.

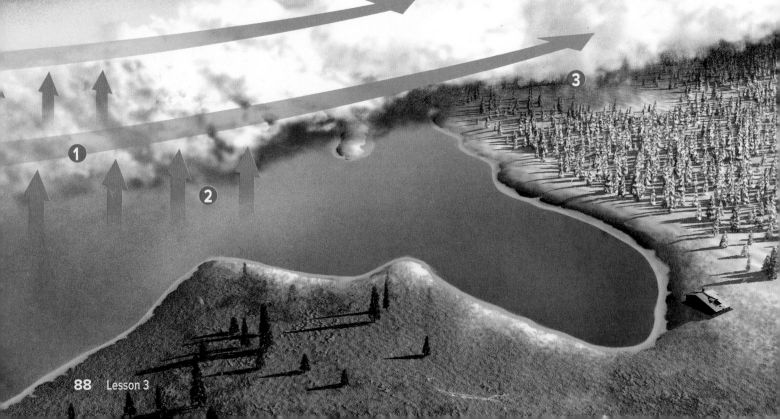

The weather is very different throughout the United States. However, weather tends to follow a pattern in an area. For example, in Seattle, Washington, rain usually falls between November and March, and daytime temperatures throughout the year are mild. Seattle has a wet, mild climate.

Data on average temperature and average precipitation help you figure out the climate of an area.

QUICK CHECK

Cause and Effect **Why do places near the Great Lakes often get a lot of snow?**

DataGraphic

United States: Average January Temperatures

The map shows the average temperatures across the United States in January. The graph shows the average rainfall in specific cities. Use the map and graph to answer the questions below.

United States: Average January Temperatures

January Average Daily Temperature

Degrees Fahrenheit	Degrees Celsius
60 to 80	16 to 27
40 to 60	4 to 16
20 to 40	-7 to 4
0 to 20	-18 to -7

— Region boundary
---- State boundary

Annual Precipitation

Think About IT

1. How do the temperatures in the northeast and southwest United States compare?

2. Which city receives more precipitation, Grand Island or Colorado Springs?

3. What part of the United States has the highest average temperature?

D EXTREME WEATHER

Some places in the United States can have extreme weather. Have you ever seen a movie called *The Wizard of Oz*? In that movie, a **tornado** picks up a girl named Dorothy and carries her off to a land called Oz. The movie is only a story, but tornadoes are real. A tornado is a strong wind that forms a funnel shape and moves over the ground very quickly, destroying everything in its path. Sometimes, tornadoes are powerful enough to pick up and move cars!

Tornadoes can happen anywhere in the United States, but they occur more often where cold air from Canada meets warm air coming up from the Gulf of Mexico. This area is called Tornado Alley, and it runs from central Texas through Oklahoma, Kansas, Nebraska, and Iowa.

Hurricanes are another kind of extreme weather. A hurricane is a storm with very strong winds and heavy rain. Hurricanes form over the warm water in the Atlantic Ocean to the south of the United States. As hurricanes move north, some of them may hit land in the Southeast.

Hurricane winds push water in front of them. The wind and water can be very dangerous and can cause terrible damage.

EVENT

In August 2005, **Hurricane Katrina** slammed into the Gulf Coast. It was one of the strongest hurricanes ever recorded to hit the United States. As a result of the storm, most of New Orleans flooded and many people died.

Rebuilding after Hurricane Katrina

Climate and Storms

There were a record number of hurricanes in the United States in 2005. One of them, Hurricane Katrina, caused extensive damage in New Orleans and other communities on the Gulf of Mexico.

It was one of the deadliest hurricanes in United States history and killed more than 1,200 people.

In 2012, Hurricane Sandy struck parts of the Atlantic coast. At the time, it was the second-costliest hurricane in United States history and had the largest diameter of any Atlantic hurricane on record.

Most scientists think that Earth's climate is growing warmer, heating the ocean waters and causing more severe storms. Scientists are studying weather patterns and learning new ways to predict hurricanes and other storms.

QUICK CHECK

Compare and Contrast What is the difference between a hurricane and a tornado?

◄ A research vehicle monitors the weather as a thunderstorm passes overhead.

Check Understanding

1. **VOCABULARY** Draw a picture to illustrate each word. Label the picture.

   tornado   rain shadow   lake effect

2. **READING SKILL** **Compare and Contrast** Use the chart to compare the temperature at the top of a mountain with the temperature at the mountain's base.

3. **Write About It** Write about the climate where you live. Then give two examples of ways people in your town have adapted to the climate.

Lesson 4

VOCABULARY

producer

capital resource

human resource

natural resource

interest

credit

READING SKILL

Compare and Contrast
Copy the chart. Fill it in with needs and wants.

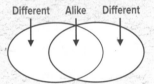

Different   Alike   Different

STANDARDS FOCUS

SOCIAL STUDIES Production, Distribution, and Consumption

GEOGRAPHY Human Systems

This boy is shopping for something he wants but doesn't need.

Our Economy

Visual Preview

How do resources affect the economic choices people make?

A Needs, wants, and scarcity are important parts of our economy.

B Businesses use natural resources, human resources, and capital resources.

C Banks loan money. People save money in a bank to earn interest.

D Businesses and consumers all play a role in our economy.

A NEEDS AND WANTS

What do you really need to live? Food? A home?
We call things like food, clothing, and shelter needs.
You can't live without them. Once you have met the most
basic needs, everything else is a want.

Wants are things you can live without. You don't need a pair of $100 sneakers to live, do you? You can buy an inexpensive pair of sneakers. Wants might make your life easier or more interesting, but you can live without them.

Scarcity

Now that you know the difference between what you need and what you want, let's talk about scarcity—when there isn't enough of what you need or want. Scarcity comes from the word scarce, which describes something that is hard to find or is in short supply. You could have a scarcity of money or a scarcity of a nonrenewable resource. For example, sometimes the world has a scarcity of oil.

When there is a scarcity of something, the price of the item usually goes up. Why? The price goes up because people will pay more for something that they want if it's hard to find.

In January, 2015, for example, the average price of a barrel of oil was $99. By October of that year, the average price of a barrel of oil dropped to $43, due in part to increased supply. The price dropped by more than half in less than a year.

QUICK CHECK

Compare and Contrast **What is the difference between needs and wants?**

During a gas shortage in New York, gas prices more than doubled at many stations. ▶

Farmer

Blacksmith

In the 1700s, people traded goods or services for things they needed.

B THE BASICS OF OUR ECONOMY

In the early days of our country, money was scarce. People grew or made just about everything they needed. Sometimes, people would grow or make a little extra of something. Then they might barter, or trade, for something they didn't have or could not grow or make.

Someone who was good at making one thing, might make them for everyone in the village in return for payment. A shoemaker might make shoes for everyone that he knew. Making shoes was that person's specialization.

People still bartered, though. The shoemaker might be paid with a couple of chickens, some soap, or a bag of grain. As businesses grew, people hired other workers to help them manufacture, or make large numbers of goods to sell.

People who make goods are called **producers**. They sell the products to consumers, the people who use them. But producers need things as well. At some point, everyone is a consumer. When you buy a hamburger, a computer game, or a movie ticket, you are a consumer, too.

Business Resource	Description
Capital Resources 	**Capital resources** are all the things businesses use to make, produce, or transport a good or service. They include computers, printers, machines, or even factories.
Natural Resources 	**Natural resources** are needed by many businesses. Farmers need soil to grow crops, computer manufacturers use metal to build their machines, and stores are heated with oil or natural gas.
Human Resources 	**Human resources** are the people who work for a business. Mail carriers are part of the human resources of the postal service. Teachers are part of the human resources of schools.

Chart Skill

How are capital resources different from human resources?

Business Resources

What would you need to run a business? Of course it depends on the kind of business you'd be running. You've learned that businesses need money to pay for all sorts of things to keep them going.

Businesses need other things to be successful. A business's spending can be broken down into three main categories— capital resources, natural resources, and human resources. The chart above shows the resources needed for a business. What kind of resource is a truck for a delivery business? What resource is the driver?

QUICK CHECK

Summarize **What are the three kinds of resources described in this section?**

Starting a business can be very expensive. In the last lesson, you read about the students who started Popcorn Mania. As you know, they needed to get capital resources to start the business.

Many business owners do the same thing the students did when they need capital resources. They go to banks to borrow money. Of course, banks are businesses. They need to make money, too! They make money by charging **interest**, or a fee, on the money they lend to people. For example, if a business owner borrows $10,000 from a bank, he or she will, over time, have to pay the bank $10,500. This includes the $10,000 loan plus $500 in interest.

Banks also provide credit cards. **Credit** lets businesses and people buy goods now and pay for them later. If you use a credit card to buy a cell phone, the bank pays the store the cost of the phone. You pay the bank at a later time. Since you are borrowing money from the bank, the bank charges you interest until the loan is paid.

Many families have savings accounts that earn interest. ▼

(c)©Hiya Images/Corbis, (bkgd)Tetra Images/PunchStock

Spending and Saving

Where does a bank get its money? In part, from families like yours. Your family might have a savings account at a bank. This is your family's turn to earn some interest. Since most banks use money in savings accounts to make loans to others, banks usually pay interest on the money in savings accounts. They're paying a small fee to your family for the use of their money.

Savings accounts are often linked to ATMs. Do you know what ATM stands for? Automated Teller Machine—a teller is a person who works at a bank. The teller gives people money from their bank accounts. Since these machines do a similar job, they are called automated tellers. You can take out or put money into these machines. Some of them even let you pay bills. To use them all you need is a bank card, a secret code, and of course money in the bank.

There are three main reasons why people open savings accounts. The first is to keep their money safe. The second is to help them save for the future. Finally, some people might save for a vacation or new roof. What would you save for?

SAVINGS BANK

Laura Leacock
2525 Sycamore Lane
Brooklyn, NY, 11222

Date: 11-03-15

| Personal Savings | 101767576 |

Account Number: ....

Deposits/Credits	Deposit $100.00
10/15	Deposit $37.00
10/25	

Interest	$100.00
	$0.07
Average Balance	
Interest paid this period	

| Account Balance | $ 137.07 |

Savings

ATMs, which are owned by the banks, do many of the same things as bank tellers.

QUICK CHECK

Compare and Contrast How is using a credit card different than using a bank card?

D CARING FOR THE ECONOMY

Circular Flow

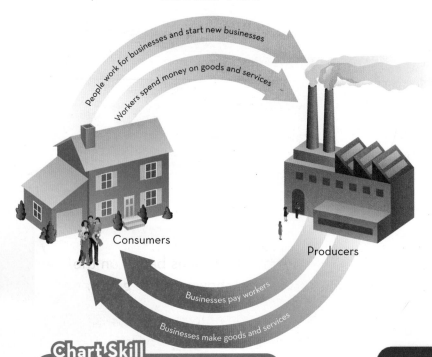

People work for businesses and start new businesses

Workers spend money on goods and services

Consumers

Producers

Businesses pay workers

Businesses make goods and services

Chart Skill

How do workers spend the money they earn?

The Circular Flow chart on this page shows how money moves through our economy.

QUICK CHECK

Draw Conclusions **How is the economy helped when businesses hire new workers?**

Just as consumers look after their money, the United States government tracks money, too. The Federal Reserve System controls banks across the country. The United States Department of the Treasury collects taxes from workers. This is how local governments get money to build highways, schools, parks, and more.

It All Works Together

Everyone works together to make the economy run smoothly. Producers make goods and services, businesses hire workers and pay them for the jobs they do, workers use their pay to buy goods and services and start new businesses.

Check Understanding

1. **VOCABULARY** Draw a chart that illustrates how individuals and businesses are affected by these vocabulary words.

   interest   credit

2. **READING SKILL** **Compare and Contrast** Use the chart to write about your needs and wants.

   Different   Alike   Different

3. **Write About It** Write a paragraph about the businesses in your community. What do they do?

(c)©Hiya Images/Corbis

Chart and Graph Skills

Read Line Graphs

VOCABULARY

graph

line graph

The number of Internet users in our country has changed over time. One way to learn how it has changed is to look at a **graph**. Graphs are diagrams that show information in a clear way. **Line graphs** show change over time.

Learn It

- The line graph shows how the number of Internet users in the United States changed between 2005 and 2014.

- Labels on the side of each graph tell you the number of people. Labels on the bottom show the year. The top graph shows every other year.

Try It

- How many Internet users were there in 2010?

- Between what two years did Internet usage decrease?

Apply It

- Write two sentences based on the information shown on the graph.

- How can line graphs help you to compare and contrast information?

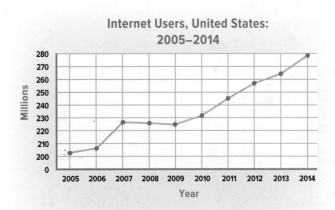

Internet Users, United States: 2005–2014

Lesson 5

VOCABULARY

constitution

legislative branch

executive branch

judicial branch

veto

municipal

READING SKILL

Compare and Contrast
Use the chart below to compare the duties of state government with those of local government.

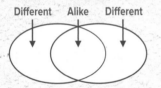

Different   Alike   Different

STANDARDS FOCUS

| SOCIAL STUDIES | Power, Authority, and Governance |
| GEOGRAPHY | Human Systems |

State and Local Governments

Local governments provide firefighters that protect our towns and cities.

Visual Preview

Why do state and local governments work together?

A State and local governments make laws and provide services.

B The three branches in state governments each have different powers.

C Local governments provide services, make laws, and collect taxes.

SHARING POWER

On the way to school, you notice that the traffic light isn't working at a busy intersection. Who should you call to get the traffic light fixed? Would you call the President to fix a traffic light?

Maybe you've heard someone say, "The government should do something about that!" What exactly is the government, anyway?

The President is just one part of the government. A government is the people and laws that run a town, county, state, or country. In the United States, government responsibilities are shared. One person, or even one group, does not run everything. States, counties, cities, and towns all have their own governments. These smaller governments create laws and provide services for smaller areas. They share power and responsibility.

Some government duties belong to the states. Others belong to towns and cities. Look at the chart to see the duties each level of government takes care of.

QUICK CHECK

Compare and Contrast How are the different levels of government the same? How are they different?

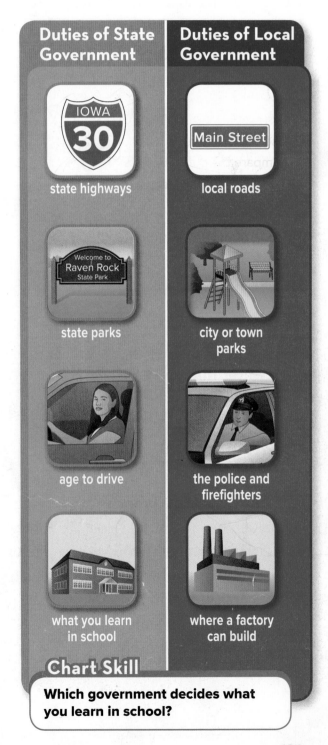

Duties of State Government	Duties of Local Government
IOWA 30 state highways	Main Street local roads
Welcome to Raven Rock State Park state parks	city or town parks
age to drive	the police and firefighters
what you learn in school	where a factory can build

Chart Skill

Which government decides what you learn in school?

101

HOW STATE GOVERNMENTS WORK

Each state has its own **constitution**, or plan of government, and laws. Running a state is a big job. The constitution of a state divides state governments into three branches, or parts. The branches work together to run the state. No branch has total control. This system of sharing power is called checks and balances.

Study the charts to see what the branches do and to see how a bill becomes a law.

QUICK CHECK

Cause and Effect **What can the state court do if it thinks a law is wrong?**

Three Jobs, Three Branches

Legislative

Executive

Judicial

The **legislative branch** makes the laws. Most legislatures have two parts—an assembly and a senate. Voters in most states elect both state senators and assembly members.

The governor is head of the **executive branch**. He or she is the highest elected state official. The governor plans the state budget and decides whether to sign a bill into law.

The **judicial branch** decides whether someone has broken the law. It also interprets laws. If the state's court believes a new law goes against the state's constitution, the court can reject the law.

How a Bill Becomes Law

1. Citizens develop an idea for a bill.

2. Members of the State Assembly or the Senate propose the bill.

3. The Assembly and the Senate vote to approve the bill.

yes
no ✓

4. The governor signs the bill. If he or she chooses not to sign the bill, it is called a **veto**.

5. If the bill is vetoed, another vote can be taken. If more than 2/3 of the assembly and the senate vote to approve it, the bill becomes a law.

Chart Skill

What is the first step in making a bill into a law?

Our country is made up of 50 states, but each state has smaller parts, usually called counties. A small state such as Connecticut has only 8 counties, while larger states have more. Arkansas, for example, has 75 counties. Each county has a government to provide services. Some county governments provide law enforcement for areas that don't have their own police department.

Cities and towns also have governments. These are called local or **municipal** governments. Some are led by mayors. Others are led by city managers, who are chosen members of the city council.

Local governments provide services and make laws. They decide how land will be used and they collect taxes. City governments provide park workers to keep the parks clean.

◀ Local government runs buses and subways.

Local government takes care of local streets, signs, and lights. ▼

Taxes

Where do governments get money for the services they provide? Most of it comes from taxes. State governments may charge taxes on people's income. Local governments tax property and sometimes income. Homeowners pay taxes on homes and land. Some states and counties have a sales tax on goods that people buy. Businesses also pay taxes.

Tax money is used for many things. It buys equipment such as fire trucks, police cars, and stoplights. Taxes also pay the salaries of people who do jobs that maintain our cities, such as city park workers and sanitation workers.

QUICK CHECK

Summarize What are some kinds of taxes that people pay?

◄ Park workers work for local government.

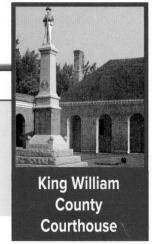
Check Understanding

1. **VOCABULARY** Write a sentence with each of the following vocabulary words.

   legislative branch   executive branch

2. **READING SKILL Compare and Contrast** Use your chart to write about your local government.

Different   Alike   Different

3. **Write About It** Write a paragraph about how governments help people adapt to where they live.

EXPLORE The Big Idea

Map and Globe Skills

Understand Latitude and Longitude

VOCABULARY

grid

latitude

longitude

degree

parallel

meridian

Every place on Earth has an "address" based on its location. To describe the address of a place, geographers use a map **grid**. Grids are lines that cross each other. The grid system is based on a set of lines called **latitude** and **longitude**. Lines of latitude measure how far north or south a place is from the equator. Lines of longitude measure distance east or west. Lines of latitude and longitude measure distance in **degrees**. The equator is zero degrees. The symbol for degrees is °.

Lines of Latitude

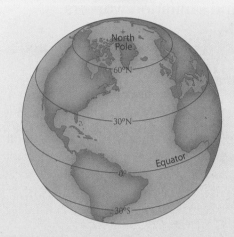

Learn It

- Lines of latitude are also called parallels. Lines of latitude north of the equator are labeled N. Lines of latitude south of the equator are labeled S.

- Lines of longitude are also called meridians. The Prime Meridian is the starting place for measuring distance from east to west. Lines of longitude east of the Prime Meridian are labeled E. Lines of longitude west of the Prime Meridian are labeled W.

- Look at Map A. Lines of longitude and latitude cross to form a global grid. It can be used to locate any place on Earth.

- To describe a location on a map, give the latitude first and the longitude second.

Lines of Longitude

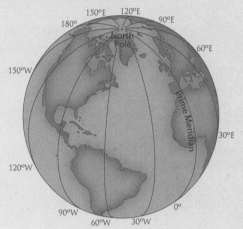

MAP A

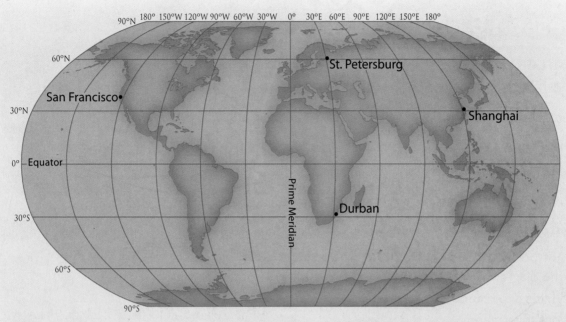

Try It

- Locate Durban, South Africa, on Map A.
  Durban is east of the Prime Meridian.
  Durban is located at about 30°S, 30°E.

Apply It

- Use Map A to locate the cities closest
  to these latitude and longitude
  addresses. Name each city.

  30°N, 120°W   60°N, 30°E

- Look at Map B. Give the latitude and
  longitude closest to Decatur.

MAP B

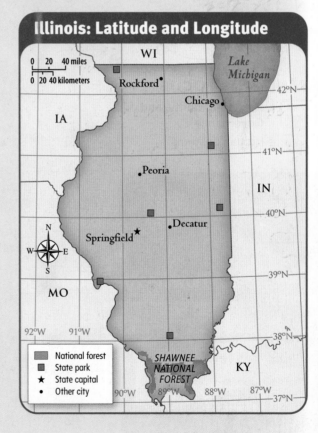

Illinois: Latitude and Longitude

Our Nation's Government

VOCABULARY

federal

democracy

citizen

reservation

sovereign

READING SKILL

Compare and Contrast
Copy the diagram. Fill it in with facts about federal and tribal government.

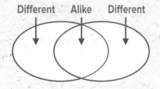

Different   Alike   Different

STANDARDS FOCUS

SOCIAL STUDIES   Power, Authority, and Governance

GEOGRAPHY   Human Systems

The United States Capitol

Visual Preview

How has the national government adapted to meet people's needs?

A The United States is a democracy. Citizens elect leaders to represent them.

B The United States government has three branches.

C Many Native Americans have their own tribal governments.

OUR NATIONAL GOVERNMENT

The United States Constitution begins with "We the People." That shows that "the people" control the government. That includes you! What are some ways that our government represents the people?

The government of the United States is called the national, or **federal**, government. It provides services for people in all 50 states and United States territories. These federal services include our United States military—the army, navy, air force, marines, and coast guard. The federal government also prints money and postage stamps. It issues passports and makes sure that food and drugs are safe for people to use.

Choosing Leaders

The United States is a **democracy**, a government that is run by its people. As soon as you turn 18, you are able to vote. You have a say in who runs the government.

Since the United States is so large, individuals do not run the country directly. Instead, the **citizens** elect representatives to pass laws in Congress. A citizen is a person who is born in a country or who has earned the right to become a member of that country by law. Citizens elect state

▲ Voting is every citizen's right and responsibility.

and local representatives, as well as the President, in national elections.

QUICK CHECK

Compare and Contrast What is the difference between a citizen and a representative?

Our national government, centered in Washington, D.C., has the same three branches that state governments have: executive, legislative, and judicial. Just like the branches of state government, each branch of the federal government has its own duties and responsibilities. Our national government also has a system of checks and balances so that one branch does not have too much power.

Executive Branch

The President is head of the executive branch and is elected for a term of four years. The President

▶ Carries out laws

▶ Leads the military

▶ Plans the national budget that tells how the government will spend its money

▶ Meets with leaders of other countries

▶ Appoints a group of advisors who help with important decisions

Legislative Branch

The legislative branch of the federal government is called the Congress. It has two parts, the Senate and the House of Representatives.

▶ The Senate has 100 senators, two from each state.

▶ The number of representatives in the House of Representatives depends on a state's population—the larger the population, the more representatives there will be in Congress.

Congress:

▶ Makes laws for our country

▶ Decides how much money to spend

Judicial Branch

The judicial branch of the federal government interprets the laws of our country.

▶ The Supreme Court is the highest court in the country.

▶ The federal judicial branch includes all the federal courts in the country.

QUICK CHECK

Summarize What does the judicial branch do?

Global Connections

The United Nations

After World War II ended, leaders from the United States and other powerful nations wanted to find a way to keep peace in the world. They formed the United Nations (UN). Member nations promise to work out their differences peacefully. The United States has been an important member of the UN from the beginning.

The UN also works to help children and to prevent and cure disease. The United Nations Children's Fund (UNICEF) is the branch of the UN that helps children around the world.

New York City

▲ The UN was formed in 1945 by 50 countries. Its headquarters is in New York City.

Teachers from UNICEF help provide education to children all over the world. ▼

(t)Purestock/SuperStock, (b)Carrie Antal/USAID

Ⓒ TRIBAL GOVERNMENT

In addition to local, state, and national governments, there are also tribal governments in the United States. Some Native American communities have tribal governments.

▲ Tribal leaders attend the White House Tribal Conference to discuss Native American affairs.

All Native Americans are citizens of the United States. They vote in local, state, and national elections, and follow United States law. However, many Native Americans live on **reservations**—land set aside for their use. These Native Americans are citizens of tribal governments. Most reservations are **sovereign**, or independent. Native Americans who live on reservations elect their own leaders and make their own laws. At the same time, they follow local, state, and national laws.

The Hopi Reservation in Arizona, for example, has a Hopi Tribal Council. This council takes care of reservation business and makes laws for the Hopi who live on the reservation. The council also works with other Native American groups, with the Arizona state government, and with the national government on issues that are important to the Hopi.

QUICK CHECK

Summarize **What do tribal governments do?**

Check Understanding

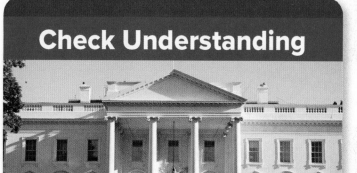

1. **VOCABULARY** Write a paragraph about our national government using the following vocabulary words.
   federal   **democracy**   **citizen**

2. **READING SKILL Compare and Contrast** Use the diagram to write about the differences between a tribal government and the national government.

3. **Write About It** Write a paragraph about how the national government affects the people of the United States.

Lesson 7

Our Democratic Values

VOCABULARY

jury

patriotism

rule of law

justice

READING SKILL

Compare and Contrast
Copy the diagram below. FIll it in with facts about our rights and responsibilities.

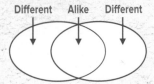

Different   Alike   Different

STANDARDS FOCUS

 SOCIAL STUDIES   Civic Ideals and Practices

GEOGRAPHY   Human Systems

Statue of Liberty

Visual Preview

What democratic values do Americans share?

A The Declaration of Independence states that all people are created equal.

B Americans value diversity and work for the common good.

C Americans value truth, equality, justice, and the rule of law.

A RIGHTS AND RESPONSIBILITIES

In 1776 people living in the American colonies decided they did not want to live under British rule any longer. They wrote a document called the Declaration of Independence. It told the world that the colonists had the right to break away from Great Britain.

The colonists knew they didn't want another government in which they didn't have a say. They asked Thomas Jefferson to write the Declaration of Independence. In it, he wrote that all people are "created equal" and share rights that no one can take from them. He said that it was the job of governments to protect these rights.

All men are created equal.
—THOMAS JEFFERSON

Three important rights that unite all Americans are "life, liberty, and the pursuit of happiness." *Life* means that we have the right to live free of violence. *Liberty* describes our right to act, speak, and think the way we please. The *pursuit of happiness* is the freedom to search for things that make us happy. Responsibilities accompany these rights.

Being a Responsible Citizen

One of our most important rights, the right to vote, is also an important responsibility. When we vote, we let our representatives and others know how we feel about things. Voters choose who will make our laws.

In addition to voting, all citizens are asked to pay taxes and follow laws. At times, citizens must serve on a jury. A jury is a group of citizens in a court of law who decide whether a person is innocent or guilty. By doing all these things and acting as a responsible citizen, Americans protect their rights and the rights of their family, community, state, and country.

QUICK CHECK

Compare and Contrast **What is the difference between the rights and responsibilities of voting?**

A group of people gathered in 1963 to hear Martin Luther King, Jr., give a speech about the rights of all Americans.

B WORKING TOGETHER

Not only do we have rights and responsibilities, but we have power as citizens. In lesson 6, you learned how a bill becomes a law. That's just one of the ways citizens work together to change things.

The Common Good

Americans also make changes by working for the common good—what is best for everyone. For example, a company wanted to build a new store in a city in Oregon. People in the community worried that the store would create too much traffic and cause pollution of nearby streams. After many long discussions with the company, the community convinced it to build elsewhere. The community worked together for the common good and won!

Organizations also work for the common good. One example is the Red Cross. It works to help people in need in the United States and around the world.

Some people work for the common good by volunteering. When you volunteer, you help others without expecting anything in return. There are many ways to volunteer. Some

(t)National Archives and Records Administration (NWDNS-306-SSM-4A-35-6)

◀ These students show their patriotism by using chalk to color a flag.

people join the Peace Corps, a group of Americans who help people around the world. Others volunteer in their own communities.

Patriotism

Working toward the common good is also part of patriotism. **Patriotism** is the respect and loyal support of one's country. You show patriotism when you wave a flag, recite the Pledge of Allegiance, or sing the national anthem. You're also being patriotic when you step in to stop someone from being treated unfairly and when you tell the truth, especially when it's difficult.

Calvin Coolidge, President of the United States from 1923 to 1929, said:

"Patriotism is easy to understand in America; it means looking out for yourself by looking out for your country."

QUICK CHECK

Main Idea and Details What are some ways you can show your patriotism?

Citizenship
Volunteering

When a tornado destroyed some houses in their town, students wanted to help. They decided to volunteer at a charity drive. They helped gather and distribute canned food along with many other items such as shampoo and soap to people in need.

Write About It Write a letter describing how you would help victims of a natural disaster such as a hurricane or tornado.

As Americans and as patriots, we value our nation's diversity. People in our country are from many different races, cultures, and ethnic groups. People have come to the United States from every continent and from every country in the world. This is one of the things that makes our country special. Look at the pie chart below to see our nation's diversity.

Americans of every age, race, and ethnicity share similar values. ▼

Justice and the Rule of Law

In a country made up of different people with different ideas and goals, Americans sometimes disagree. When we do, we rely on laws for solutions. Americans believe in the **rule of law**. All of us, even the President, are ruled by our laws. Laws apply to all people equally. **Justice**, or fair treatment, is an important value in our laws. If Americans believe they have been treated unfairly, they can go to court and seek justice.

Truth is an American value, too, and an important part of our laws. We must tell the truth in court, so that no one goes to jail because of lies. We must tell the truth in business, so people are not cheated out of their money. Our government must also be truthful, so voters can make decisions based on facts they can trust.

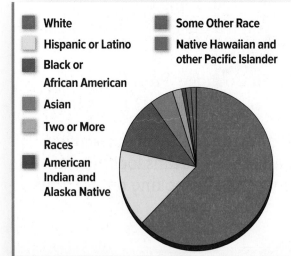

United States Cultural Groups, 2010

- White
- Hispanic or Latino
- Black or African American
- Asian
- Two or More Races
- American Indian and Alaska Native
- Some Other Race
- Native Hawaiian and other Pacific Islander

Chart Skill

What is the largest cultural group in the United States?

monkeybusinessimages/iStock/Getty Images

◄ Martin Luther King, Jr. and his wife Coretta Scott King fought for fairness for Americans of all races.

Fighting for Fairness

Treating people equally is an American value. It's also stated in the Declaration of Independence. There have been many times in our history when some Americans were not treated fairly. Native Americans had land taken from them. Africans were brought here in slavery. German and Japanese Americans faced discrimination during the world wars.

Throughout our history, however, people have stood up to fight for equality. Responsible and patriotic Americans have demanded that our country live up to its values.

QUICK CHECK

Main Idea and Details **Why is truth an important American value?**

Check Understanding

1. **VOCABULARY** Write one sentence for each vocabulary word.

   justice   patriotism

2. **READING SKILL** **Compare and Contrast** Use the chart to write a sentence about your responsibilities.

3. **Write About It** Write a paragraph about how people's idea of the common good might differ from place to place in our country.

Vocabulary

Copy the sentences below. Use the list of vocabulary words to fill in the blanks.

region **precipitation**

profit **interest**

1. When banks lend money, they charge ____.

2. ____ is moisture that falls to the ground as rain, sleet, hail, or snow.

3. An area with common features is a ____.

4. ____ is money a business earns after it pays for all its costs.

Comprehension and Critical Thinking

5. What has caused erosion in the Appalachian Mountains?

6. Why does a bank charge interest on the money it lends?

7. **Critical Thinking** Why do state and local governments have different jobs and responsibilities?

8. **Reading Skill** What is the difference between weather and climate?

Skill

Use Line Graphs

Write a complete sentence to answer each question.

9. How has the population of Tennessee changed?

10. About how much has the population brown between 1960 and 2010?

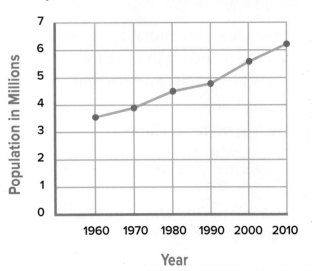

Population of Tennessee, 1960–2010

Test Preparation

Read the passage. Then answer the questions.

> The United States is a large country, and one place in our country can be very different from another. For example, Florida has very different landforms and climate than Alaska. The two states also have different natural resources.
>
> States that are near each other usually have a lot in common. Both Iowa and Nebraska are in the Great Plains. Arizona and New Mexico share desert areas. To help us understand our country more easily, we can divide states into regions. A region is an area with common features that set it apart from other areas. Regions are based on things such as shared landforms and climate.

1. What is the main idea of this passage?

A. Iowa and Nebraska are neighbors.

B. We divide our country into regions to make it easier to understand.

C. The United States is a large country.

D. Florida is warmer than Alaska.

2. Based on the passage, which conclusion can you draw?

A. Florida and Alaska are in the same region.

B. All states in the same region have desert areas.

C. States that are in the same region usually have different climates.

D. Arizona and New Mexico are probably in the same region.

3. What does the passage say about Florida and Alaska?

A. The states have natural resources.

B. Florida and Alaska have different resources, climate, and landforms.

C. Florida and Alaska are states.

D. The two states share landforms.

4. Describe why it might be important to protect the different landforms of the United States.

The Big Idea Activities

How do people meet their needs?

Write About the Big Idea

Expository Essay
Use your Unit 2 foldable to help you write an essay. Answer the Big Idea question—How do people meet their needs? Write an essay about one of the regions of the United States. Your essay should answer the Big Idea question. You may choose to describe the region's geography, climate, and resources.

Travel Advertisement

Work in a small group to create a colorful and exciting brochure or poster for a region of the United States.

1. Each group should chose a region of the United States to promote.

2. Consider including information about the region's climate, natural resources, tourist attractions, cities, or national parks.

3. You may draw pictures or create a collage from newspapers or magazines.

4. Each member of the group should present some information about the region.

(tl)©Monashee Frantz/age fotostock

Unit 3

EXPLORE The Big Idea

Essential Question
What causes a region to change?

FOLDABLES™
Study Organizer

Main Idea and Details
Use a layered book foldable to take notes as you read Unit 3. The title of the foldable should be **The Northeast**. Label the three tabs **Geography**, **Economy**, and **People**.

People
Economy
Geography
The Northeast

LOG ON
For more about Unit 3 go to
connectED.mcgraw-hill.com

The Northeast

PEOPLE, PLACES, AND EVENTS

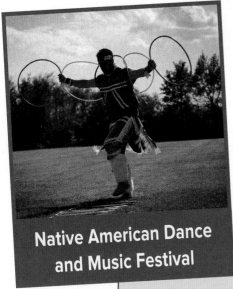

Native American Dance and Music Festival

The Iroquois People

The Eastern Woodlands were once home to many groups of Native Americans. One large group, **the Iroquois people**, partnered with five Native American groups.

Today visit the Ganondagan State Historic Site and attend the **Native American Dance and Music Festival**.

Immigrants

Ellis Island

The United States began to grow rapidly in the late 1800s. **Immigrants** arrived looking for a better life. After 1892, most immigrants entered the United States through the immigration center on **Ellis Island** in New York harbor.

Today you can visit Ellis Island and learn about immigration.

(tl)Design Pics/Darren Greenwood, (tr)©iStockphoto.com/SkyF, (bl)Library of Congress, Prints and Photographs Division [LC-DIG-nclc-05054], (br)Ron Chapple Stock/Alamy

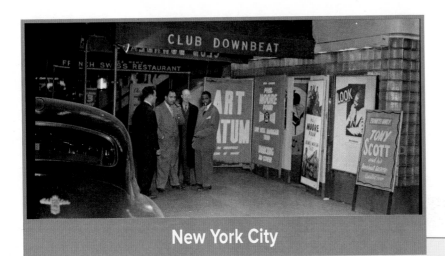

New York City

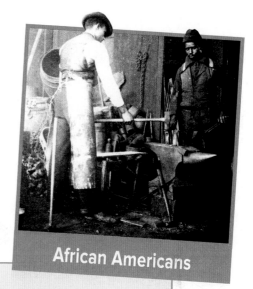

African Americans

In the early 1900s, thousands of **African Americans** moved north in the Great Migration to find work. Many settled in Newark, New Jersey, and **Harlem in New York City**.

Today you can learn more about African American communities at the Anacostia Community Museum in Washington, D.C.

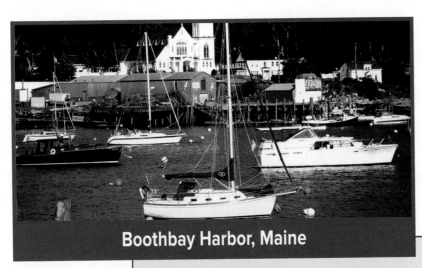

Boothbay Harbor, Maine

Annual Fisherman's Festival

Along much of the Northeast coast, small villages and towns grew out of the fishing industry. One of these is **Boothbay Harbor, Maine**.

Today you can celebrate Boothbay Harbor's heritage as a fishing village during the **Annual Fisherman's Festival**.

(tl)William P. Gottlieb/Ira and Leonore S. Gershwin Fund Collection, Music Division, Library of Congress [LC-GLB13-0833], (tr)Library of Congress, Prints and Photographs Division [LC-USZ62-101316], (bl)©Digital Vision/Getty Images, (br)Willard/Getty Images

Northeast Region

The Northeast is home to exciting places like our nation's capital.

1 Snowboarding is a popular winter activity in the mountains of the Northeast.

6 Pennsylvania is home to one of the world's largest chocolate factories—Hershey's Chocolate World.

5 Cape Cod, Massachusetts, is a popular destination.

Lak Eri

2 About 12 million tourists visit Niagara Falls every year.

3 Maine produces 75 percent of the lobster caught in the United States.

Allagash Wilderness Waterway

CANADA

Lake Ontario

St. Lawrence River

ADIRONDACK MOUNTAINS

Lake Placid

1

Montpelier

ME

Augusta

3

White Mountain National Forest

VT

NH

Concord

2

Allegheny National Forest

NY

Albany

Hudson River

ATLANTIC OCEAN

Boston

MA

Cape Cod

5

Hartford

Providence

CT

RI

4 The Statue of Liberty is a symbol of freedom around the world.

APPALACHIAN MOUNTAINS

PA

Susquehanna R.

Hershey's Chocolate World

6

Harrisburg

Statue of Liberty

Long Island

4

New York

Trenton

NJ

Pine Barrrens

Potomac River

MD

Dover

Washington, DC

Annapolis

DE

Delaware Bay

N

W E

S

0   50   100 miles

0   50   100 kilometers

Chesapeake Bay

Photographed by MR.ANUJAK JAIMOOK/Getty Images, (tr)lynx/iconotec.com/Glow Images, (br)Image Source/Getty Images

The Geography of the Northeast

VOCABULARY

glacier

bay

fuel

fall line

tourist

READING SKILL

Main Idea and Details
Copy the chart below. Fill it in with details about how the Northeast was formed.

Main Idea	Details

STANDARDS FOCUS

SOCIAL STUDIES — People, Places, and Environments

GEOGRAPHY — The Uses of Geography

Visual Preview

How has the geography of the Northeast affected the region?

A Animals and plants live in the Northeast, which was shaped by glaciers.

B Cities grew around bays because they provided protection for ships.

C The Northeast has many natural resources that include forests and water.

D The Northeast has four seasons.

Ⓐ THE NORTHEAST LONG AGO

The 11 states that make up the Northeast share a rich geography,
sprinkled with mountains, hills, lakes, rivers, and forests.
Most of them were formed long ago.

The world's oldest chain of mountains, the Appalachians, stretches from Maine in the North to Alabama in the South. Year after year of wind, water, and ice eroded the mountains' sharp and pointed peaks into rolling hills. The Appalachians saw a good deal of bad weather many years ago. Today the Northeast still experiences harsh weather.

The Ice Was Here

Once, much of northern North America was covered with large, moving sheets of ice called **glaciers**. In some places, these glaciers were as much as one mile thick. As they moved south, the glaciers flattened the land, crushed boulders, and dug giant holes in the ground.

When the climate warmed, the ice melted. The holes filled with water and became Lake Ontario, Lake Erie, and the Finger Lakes of New York State. Now, many animals and plants live in these areas.

QUICK CHECK

Main Idea and Details **How were the Appalachian Mountains shaped?**

Plants and Animals of the Northeast

White Oak Tree

Mallard Duck

New England Aster

Blue Crab

Common Buttercup

Moose

A RICH LAND

The Northeastern coastline is dotted with **bays**. Bays are areas where the ocean is partly surrounded by land. This creates sheltered places called harbors, where ships can be safe from storms. Early settlers anchored their ships in these harbors. Over time, large cities including Baltimore, Maryland, and New York City, grew around these harbors.

Forests

At one time, forests carpeted the Northeast. They were a valuable resource for Native Americans and European settlers. Native Americans used tree trunks to build homes and carve canoes. European settlers used trees to build homes and ships. Both groups burned wood as **fuel**, something that produces energy.

New York Harbor and Manhattan

(bkgd) TongRo Image Stock/Alamy

Over time, many Northeastern forests were replaced by roads, farms, and towns, but trees are still an important resource in the region. The two main types of trees that grow in the Northeast are broadleaf trees, which lose their leaves each winter, and needle-leaf trees (also known as evergreens) which keep their leaves all year long. The maple is a broadleaf tree, and the spruce and pine are needle-leaf trees.

QUICK CHECK

Summarize **Where did early settlers anchor their ships?**

PLACES

Adirondack State Park is home to the largest "old growth" forest in the Northeast. An old growth forest is one in which the trees have never been cut down. Many animals, including black bears, live in old growth forests.

Black Bear in a Park

Spruce needles and cones

Maple leaf

▲ Maple syrup comes from Maple trees, which are found throughout the Northeast.

MOUNTAINS AND WATER

We've talked so far about forests and coastlines. Do you want to know what else is in the Northeast? Mountains, lots of them! Almost every Northeastern state has mountains. The Appalachian Mountains include smaller mountain ranges, such as the Green Mountains of Vermont and the Adirondack Mountains, which extend from Canada to New York.

There's a lot of water, too. Many rivers flow down these mountains. On the east side of the mountains, in areas where the land suddenly drops, then flattens into a plain, the flowing rivers turn into splashing waterfalls. Keep an eye out for these **fall lines** where land drops sharply to lower land below. You may see a waterfall!

Niagara Falls is a set of three separate waterfalls on the border between the United States and Canada.

Photographed by MR.ANUJAK JAIMOOK/Getty Images

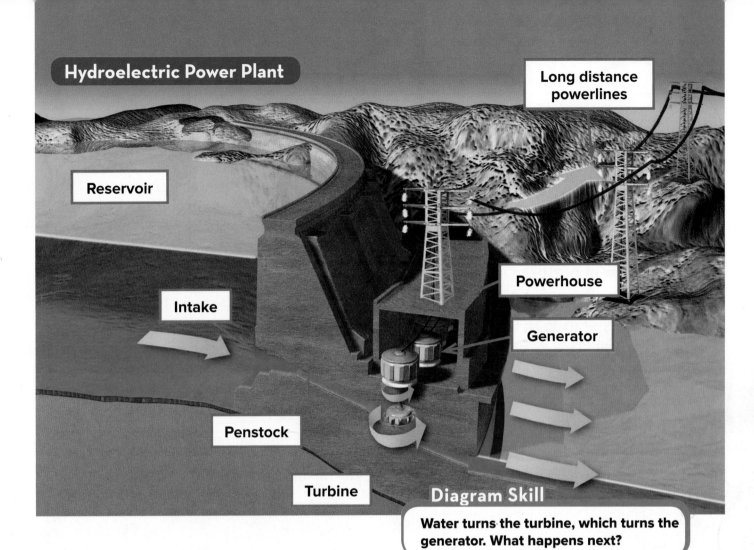

Hydroelectric Power Plant

Reservoir

Long distance powerlines

Intake

Powerhouse

Generator

Penstock

Turbine

Diagram Skill

Water turns the turbine, which turns the generator. What happens next?

All this water is used as a resource to produce energy for machines. Settlers used waterfalls to turn the wheels of their mills that ground grain. Water power is still used to run machines, such as those that create electricity.

The mountains and waters of the Northeast provide other resources, too. The mountains contain minerals such as coal. The region's bays and lakes, and of course the Atlantic Ocean, also offer resources—foods such as fish, crabs, and lobsters.

QUICK CHECK

Summarize What are some resources found in the Northeast?

Clams can be found along the coast of the Northeast. ▼

D CLIMATE OF THE NORTHEAST

The Northeast has four seasons, but there are differences in the seasons within the region. At high elevations, such as the mountains of Maine, the climate is colder than in lower areas. In southern areas, such as coastal Maryland, the climate is warmer than in northern areas.

One thing all the states in the region share is precipitation in the form of snow and rain. The precipitation keeps the rivers full and forests and farmlands growing.

Much of the precipitation comes from storms that strike the region in the fall and winter. These are known as "nor'easters" (that's short for north-eastern). Lighthouses were built all along the northeastern coastline to help sailors see the land at night during storms and fog.

Portland Head Light, a lighthouse near Portland, Maine, opened in 1791.

Fall Colors

In early fall, temperatures drop, and daylight hours shorten. These changes cause the green leaves of broadleaf trees to turn brilliant shades of orange, red, yellow, and brown. Many **tourists**, or people who travel to visit other places, travel to the Northeast each fall to see the colorful changing leaves.

QUICK CHECK

Compare and Contrast **How is the climate in coastal Maryland different from the climate in the mountains of Maine?**

Check Understanding

1. **VOCABULARY** Write a sentence for each of the vocabulary words.

   glacier   fuel   fall line

2. **READING SKILL Main Idea and Details** Use the Main Idea chart to write about the geography of the Northeast.

Main Idea	Details

3. **Write About It** Write a paragraph about how European settlers' use of forests caused the region to change.

134 Lesson 1   (t)Siede Preis/Getty Images; (b)Design Pics/Bilderbuch; (br) TongRo Image Stock/Alamy

Map and Globe Skills

Compare Maps at Different Scales

VOCABULARY

map scale

small-scale map

large-scale map

Maps can't show places in the size they are on Earth. Instead, they use a **map scale** to tell you the actual size of an area on the map.

Map A is a **small-scale map**. It covers a large area, but can't include many details. Map B is a **large-scale map**. It shows many details of a smaller area.

Learn It

- Map A shows Maine. It shows a large area without many details. This is a small-scale map.

- Map B shows Acadia National Park on Maine's coast. It shows a smaller area with more details and information. It is a large-scale map.

Try It

- Which map shows the largest area?

- Using the scale on Map A, measure the distance from Seal Harbor to Swans Island. Do the same with Map B, using the scale on Map B. What did you find?

Apply It

- Compare a map of the United States with a map of your state. Which map is a small-scale map? Which is a large-scale map?

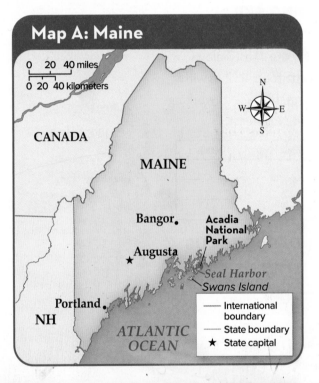

Map A: Maine

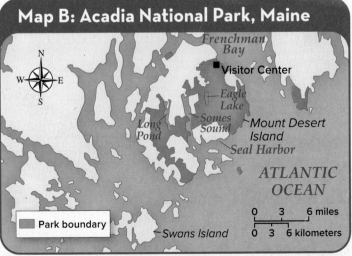

Map B: Acadia National Park, Maine

The Economy of the Northeast

Cranberries are important to the economy of the Northeast.

VOCABULARY

industry

service

urban

suburban

megalopolis

READING SKILL

Main Idea and Details
Copy the chart below. As you read, fill it in with information about working in the Northeast.

Main Idea	Details

STANDARDS FOCUS

SOCIAL STUDIES — Production, Distribution, and Consumption

GEOGRAPHY — Environment and Society

Visual Preview

How have people of the Northeast adapted to make a living?

A Many people still earn a living in the Northeast by fishing and farming.

B People in the Northeast worked in manufacturing long ago.

C Many people in the Northeast work in service jobs.

D Most people in the Northeast live and work in cities and suburbs.

A   USING RESOURCES

Most people in the Northeast live in or near cities. That's because manufacturing became an important part of the region's economy in the 1800s. Before that, most people depended on the natural resources in the region to make a living.

How do people in the Northeast make a living? Many people in the Northeast work in offices, but some people still make a living from the region's natural resources.

Along the coast from Maine to Maryland, fishing, trapping lobster and crabs, or digging for clams and oysters is still a full-time job. Further inland, people use the Northeast's rich land to earn a living. Each state in the region grows a wide variety of fruits and vegetables.

The Northeast's grassy areas provide food for cows. Dairy farmers use cow's milk to produce milk products, cheeses, and yogurt. Dairy farming is big business in Pennsylvania, New Jersey, Vermont, Connecticut, and New Hampshire. Look at the map to see where some of the items are grown.

Products of the Northeast

ME
VT NH
NY
MA
RI
PA
CT
NJ
MD
DC DE

Trees, plants, flowers		Legumes
Dairy		Maple syrup
Fruit		Vegetables, Mushrooms

Map Skill

LOCATION **In what states are fruits grown?**

QUICK CHECK

Main Idea and Details What do the Northeast's grasslands do for its economy?

B BUILDING FACTORIES

Did you know that people used to make almost everything they needed themselves? From hats to shoes and clothes to homes, if you needed it, you had to make it yourself. People even wove their own cloth.

In the late 1700s, some people in England discovered how to build machines that wove lots of cloth all at once. That meant people could buy cloth instead of making it.

Early Factories

In 1789 a man named Samuel Slater wrote the plans for one of these machines. He brought the plans to Rhode Island. Textile, or cloth, factories were soon being built all over the Northeast. Other businesses began to use the same ideas as

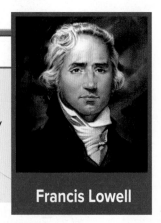

PEOPLE

In 1813, **Francis Lowell** built a textile factory in Massachusetts. The factory town built nearby was the first planned town for workers.

Francis Lowell

the textile factories to produce paper, tin, and other goods.

Many people left their homes to look for work at these new factories. Lucy Larcom began working in a Lowell textile mill when she was only 11. Lucy, like many young girls, worked to help support her family. Read what she had to say about her experience.

A town was built near the Lowell factory in Massachusetts so workers could live near the factory.

Mill

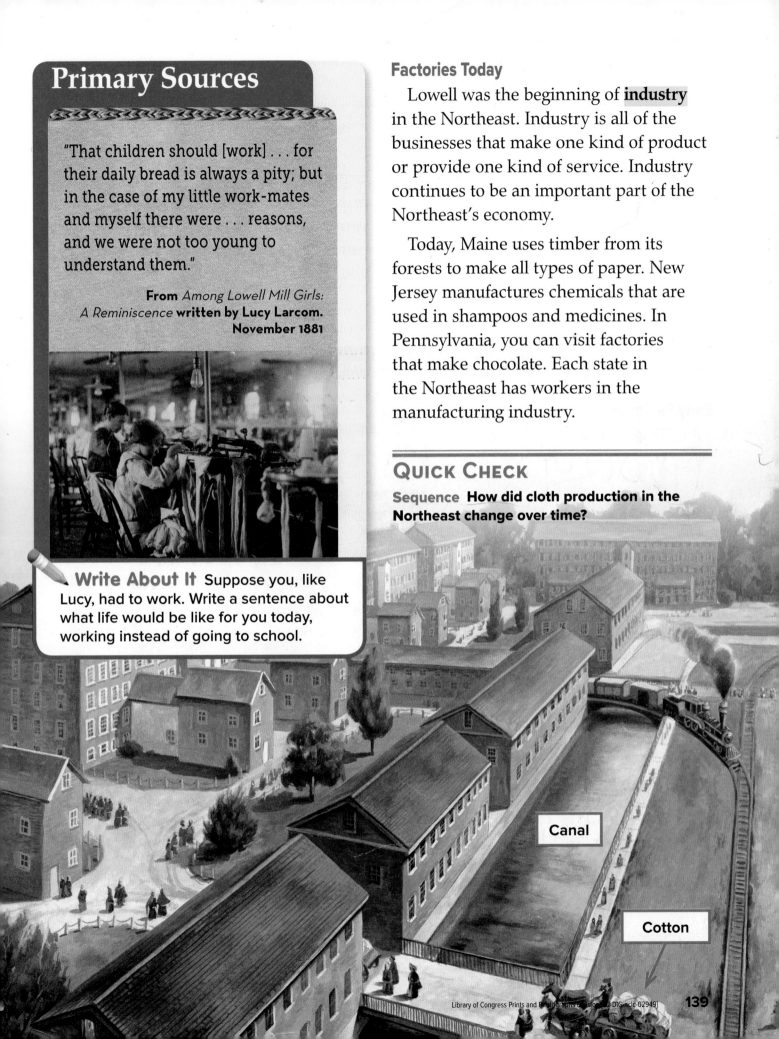

Primary Sources

"That children should [work] . . . for their daily bread is always a pity; but in the case of my little work-mates and myself there were . . . reasons, and we were not too young to understand them."

From *Among Lowell Mill Girls: A Reminiscence* **written by Lucy Larcom. November 1881**

Write About It Suppose you, like Lucy, had to work. Write a sentence about what life would be like for you today, working instead of going to school.

Factories Today

Lowell was the beginning of **industry** in the Northeast. Industry is all of the businesses that make one kind of product or provide one kind of service. Industry continues to be an important part of the Northeast's economy.

Today, Maine uses timber from its forests to make all types of paper. New Jersey manufactures chemicals that are used in shampoos and medicines. In Pennsylvania, you can visit factories that make chocolate. Each state in the Northeast has workers in the manufacturing industry.

QUICK CHECK

Sequence How did cloth production in the Northeast change over time?

Canal

Cotton

C SERVING OTHERS

So far, you've read about the goods, or products, of the Northeast's agriculture and manufacturing industries. Many people in the Northeast don't produce goods or food. Instead, they provide a **service.** All the jobs that people do to help others are service jobs. As a matter of fact, many people in the United States provide services.

When you buy a snack at the local store, the person behind the counter provides a service. Your doctor and dentist also provide services when they help you keep your body and teeth healthy. Your teacher provides a service, too—he or she helps you learn new things.

Service Workers in the Northeast

People in Millions

3

2

1

0

Protective Services

Retail and Wholesale Trade

Restaurant

Jobs

(l)Kris Timken/Getty Images, (c)Blend Images/Alamy, (r)Stewart Cohen/DreamPictures/Blend Images LLC

What about when you go to a bike repair shop? The person who fixes your bike is providing a service, too. Throughout the region and the country, service workers provide services we can't or don't have the time to do ourselves.

Instead of having to make our own clothes and grow our own food as people did in the past, we rely on people who work in manufacturing and agriculture to provide these for us. All we need to do is to buy them from someone who works in a service job. Look at the chart below. Which two industries have about the same number of service workers?

QUICK CHECK

Summarize **What are some service jobs in the Northeast?**

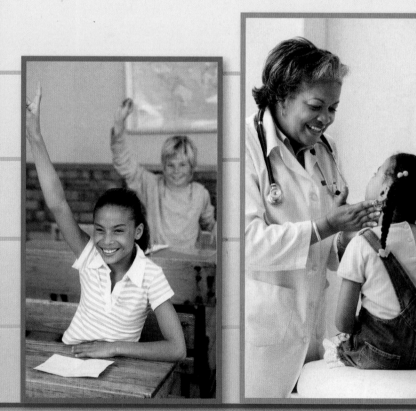

Chart Skill

What industry has the most service providers in the Northeast?

Education   Healthcare   Other

(l)©Tomas Rodriguez/Corbis/Glow Images, (c)©Jose Luis Pelaez Inc/Blend Images LLC, (r)Rob Melnychuk/Digital Vision/SuperStock

e Northeast has less land than any
region in the United States, but
one in every six people lives in the
heast. Where do all the workers live?

and Suburbs

e Northeast has a number of areas
re urban. Urban means "of the
—in other words, all cities are urban
rs.

The first big Northeast cities began as
ports, or harbors, where ships landed
with goods to trade. Trade with Europe
was important to the early settlers and
to the young United States. Eventually,
these trading ports grew into cities. Later,
the growing populations of city ports
made them good places to build factories.
Not only did they have a large supply of
workers, but their location along harbors
made it easy to ship goods to other
places.

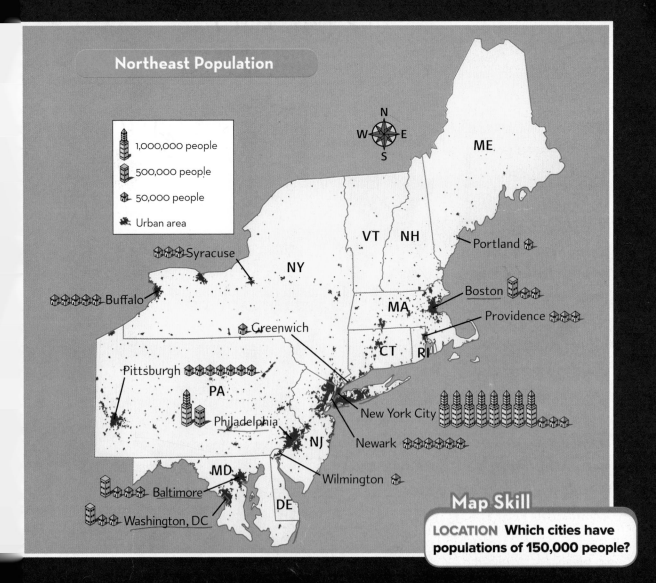

Northeast Population

1,000,000 people

500,000 people

50,000 people

Urban area

Syracuse

Buffalo

Greenwich

Pittsburgh

Philadelphia

Baltimore

Washington, DC

ME

VT NH

Portland

NY

Boston

MA

Providence

CT RI

New York City

PA

Newark

NJ

Wilmington

MD

DE

Map Skill

**LOCATION Which cities have
populations of 150,000 people?**

The Northeast's megalopolis is so big that it can be seen from space at night.

Today, many people in the Northeast live in suburban areas. A suburb is a community near a city. If you look closely, you can even see the word "urban" in suburban. Suburbs developed because people wanted to live in less crowded spaces, but near a city.

Bigger than a City

Together, a city and its suburbs form a metropolitan area. Some cities themselves are the suburbs of larger cities. For example, the city of Newark, New Jersey, is part of New York City's metropolitan area. A few Northeast metropolitan areas have grown so large they overlap. These overlapping metropolitan areas form a megalopolis—a single huge metropolitan area. One megalopolis runs from Boston to Washington, D.C.

QUICK CHECK

Summarize **What did the first Northeast cities look like?**

Check Understanding

1. **VOCABULARY** Write a paragraph about the economy of the Northeast using these words.

   urban   suburban   megalopolis

2. **READING SKILL Main Idea and Details** Use the Main Idea chart to write about the different types of factories in the Northeast.

Main Idea	Details

3. **Write About It** Write a sentence about how factories in the Northeast helped cause the region to grow.

The People of the Northeast

VOCABULARY

culture

diverse

READING SKILL

Main Idea and Details
Copy the chart below. As you read, fill it in with information about people of the Northeast.

Main Idea	Details

STANDARDS FOCUS

SOCIAL STUDIES Culture

GEOGRAPHY The Uses of Geography

The Northeast is a diverse region.

Visual Preview

What is important to the culture of the Northeast?

A Native Americans are an important part of Northeast culture.

B Immigrants contribute to the rich diversity of the Northeast.

C Northeasterners hold festivals to celebrate their heritage.

D The Northeast has many activities to explore.

A MANY WAYS OF LIFE

For hundreds of years, people from all over the world have settled in the Northeast. These immigrants brought their ways of life with them and helped to enrich the region.

What does your family do during holidays? What language do you speak at home? What foods do you eat? All of this and more is part of your **culture**. Culture includes a people's history, language, religion, and customs, or ways of doing things. It also includes a people's stories, songs, and jokes.

The cultures that came to the Northeast were a rich mix. Each culture brought its foods, ways of having fun, and styles of music and art. This joining of cultures has shaped life in the Northeast region.

First Northeasterners

The first people in the Northeast were Native Americans. The Iroquois and the Lenape are two of the many Native American groups in the region. They grew maize, beans, and squash for food. They also ate wild plants. The Iroquois knew about maple syrup and tapped maple trees to get the syrup. Native Americans also hunted deer and other wild animals. They used deer hides to make their clothing.

QUICK CHECK

Main Idea and Details **Describe Native Americans of the Northeast.**

Many Chinese immigrants came to the United States in the 1800s. ▼

▲ Irish immigrants have greatly influenced the Northeast.

B IMMIGRANTS THEN AND NOW

In the early 1600s, Native Americans encountered people who had sailed from England. These settlers came for a better life.

Settlers came from the Netherlands and Sweden, too. Johan Printz, the leader of a Swedish settlement in Pennsylvania, had this to say about the New World:

> "This is a very lovely country with everything a person can wish himself on this earth."
>
> JOHAN PRINTZ

Soon, more and more people came to settle in what they called the "New World." These new settlers slowly pushed out most of the Native Americans who had lived in the area. By 1750, the English had settled in colonies throughout the region. Eventually, other Europeans found homes in the Northeast. People from Sweden moved to Delaware, while New York was settled by people from the Netherlands. Many Germans made their homes in Pennsylvania.

Africans were another important group of people to arrive in the 1600s. Most came against their will as enslaved workers, but some Africans came as servants who would be free men and women after a period of time.

▲ People of Hispanic origin are a large part of the rich cultural heritage of the Northeast.

Many Africans, like this Ethiopian family, are enriching the Northeast's cultural diversity. ▼

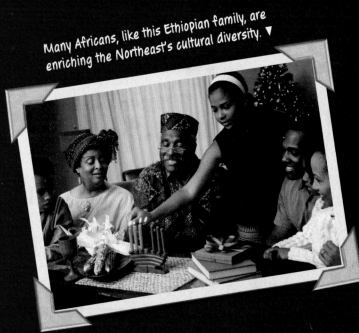

EVENT

The **Amish left Europe** in the early 1700s in search of religious freedom. They first settled in Pennsylvania. Today there are Amish communities in 22 states around the country.

Amish School Boys

Ellis Island and People Today

As the Northeast grew, its people became more diverse. Diverse means that there is a variety.

From about 1892 to 1954, immigrants from around the world came to the Northeast and stopped at Ellis Island in New York City's harbor. There, officials tried to make sure that only healthy people entered the United States.

In recent years, people from China and other Asian nations have moved to the Northeast. Others have come from Mexico and the Dominican Republic.

Wherever they came from, people arrived in the Northeast looking for a better life and a better future. They brought with them their culture and ideas and shared them with others.

QUICK CHECK

Summarize **Why did many immigrant groups come to the Northeast?**

C CELEBRATING CULTURES

People in the Northeast are proud of the many cultures that make up their region. One way to show pride in your culture is by sharing it with others. Many groups do this by having festivals. These festivals are full of tasty foods, music, and lively dancing.

Festivals For Everyone

One of the largest of these celebrations is Saint Patrick's Day. Irish Americans celebrate the day by attending one of the many parades in the region. Towns with large German-American populations celebrate the fall harvest during Oktoberfest. At Oktoberfest, people eat bratwurst, a type of sausage, and dance to music played on an accordion.

EVENT

Every year, Philadelphia, Pennsylvania, hosts **the Mummers Parade** on New Year's Day. The parade grew out of European customs brought to the city by early settlers.

Mummers Parade

Other cultural groups hold festivals, too. Poughkeepsie, New York, holds a Greek festival with dancing and Greek foods, such as spanakopita, a spinach and feta cheese pie. Each spring, a Japanese festival called Sakura Matsuri, part of the National Cherry Blossom Festival, is held in Washington, D.C. Visitors can taste Japanese food and learn the Japanese art of paper folding, or origami. On Labor Day weekend, Scranton, Pennsylvania, holds La Festa Italiana. This is a celebration of Italian culture, music, and food.

The koto is a traditional Japanese stringed musical instrument and is an important part of their festivals. ▼

QUICK CHECK

Draw conclusions **Why do cultural groups in the Northeast hold celebrations?**

Global Connections

New York City's Caribbean Festival

One of the world's largest festivals happens each Labor Day weekend in Brooklyn, New York. It's the West Indian American Day Carnival and Parade.

The popular festival celebrates the cultures of the West Indies. These islands in the Caribbean Sea include Jamaica, Trinidad and Tobago, St. Kitts, and Barbados, among others. Many people in the Northeast were born in the West Indies or have parents or grandparents who were. At the festival, they and others can enjoy the dances, music, art, and food of the West Indies.

The festival begins at two in the morning with a parade. Festival-goers wear costumes and walk through the streets of New York City to the music of steel drums. Later in the day, people enjoy foods such as fried fish, coconut bread, and a leafy vegetable called callaloo.

Dancers wear elaborate costumes during the West Indian Day Parade. ▼

Brooklyn, NY

▲ People play steel drums during the West Indian Day parade.

Citizenship
Working for the Common Good

What are some ways that kids can work for the common good? Some students in New York decided to get involved in a project that would make their neighborhood more beautiful. They found an organization that would help them make positive changes in their environment by creating open spaces with trees and flowers. These kids helped to create an open garden where anyone could gather.

Write About It Write about how you could work for the common good.

You've read about the diverse cultures of the people of the Northeast and about their celebrations. The region is also full of places to visit.

If you like the outdoors, it's a fantastic place to be. You can hike in the mountains or sail along the region's coast.

Perhaps you enjoy seeing exhibits at museums. You can talk to dolphin trainers at the National Aquarium in Baltimore, Maryland, or view fine art at many museums in the region. If you want to see a replica of America's first submarine, "the Turtle," head to the United States Navy's Submarine Force Museum in Groton, Connecticut.

Sailing on Lake Champlain in Vermont

(l)Hero Images/Getty Images, (bkgd)Amy Riley/iStock/Getty Images

A woman watches a large shark at the National Aquarium in Baltimore, Maryland.

Culture and Environment

For music, you can go to Tanglewood in Lenox, Massachusetts. It's the summer home of the Boston Symphony Orchestra. One musician who has played at Tanglewood is Yo Yo Ma, a cellist. Like many Northeasterners, Yo Yo Ma is interested in learning how the world's cultures have mixed to create beautiful music.

People in the Northeast enjoy their environment so much that many work to keep it clean and healthy. Read p.150 to see how some kids worked for the common good of the Northeast.

QUICK CHECK

Summarize What are some of the things that people in the Northeast can do for fun?

Check Understanding

1. **VOCABULARY** Write a sentence that uses each of these vocabulary words.

   culture   diverse

2. **READING SKILL Main Idea and Details** Use the chart to write about places to explore in the Northeast.

Main Idea	Details

3. **Write About It** Write a paragraph about how the population of the Northeast has changed over time.

EXPLORE The Big Idea

Review and Assess

Vocabulary

Copy the sentences below. Use the list of vocabulary words to fill in the blanks.

glacier   **megalopolis**

fall line   **cultures**

1. The ___ is where mountains flatten into a plain.

2. Two or more metropolitan areas that overlap form a ___.

3. A ___ is a moving sheet of ice.

4. The people of the Northeast come from many different ___.

Comprehension and Critical Thinking

5. What is the difference between broadleaf and needle-leaf trees?

6. What kinds of resources can be found in the Northeast?

7. **Critical Thinking** Why were cities built near harbors?

8. **Reading Skill** What places in the Northeast would you most enjoy visiting? Explain why using the main idea and details.

Skill

Compare Maps at Different Scales

9. What is the difference between a large-scale map and a small-scale map?

10. Look at the maps on this page. Which map is a large-scale map?

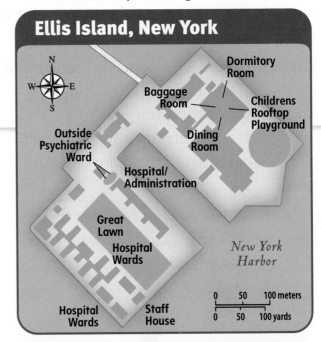

Ellis Island, New York

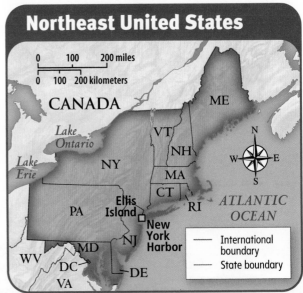

Northeast United States

# Test Preparation

Read the paragraphs. Then answer the questions.

> New Hampshire's newest state forest . . . was purchased by The Nature Conservancy . . . . It . . . will never be developed . . . It will always be open. . . . [and] it provides an ideal habitat for an endangered plant species called the northeastern bulrush.
>
> This is good news. Teachers use the land for forestry, science, and other subjects. Students tap trees, while environmental science students measure the effects of ozone pollution on white pine. Gym classes go snow-shoeing and hiking in the forest, and the schools' cross-country ski team trains on its trails.

1. What is the main idea of the passage?

   A. New Hampshire has beautiful forests.

   B. Teachers use land for forestry and science.

   C. The Nature Conservancy bought the forest to provide a habitat for the northeastern bulrush.

   D. The state forest will provide habitat for an endangered species and provide students a place to learn.

2. Why is it important to have undeveloped land? What does it provide the community?

3. Which of the following statements is an opinion?

   A. The northeastern bulrush is an endangered plant species.

   B . The Nature Conservancy is the newest state forest in New Hampshire.

   C. The Nature Conservancy bought the newest state forest.

   D. New Hampshire has beautiful state forests.

4. List reasons why it is important to provide habitat for plants and animals that are endangered.

The Big Idea Activities

What causes a region to change?

Write About the Big Idea

Expository Report

Recall what you learned about the geography, economy, and people of the Northeast in Unit 3. Review your notes in the completed foldable.

Use the information from your foldable and other sources to write a report. Your report should end up being several paragraphs. The topic of your report will explain what caused the Northeast to change over time.

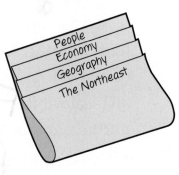

People
Economy
Geography
The Northeast

Plan a Bike Trip

Suppose you are a travel agent. Your newest client wants you to plan a bike trip. Work with a partner to plan a trip through part of the Northeast.

1. Research areas of the Northeast that might be best suited to a bike trip.

2. Use a map to figure out the best routes.

3. Create a presentation for your client. It should include pictures and descriptions, and even a map, of the trip you are suggesting.

4. You may draw pictures or create a collage from newspapers or magazines.

5. Present your trip to your class. Be sure to explain why you chose the particular route you selected.

(tl)©Comstock Images, (b)Cernan Elias/Alamy

Unit 4

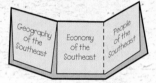

Essential Question
How do people affect the environment?

FOLDABLES
Study Organizer

Summarize
Use a three-tab book foldable to take notes as you read Unit 4. Label the three tabs **Geography of the Southeast**, **Economy of the Southeast**, and **People of the Southeast**.

Geography of the Southeast | Economy of the Southeast | People of the Southeast

LOG ON
For more about Unit 4 go to connectED.mcgraw-hill.com

The Southeast

©Linda Richards/Alamy **155**

PEOPLE, PLACES, AND EVENTS

Sequoyah

Sequoyah Birthplace Museum

Sequoyah was a Cherokee silversmith who lived in Tennessee. He spent 12 years creating an alphabet that allowed the Cherokee to write their language for the first time.

Today you can visit the **Sequoyah Birthplace Museum** in Vonore, Tennessee.

Louis Armstrong

New Orleans Jazz and Heritage Festival

Louis Armstrong began his career in New Orleans and became a world famous trumpet player.

Today you can hear many famous musicians play at the **New Orleans Jazz and Heritage Festival**.

(tl)Library of Congress Prints and Photographs Division [LC-USZC4-2566], (tr)Jerry Whaley/Alamy, (bl)William P. Gottlieb/Ira and Leonore S. Gershwin Fund Collection, Music Division, Library of Congress [LC-GLB23-0015], (br)©Erica Simone Leeds

Selma, Alabama

Voting Rights

Citizens from all over the United States protested the unfair treatment of African Americans by walking in a march from **Selma, Alabama,** to Montgomery, Alabama and supporting **voting rights for** African Americans.

Today you can walk the National Historic Trail that follows the path protesters walked between Selma and Montgomery.

Pony Penning

Barrier Islands

Barrier islands form when ocean waves deposit sand along a coast. Assateague Island, one of the most famous of the barrier islands in the Southeast, is known for its population of wild horses.

Today at the annual **Pony Penning**, you can watch the horses swim to the mainland where the young horses are sold.

Southeast Region

People enjoy all sorts of outdoor activities in the warm Southeast.

1 Country music often includes fiddles. Nashville, Tennessee, is home to the Country Music Hall of Fame and Museum.

OZARK PLATEAU

Arkansas River

★Li Ro

OUACHITA MOUNTAINS

Vicksburg National Millitary Park

Red River

6 The White Magnolia is the state flower of both Mississippi and Louisiana.

Ja

LA

Bato Roug

G

5

Lacassine National Wildlife Refuge

5 The Mississippi is one of the longest rivers in the United States. Steamboats like this one carry tourists up and down the river.

(t)Creatas/SuperStock, (c)Robert Campbell/SuperStock, (b)GoodShoot/PunchStock

2 The grassy farms of the Southeast are a great place to raise horses. At horse shows, riders and their horses compete for prizes.

Potomac River

Charleston

Assateague Island

Ohio River

2 Louisville

Frankf[o]

WV

VA

Richmond

KY

Chesapeake Bay

APPALACHIAN MOUNTAINS

Cape Hatteras

Nashville **1** TN

Tennessee River

Raleigh

NC

PIEDMONT

Ocracoke Island

N
W   E
S

Memphis

MS

Columbia

SC

ATLANTIC COASTAL PLAIN

0   100   200 m
0   100   200 kilometers

Alabama River

Atlanta

AL

GA

Savannah River

6

Chattahoochee River

Montgomery

De Soto National Forest

Okefenokee Swamp

ATLANTIC OCEAN

COASTAL PLAIN

Tallahassee

4 Mobile Bay

Mississippi River Delta

Gulf of Mexico

FL

Cape Canaveral

Lake Okeechobee

Big Cypress National Preserve

The Everglades

3

Miami

4 Conch is an ingredient in southeastern chowders and gumbos. The shell is also a popular decorative item.

Florida Keys

Straits of Florida

3 Flamingoes live in Everglades National Park. They thrive in wetland environments.

(t)Purestock/SuperStock, (bl)Comstock Images/Getty Images, (br)Kateryna Potrokhova/iStock/Getty Images Plus/Getty Images

159

Lesson 1

VOCABULARY

source

mouth

wetland

peninsula

levee

READING SKILL

Summarize

Copy the chart . Fill it in with details about the geography of the Southeast.

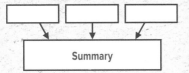

Summary

STANDARDS FOCUS

SOCIAL STUDIES — People, Places and Environments

GEOGRAPHY — Physical Systems

The Geography of the Southeast

Visual Preview

How does the Southeast's geography affect the region?

A The Southeast has many water-loving animals in its rivers and wetlands.

B Islands form in different ways.

C Some parts of the Southeast are hit by big storms.

D Walls are built along rivers in the Southeast to help prevent flooding.

160 (bcl)Tetra images RF/Getty Images, (bcr)©Stocktrek Images/Alamy, (br)NOAA/Department of Commerce

A   RIVERS AND WETLANDS

*The Southeast has a little of everything—mountains, rolling hills,
a broad coastal plain, and many islands. Most of all,
the region has plenty of water!*

The Mississippi River is the second longest river in North America. It runs 2,350 miles from its **source**, or beginning, in Minnesota to its **mouth**, or end, at the Gulf of Mexico in Louisiana.

A Region of Wetlands

Much of the Southeast is low, flat land. When rain falls, it does not always drain away. As a result, the Southeast has a lot of **wetlands**, or areas where water is always on or close to the surface of the ground.

In the past, people often drained wetlands so they could build on the land. Now we know that wetlands are valuable. They act like giant sponges

PLACES

The **Okefenokee Swamp** covers more than 430,000 acres in Georgia. You can take a boat tour, but watch out for alligators!

Okefenokee Swamp

that help control floods. Wetlands also act as filters. As water flows through them, the wetland soils remove pollution from the water. Many plants and animals live in the wetlands of the Southeast.

QUICK CHECK

Summarize How are wetlands valuable?

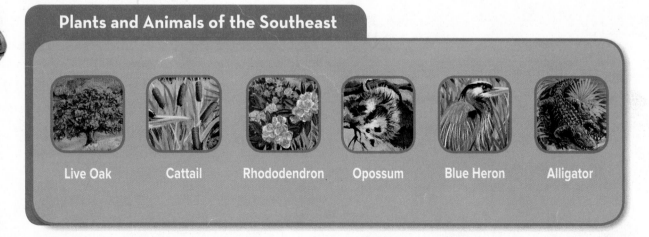

Plants and Animals of the Southeast

Live Oak   Cattail   Rhododendron   Opossum   Blue Heron   Alligator

B LANDFORMS IN THE SOUTHEAST

Look at the map on pages 158-159. Which bodies of water border the Southeast states? You can see that the Southeast has miles of coastline. The land along the coast is low and flat. In some places, this flatland stretches for many miles inland. The land is rich and good for farming.

Find Florida on the map. Florida is a **peninsula**, or an area of land that is surrounded by water on three sides.

Hills and Mountains

As you move inland from the coast, you come to gently rolling hills. These hills are called the Piedmont, or foothills.

(bkgd) PhotoAlto

Next are the Appalachian Mountains. These mountains have been worn down by erosion over millions of years. They are not as high as mountains that formed more recently. At 6,684 feet, Mount Mitchell in North Carolina is the highest peak in the Appalachian Mountains. The Appalachian Mountains run through the Northeast and Southeast. Which states do they run through in the Southeast?

Islands

The Southeast also has plenty of islands. Did you know that islands can be formed in different ways? You can read about how three different islands were formed in the chart below.

QUICK CHECK

Summarize What are the landforms in the Southeast?

Islands in the Southeast

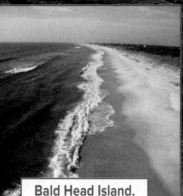

Bald Head Island, North Carolina

Barrier islands form as ocean waves drop tons of sand along the coast. They act like barriers, or walls, to protect the mainland from the ocean waves.

Miami Beach, Florida

Miami Beach and the Florida Keys are made from the bones of coral, a tiny sea animal. As the coral grows together, it may rise above the ocean's surface.

Puerto Rico

The island of Puerto Rico formed when underground rocks were pushed together and forced upwards.

Chart Skill

Which island was made by waves dropping sand along a coast?

These horses live on a farm in the Appalachian Mountains in West Virginia.

If you like warm weather, you'll love the Southeast. Most of the Southeast has a climate of warm or hot summers and mild winters. Near the Gulf of Mexico, the climate is usually warm and humid. Humid air holds lots of moisture.

During the day, sunlight warms both water in the Gulf of Mexico and nearby land. Sunlight warms land faster than it warms water. As the ground warms, it heats the air above it. The warm air rises, and cooler air from over the water moves to replace it. A sea breeze blows from the water toward the land.

As night falls, land cools faster than water. Warm air rises over the water. Cooler air from over the land moves to replace it. A land breeze blows from the land towards the water.

The Gulf of Mexico affects the climate | by cooling the land in summer and warming it in winter. In the summer, water stays cooler longer than land does, so cool breezes blow off the Gulf onto the nearby land. In winter, the water is warmer than the land, so the breezes from the water onto the land bring warm air.

Air Movement in Sea and Land Breezes

sea breeze, day

land breeze, night

KEY

warm air

cold air

In the northern part of the Southeast region, especially in the Appalachian Mountains, it is usually cooler than in the deep South. In winter, there may even be some snow in the mountains of West Virginia, Tennessee, and North Carolina—but it never lasts for long.

The entire region gets rain, but there are also sunny days. In fact, Florida's nickname is the "Sunshine State."

Storm Season

Sometimes the weather in the Southeast is not so pleasant. Coastal areas in the Southeast may be hit by hurricanes in the late summer and fall. Hurricane winds and waves may cause floods and damage buildings and trees.

QUICK CHECK

Summarize **What is the climate of the Southeast?**

▲ Hurricane Katrina was the third-strongest hurricane that has ever hit the United States.

These brown pelicans live along the Florida coast.

Since much of the Southeast is low land, heavy rains can cause floods. To prevent floods, people have built **levees**, or large walls, along the shores of some rivers to keep the rivers from overflowing.

Hurricane Damage

Hurricane Katrina hit land near New Orleans, Louisiana, in 2005. Levees that held back water from a nearby lake were broken. Water rushed in and flooded part of the city. Some people lost their lives, and many people lost their homes. The hurricane's winds also did millions of dollars worth of damage to towns along the Mississippi and Alabama coasts.

Levees along the Mississippi River in Louisiana prevent flooding. ▼

Scientists worry that there may be more and stronger hurricanes in the future, because the world's climate seems to be getting warmer. Engineers and scientists keep looking for ways to prevent future storms from causing so much damage.

QUICK CHECK

Make Inferences **What damage may happen when rivers overflow?**

Check Understanding

1. **VOCABULARY** Write a postcard to a friend that uses the following vocabulary words.

   source   mouth levee

2. **READING SKILL** Summarize
   Use the Summarize chart to write about the geography of the Southeast.

3. **Write About It** Write a paragraph about what the people in the Southeast have done to prevent flooding.

levee

(c) PhotoAlto, (b)NOAA/Department of Commerce

Chart and Graph Skills

Read Circle Graphs

VOCABULARY

graph

circle graph

A **graph** is a drawing that helps you compare information by showing the relationship between things. The graph shown here is a **circle graph**. Circle graphs show how parts of something fit into the whole. Because each part looks like a slice of pie, a circle graph is sometimes called a pie graph.

Learn It

- The title of the graph tells you what is shown in the graph. This circle graph shows the U.S. states that produce the most grapefruit.

- The labels tell you what each slice represents. You can see that the yellow slice stands for the percentage of grapefruit that is grown in Texas.

- A larger slice means more grapefruit is grown in that state.

Leading U.S. States in the Production of Grapefruit (October, 2015)

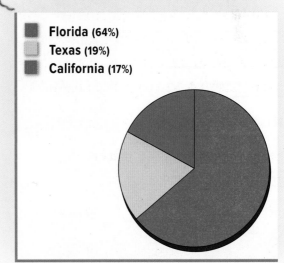

- Florida (64%)
- Texas (19%)
- California (17%)

Try It

- Compare the slices. Which state grows the most grapefruit?

- Which state grows more grapefruit—California or Texas?

- Which state grows the least grapefruit?

Apply It

- Make a circle graph that shows how much time you spend on each of the following activities during one day: sleeping, eating, school, watching TV, playing sports, doing homework, and other activities.

The Economy of the Southeast

Lesson 2

VOCABULARY

renewable resource

petroleum

refinery

nonrenewable resource

READING SKILL

Summarize

Copy the chart below. As you read, fill it in with information about the economy of the Southeast.

Summary

STANDARDS FOCUS

SOCIAL STUDIES Production, Distribution, and Consumption

GEOGRAPHY Environment and Society

The Southeast has rich natural resources of farmland, forests, and minerals.

Visual Preview

How have people affected the economy of the Southeast?

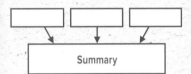

A Crops such as cotton and timber are grown on farms in the Southeast.

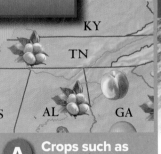

B Coal is one of the mineral resources in the Southeast.

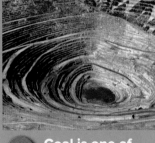

C Factories in the Southeast make many products.

D In the Southeast, many people work in the service industry.

(bcl)Royce Bair/Getty Images, (bcr)Monty Rakusen/Getty Images, (br)Jack Hollingsworth/Blend Images LLC, (bkgd)Pictor,Robert Llewellyn/ImageState/Alamy

A   A RICH LAND

What do you need for farming? Rich soil, plenty of rain, and sunlight are important. The Southeast has all of these, along with short, mild winters.

When the first settlers from Europe came to the Southeast, they began to grow crops. The first crops were indigo (a plant used to make a dark blue dye) and tobacco. Later they began to grow rice and cotton. By the middle of the 1800s, cotton was the most important crop grown in the Southeast. It was sold to factories in Great Britain and in the Northeast.

Farm Products Today

Cotton is not as important to the Southeast's economy today. Almost every state in the Southeast, however, still grows some cotton.

For centuries, tobacco was a crop that American colonists in the Southeast could sell. Due to health concerns, fewer people today smoke cigarettes. As a result, there's less demand for tobacco. Farmers in these states are now growing other crops. North Carolina is known for growing sweet potatoes, Georgia for peaches and pecans, and Florida for oranges.

QUICK CHECK

Summarize What crops are grown in the Southeast today?

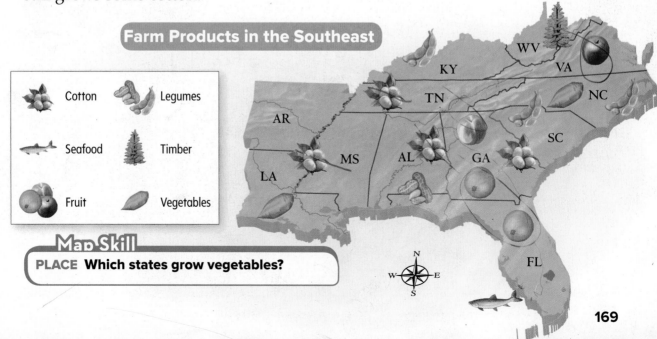

Farm Products in the Southeast

- Cotton
- Legumes
- Seafood
- Timber
- Fruit
- Vegetables

Map Skill

PLACE Which states grow vegetables?

NATURAL RESOURCES

In addition to its rich soil and good climate, the Southeast has other natural resources that include trees, oil, and coal. As trees are cut down and used for lumber, they can be replaced by planting new trees. Natural materials that can be replaced are called **renewable resources**.

Other resources, such as coal, are found underground. People have been burning coal as fuel for thousands of years. Most of the coal mined in the United States is used to run power plants that make electricity.

Petroleum, or oil, is another important underground resource. To reach oil, workers drill deep into the ground. The oil is pumped to the surface, where it is shipped to oil **refineries**. A refinery is a factory that turns the oil into useful products such as gasoline and heating oil.

This is a copper mine in Utah. ▼

Problems with Natural Resources

Coal and oil are both **nonrenewable resources**, or natural materials that can't be replaced. Both took millions of years to form. Once the coal or oil is used up, it is gone forever. However, we are not going to run out of coal soon. We have enough to last about 250 years.

Burning coal to run power plants puts pollution into the air, including a gas called carbon dioxide. Many scientists think that too much of this gas in the air is causing the world's climate to get warmer.

Another problem with coal is the way it is mined. In the past, mines were deep underground. Today coal companies find strip mining easier and cheaper. You can see, by looking at the diagram below, how strip mining destroys forests and changes the land. Whether coal is worth the problems it causes is something people must decide.

QUICK CHECK

Compare and Contrast How are renewable and nonrenewable resources different?

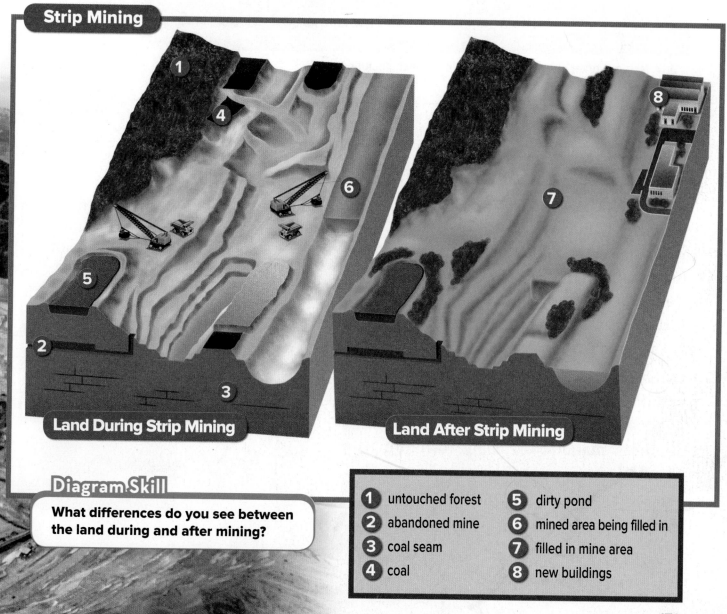

Strip Mining

Land During Strip Mining

Land After Strip Mining

Diagram Skill

What differences do you see between the land during and after mining?

1 untouched forest	**5** dirty pond
2 abandoned mine	**6** mined area being filled in
3 coal seam	**7** filled in mine area
4 coal	**8** new buildings

▲ Furniture is made throughout the Southeast.

▲ A factory worker checks a car engine in this manufacturing plant.

Ⓒ MANUFACTURING AND TECHNOLOGY

Are you wearing a shirt made of cotton? Perhaps the cotton was grown and the cloth was made in the Southeast. For many years, textile manufacturing was an important industry, especially in North Carolina. Currently, more and more textiles are being made in other countries.

As textiles have become less important to the Southeast's economy, electronics and the computer industry have become larger industries. Today factories in the Southeast manufacture paper, furniture, chemicals, cars, and soft drinks. These factories provide employment for many people.

EVENT

On August 5, 2011, the Juno spacecraft launched from Cape Canaveral, Florida. **Juno will orbit Jupiter**, studying the planet and searching for clues to how it formed.

Juno Lifts Off

(tl)Monty Rakusen/Getty Images, (tr)Tetra Images/Getty Images, (b)Bill Ingalls/NASA

DataGraphic
Jobs in the Southeast

The circle graph shows the number of people employed in each kind of industry in the Southeast. The bar graph shows the percent of service jobs for each Southeast state. Both graphs show that over fifty percent of the jobs in the Southeast are service jobs.

Employment in the Southeast

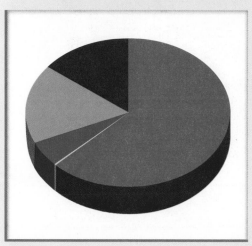

- Service Jobs
- Farming, Fishing, Forestry
- Construction
- Production, Transportation
- Other

Service Jobs in the Southeast

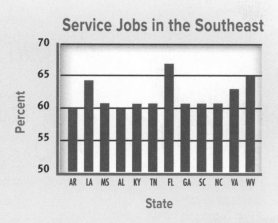

Talk About It

1. Are more people in the Southeast employed in construction or in production and transportation?

2. Which state has the largest percentage of workers in the service industry?

3. Which industry in the Southeast employs the most people?

Technology

Technology research is another important part of the Southeast's economy. Much of this research takes place at universities near Raleigh and Durham in North Carolina. Scientists there study everything from dinosaur eggs to the Mars space flights. Florida and Alabama also have important centers for space research.

QUICK CHECK

Main Idea and Details **What are some products made in the Southeast?**

173

While tourists are enjoying the beaches in the Southeast, they need services that include food, housing, transportation, and renting sports equipment.

D — SERVING PEOPLE

Do you know what a snowbird is? It's a type of bird, but it is also a nickname for people who live in the North during the summer and in the South during winter. Some "snowbirds" stay in the South for the whole winter while others visit for only a short time. In recent years, many people have moved to the Southeast to live year-round.

Each year millions of snowbirds and other tourists visit the Southeast. They enjoy the beaches, national parks, theme parks, and famous places such as Colonial Williamsburg in Virginia. Florida alone attracts about 40 million tourists a year.

Serving Visitors

Of course, serving these visitors creates thousands of jobs. Some people work at attractions and theme parks, while other people work in hotels, restaurants, ground and air transportation, and all the other businesses that vacationers need.

QUICK CHECK

Make Generalizations **Why is the Southeast a popular place to visit in the winter?**

Check Understanding

1. **VOCABULARY** Make a brochure that explains the difference between the following vocabulary words.

   renewable resource

   nonrenewable resource

2. **READING SKILL** Summarize Use the chart to write a paragraph about the natural resources of the Southeast.

   Summary

3. **Write About It** Write a paragraph about how mining for coal has changed the environment of the Southeast.

Lesson 3

VOCABULARY

dialect

segregation

READING SKILL

Summarize

Copy the chart. Fill it in about the people of the Southeast.

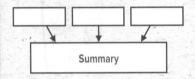

Summary

STANDARDS FOCUS

SOCIAL STUDIES — Culture

GEOGRAPHY — The Uses of Geography

A parade float travels through a crowd in New Orleans, Louisiana.

Visual Preview

How do people of the Southeast shape the region's culture?

A The Cherokee and other Native Americans live in the Southeast.

B People from around the world came to the Southeast.

C The civil rights movement brought many changes to the Southeast.

D Music is an important part of the Southeast's culture.

A NATIVE AMERICANS

The first people to live in the Southeast were Native Americans, including the Choctaw, Creek, Seminole, and Cherokee. They grew tobacco and "the three sisters"—corn, beans, and squash.

The Cherokee were one of the largest groups of Native Americans. Their lands stretched from Ohio to Alabama. Sequoyah was a Cherokee leader. He invented a way to write the Cherokee language.

Trail of Tears

In the 1830s, the United States government forced the Cherokee off their lands so that European settlers could live there. The Cherokee were forced to walk hundreds of miles to what is now Oklahoma. The journey they made was called the Trail of Tears, because so many Cherokee died on the way due to illness, hunger, or exhaustion.

Today, the Cherokee live in many places in the United States, including the Southeast. You can visit Oconaluftee Village in North Carolina to see how a typical Cherokee village would have looked 250 years ago.

PEOPLE

Sequoyah used letters from English, Greek, and Hebrew to make a system of 85 symbols that represented all the sounds in the Cherokee language.

Sequoyah

QUICK CHECK

Summarize Why were the Cherokee forced off their lands?

Native Americans from the Southeast make beautiful bead-work like this cap, along with clay pots, and grass baskets.

(t)Library of Congress Prints & Photographs Division [LC-USZC4-2566], (b)The George F. Landegger Collection of Alabama Photographs in Carol M. Highsmith's America, LOC, Prints and Photographs Division[LC-DIG-highsm-08972]

Have you ever visited St. Augustine, Florida? It was settled by Spanish explorers in 1565. That makes it the oldest continuously lived-in European settlement in this country. Besides Florida, the Spanish explored other parts of the Southeast.

English explorers also came to America. In 1607 they built a colony in Jamestown, Virginia. They eventually built more colonies along the Atlantic Coast. The English colonists learned how to grow tobacco from Native Americans in the area. Later, people from Ireland and Scotland settled in the Appalachian Mountains of Virginia and North and South Carolina. They brought their songs and music, which you can still hear today.

Africans are another group of people whose culture, music, and food are part of the Southeast. Many Africans came to the region unwillingly. Most had been kidnapped and enslaved. They were forced to work on farms in the South.

French Settlers in the Southeast

Some French people settled in Louisiana. Others settled a colony in Canada called Acadia. When the British forced the Acadians out of Canada, many of them fled to Louisiana. Their descendants today are known as Cajuns.

Gullah is a special dialect spoken by people on the Sea Islands of Georgia and South Carolina. It is a combination of English and words from different African languages. One aspect of **Gullah culture** is weaving baskets from seagrasses.

Gullah baskets

The language, customs, and food of all of these cultures became part of the culture of the Southeast. Gumbo, a popular food in the Southeast, is a blend of ingredients from different cultures. You can read below what writer John T. Edge says about Southern food.

QUICK CHECK

Summarize **Which immigrant groups came to the Southeast?**

French culture is still seen in Louisiana, especially in New Orleans, where many people speak a **dialect** of French. A dialect is a form of a language spoken in a certain place by a certain group of people. One dialect is called Louisiana Creole.

Primary Sources

"Food tells us who we are, tells us something about our social, political, and economic ways . . . Food is one of the great shared creations of the South."

John T. Edge

Write About It Write a sentence about what John T. Edge meant when he said that food is one of the great shared creations of the South.

Supporters of the civil rights movement organized freedom marches in peaceful protest for equal rights.

© CHANGING TIMES

The American Civil War in the 1860s brought an end to slavery. Changes to the United States Constitution made former enslaved peoples citizens and gave them rights. African Americans still faced unfair treatment and discrimination.

Segregation, or the practice of keeping racial groups separate, was a part of daily life in America. This meant that African American children attended different schools from white children. It also meant that African Americans were not allowed to eat in the same restaurants, ride in the same railway cars, stay at the same hotels, or join the same clubs as white people.

In the late 1950s and 1960s, people began working to give all Americans equal rights. This became known as the civil rights movement. Martin Luther King, Jr., Ralph Abernathy, and Rosa Parks were leaders in this movement. African Americans and other supporters of the civil rights movement held many peaceful protests and marches.

Every American citizen must have an equal right to vote.

—LYNDON BAINES JOHNSON

(t)Library of Congress Prints and Photographs Division [LC-DIG-ppmsca-03128], (b)Library of Congress Prints and Photographs Division [LC-USZ62-13036]

Young people played an important role in the movement. In 1957 nine African American students started attending a high school in Arkansas that had previously had only white students. In North Carolina and Tennessee, African American college students protested by holding "sit-ins." They would sit at a segregated lunch counter until they were served or until the store closed.

The Civil Rights Movement was successful. In 1964 and 1965, President Lyndon Johnson signed two new laws that protected the rights of all Americans. The Civil Rights Act of 1964 made it illegal to treat people differently because of their race, origin, religion, or gender. The next year, the Voting Rights Act of 1965 was passed. This law outlawed practices, like special taxes and tests, that had been used to prevent African Americans from voting.

Celebrating Freedom

In many places in the Southeast, African Americans hold a festival every year on June 19th. These "Juneteenth" festivals celebrate the day the end of slavery was announced in Galveston, Texas.

Citizenship

Being Informed

Lois heard that some towns celebrate a festival called Juneteenth every June 19th. She decided to find out more about it. She learned that "Juneteenth" celebrates the day that many enslaved people learned they were free. Today Juneteenth celebrations include African dancers and drummers, drama, storytelling, and great food. Lois decided to write to her town board to see if her town could start a Juneteenth celebration, too.

QUICK CHECK

Main Idea and Details **What was the civil rights movement?**

✏ **Write About It** Write a paragraph about a festival that is celebrated in your town.

The Southeast has a rich musical history. It is home to several different musical styles.

Music in the Southeast

Bluegrass is a type of folk music played on fiddles, banjos, and guitars. It traces its roots to the Irish and Scots who settled in the Appalachian Mountains.

Blues is a style of music that was developed by W.C. Handy and other African Americans in Louisiana and Mississippi. Today, blues music is popular around the world.

Jazz music is based on African and European music styles. Jazz began in New Orleans, where a Jazz Festival is still held every year. Louis Armstrong was a famous jazz trumpet player from New Orleans.

The Cajuns of southern Louisiana have a special style of music that uses the fiddle. Zydeco, a musical style that uses the accordion, came from the same area.

Did you know that rock and roll music also started in the South? It combined country, jazz, and African American rhythms. In 1954 a young man from Memphis, Tennessee, made his first record. You may have heard of him— Elvis Presley! He became a well-known entertainer and helped make rock and roll famous.

◄ The banjo is an important instrument in bluegrass music.

(bl)Don Bayley/Getty Images, (bkgd)Library of Congress Prints and Photographs Division [LC-USZ62-127236]

Soul Music

Soul music is based on African American church songs combined with blues. Aretha Franklin, who was born in Memphis, Tennessee, is known as "The Queen of Soul" because of her popular songs.

Elvis Presley was a famous rock and roll artist. ▶

QUICK CHECK

Summarize What musical styles developed in the Southeast?

▲ Jazz musician Louis Armstrong was famous for playing his trumpet.

Check Understanding

1. **VOCABULARY** Write a sentence using these vocabulary words.

   dialect   segregation

2. **READING SKILL Summarize**
   Use the chart to write about what one group of newcomers added to the culture of the Southeast.

3. **Write About It** Write a paragraph about how different ethnic groups can affect a region's culture.

Vocabulary

Copy the sentences below on a separate sheet of paper. Use the list of vocabulary words to fill in the blanks.

wetland   **renewable resource**

levee   **nonrenewable resource**

1. A __ is a wall built to prevent floods.

2. Petroleum is a __.

3. A swamp is an example of a __.

4. Trees are a __.

Comprehension and Critical Thinking

5. Describe the climate of the Southeast.

6. **Reading Skill** What are the three types of islands found in the Southeast? Summarize.

7. **Critical Thinking** What makes the Southeast an excellent region for agriculture?

8. **Critical Thinking** How are petroleum and coal alike?

Skill

Read Circle Graphs

Write a complete sentence to answer each question.

9. How many different sources of electricity does the circle graph show?

10. Which source provides the most electricity in the United States?

Sources of Electricity in the United States

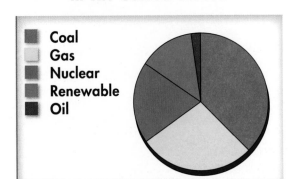

- Coal
- Gas
- Nuclear
- Renewable
- Oil

Test Preparation

Use the map and what you already know to answer the questions.

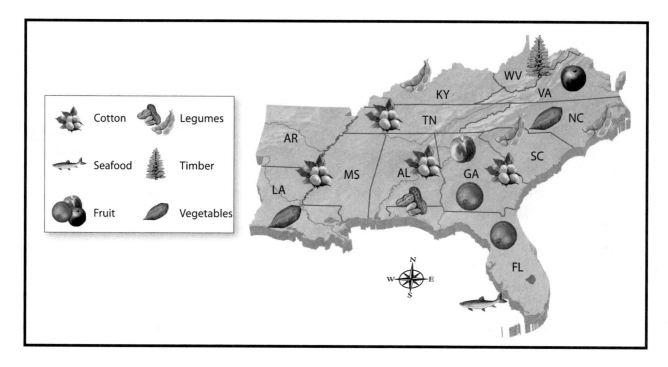

1. Which of the following states produce more than one fruit?

   A. Arkansas

   B. Georgia

   C. West Virginia

   D. Tennessee

2. Why is the Southeast a leading producer of oranges?

   A. Oranges grow well in warm climates.

   B. The orange is the official state fruit in several Southeast states.

   C. Native Americans taught settlers to grow oranges.

   D. There is a large demand for juice.

3. Which product is grown in four states in the Southeast?

   A. oranges

   B. cotton

   C. rice

   D. indigo

4. At one time, cotton and tobacco were important crops in the Southeast. Today, agriculture is more varied. Some people feel the variety is better. What is your opinion? Why?

5. Which states in the Southeast would be more likely to have fishing as an industry?

How do people affect the environment?

Write About the Big Idea

Narrative Essay

In Unit 4, you read about the geography, economy, and people of the Southeast. Review the notes in the completed foldable.

FOLDABLES
Study Organizer

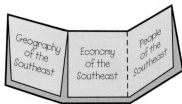

Geography of the Southeast | Economy of the Southeast | People of the Southeast

Begin your essay with an introductory paragraph describing the environment in the Southeast.

Write a paragraph describing how the geography, economy, and people of the Southeast affect the environment. The final paragraph should summarize the main ideas of the essay.

Give a News Report

Work with a partner to give a report about the issue you have researched, as if you were an anchorperson interviewing an environmentalist on a TV news show. Here's how to do your presentation:

1. Research an environmental issue such as coal mining or overfishing, that may affect the Southeast region.

2. Choose an issue to present.

3. Write a presentation. Come up with questions to discuss during the interview. Give the questions to your partner so he or she can prepare answers.

4. Draw illustrations or graphs to use as examples of the problem.

5. Present your interview to the class. Be sure to explain why the issue is important and what people are trying to do about it.

EXPLORE The Big Idea

Essential Question
How do natural resources affect a region's growth?

FOLDABLES Study Organizer

Draw Conclusions
Make a trifold book foldable to take notes as you read Unit 5. Label the three tabs **Geography**, **Economy**, and **People**.

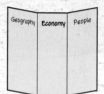

Geography	Economy	People

LOG ON For more about Unit 5 go to connectED.mcgraw-hill.com

The Midwest

PEOPLE, PLACES, AND EVENTS

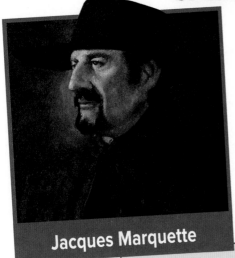
Jacques Marquette

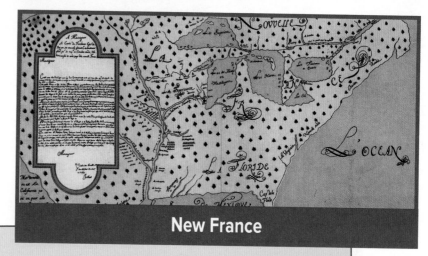
New France

French explorers **Jacques Marquette** and Louis Jolliet explored the area of the Mississippi River in 1673. They called the area **New France**.

Today you can learn more about the Mississippi River and its explorers at the National Mississippi River Museum and Aquarium in Dubuque, Iowa..

Laura Ingalls Wilder

Wilder's Log Cabin

If you ever read a book called *Little House on the Prairie,* you read about **Laura Ingalls Wilder's** life on the frontier.

Today you can visit **Wilder's Log Cabin** in Pepin, Wisconsin.

Lincoln Home National Historic Site

Abraham Lincoln

Our sixteenth President, **Abraham Lincoln**, was born and raised in Springfield, Illinois. Lincoln's parents were among the first settlers to move to the Midwest.

Today you can visit the **Lincoln Home National Historic Site** to learn more about Abraham Lincoln.

The Great Lakes

Bill Hartwig

The Great Lakes are five gigantic lakes in the Midwest. **Bill Hartwig** of the National Wildlife Refuge System is one of the many people who work to keep the Great Lakes clean.

Today the Great Lakes are the largest group of freshwater lakes in the world. They're so big you can see them from space!

Midwest Region

Midwest

The Midwest is home to both important and fun places to visit.

1 Mount Rushmore honors Presidents Washington, Jefferson, T. Roosevelt, and Lincoln. Each head is about 60 feet tall.

e akawea

ND
Bismarc

SD
ake Oahe

0   100   200 kilometers

1 BLACK HILLS   Pie

BADLANDS

N
W   E
S

NE

KS

Arkan River

5 The American Bison was very important to Native Americans. Today there are about 400,000 in the United States.

(tr)©JUPITERIMAGES/Thinkstock/Alamy, (b)dmbaker/Getty Images

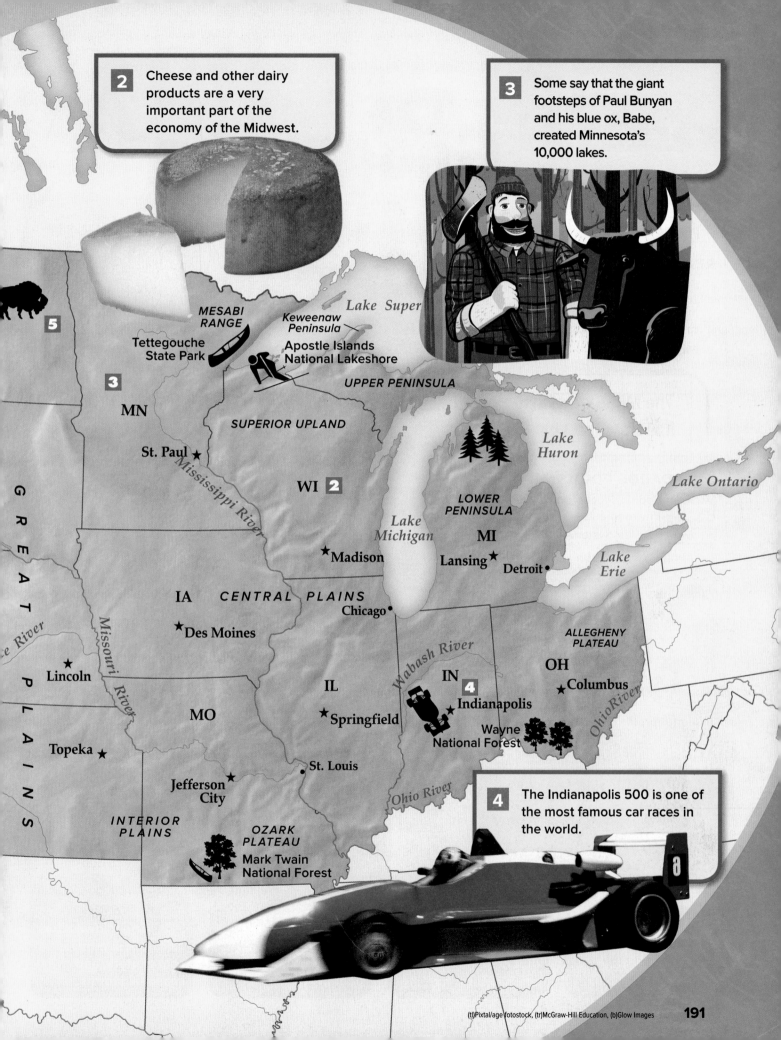

2 Cheese and other dairy products are a very important part of the economy of the Midwest.

3 Some say that the giant footsteps of Paul Bunyan and his blue ox, Babe, created Minnesota's 10,000 lakes.

5

MESABI RANGE

Lake Super

Keweenaw Peninsula

Tettegouche State Park

Apostle Islands National Lakeshore

UPPER PENINSULA

3

MN

SUPERIOR UPLAND

St. Paul ★

Mississippi River

WI **2**

Lake Huron

LOWER PENINSULA

Lake Michigan

MI

Lansing ★

Detroit •

Lake Ontario

Madison ★

Lake Erie

G R E A T   P L A I N S

e River

Missouri River

IA   CENTRAL   PLAINS

★ Des Moines

Chicago •

Wabash River

ALLEGHENY PLATEAU

OH

Lincoln ★

IN **4**

Columbus ★

IL

Indianapolis

MO

★ Springfield

Wayne National Forest

Topeka ★

St. Louis •

Ohio River

Jefferson City ★

Ohio River

4 The Indianapolis 500 is one of the most famous car races in the world.

INTERIOR PLAINS

OZARK PLATEAU

Mark Twain National Forest

8

VOCABULARY

fertile

prairie

READING SKILL

Draw Conclusions

Copy the chart. Use it to draw conclusions about the Mississippi River.

Text Clues	Conclusion

STANDARDS FOCUS

SOCIAL STUDIES — People, Places, and Environments

GEOGRAPHY — Physical Systems

The Geography of the Midwest

Visual Preview

How have the Great Lakes affected the Midwest?

A The Great Lakes make a good home for plants and animals.

B The Midwest has many rivers that help make the soil fertile for farming.

C The Midwest has plains, hills, mountains, and badlands.

D The Midwest has hot summers, cold winters, and seasonal storms.

(bcr)©Carol Wolfe, photographer, (br)crisserbug/Getty Images

A LAND FORMED BY WATER

The 12 states in the Midwest region are in the middle of the United States. This region is known as the Heartland of America. Many amazing plants and animals make this region unique and beautiful.

The Midwest region sits between the Appalachian Mountains and the Rocky Mountains. Although there are no oceans in the Midwest, there's plenty of water. Thousands of years ago, huge glaciers covered parts of the Midwest. As these gigantic sheets of ice moved slowly across the region, they flattened the land and carved out giant holes. When the glaciers melted, they filled the holes with water.

Today the holes created by the glaciers are called the Great Lakes. Lake Superior, Lake Michigan, Lake Huron, and Lake Erie are in the Midwest. Lake Ontario is in the Northeast. Thousands of smaller lakes were also formed by the glaciers. Minnesota, for example, has 22,000 lakes. All of these lakes make a good home for the region's plants and animals.

The plants and animals of the Midwest have adapted to different landforms. They have also adapted to hot summers and cold winters.

Plants and Animals of the Midwest

Foxglove Beard Tongue

White-tailed Jackrabbit

Prairie Cone Flower

Burrowing Owl

Black-eyed Susan

Red-tailed Hawk

QUICK CHECK

Draw Conclusions **Where did the water in the Great Lakes first come from?**

B FLOWING RIVERS

When the glaciers melted thousands of years ago, they created rivers. These rivers carried soil from the north and brought it south. The soil was **fertile**, or filled with vitamins and minerals that plants need to grow. Many of the states in the Midwest, such as Iowa and Ohio, now have lots of fertile soil. Fertile soil lets farmers produce crops that are healthy.

Several big rivers run through the region. More than half of the Mississippi River is in the Midwest. The Ohio River creates a southern border for Ohio, Indiana, and Illinois. The Missouri River flows into the Mississippi from the west. The Missouri is more than 2,300 miles

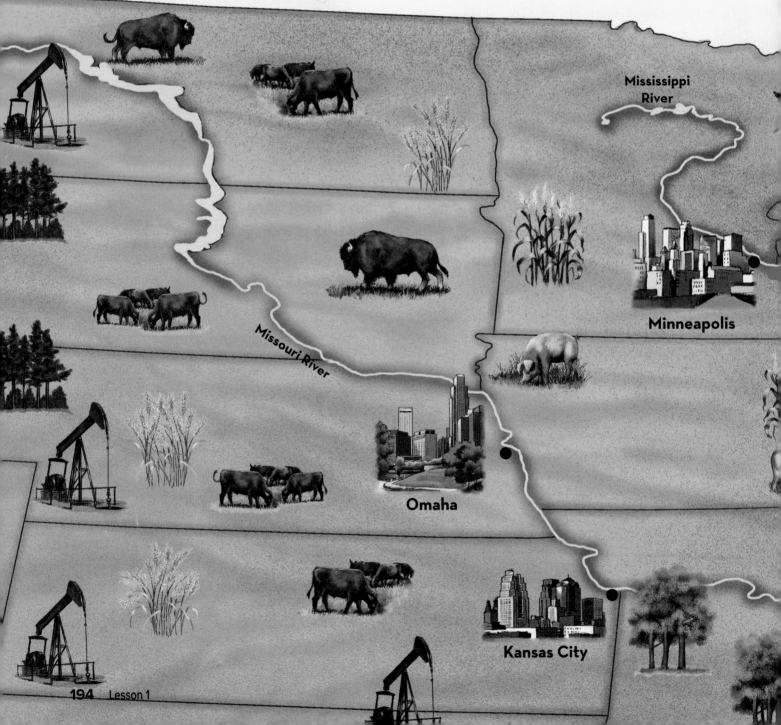

Mississippi
River

Missouri River

Minneapolis

Omaha

Kansas City

Samuel Clemens

long. This river has been nicknamed the "Big Muddy" for the amount of dirt it carries in its waters. To get an idea of how much water is in the Midwest, take a look at the map below. You can see that many of the region's cities were built along river banks.

QUICK CHECK

Summarize **How did glaciers improve Midwestern soil?**

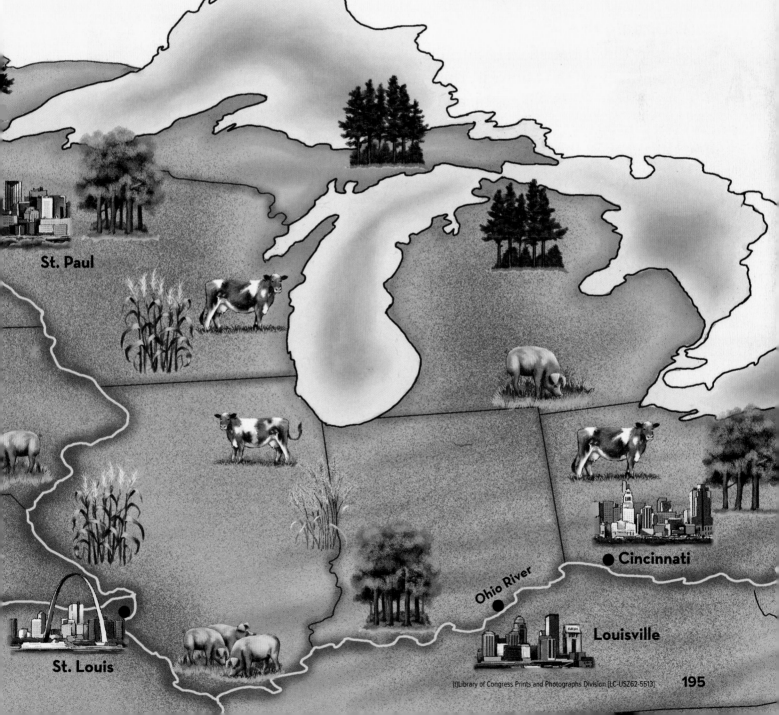

St. Paul

Cincinnati

Ohio River

Louisville

St. Louis

C LANDFORMS OF THE MIDWEST

The Midwest is mostly flat land. There are very few hills or mountains. When glaciers moved down the region, they flattened hills and filled valleys with dirt. This created plains, or flat lands covered by grasses and wildflowers. Plains covered by grasses and wildflowers are called **prairies**.

Mountains and Hills

Glaciers didn't flatten all of the hills and mountains in the Midwest. There are hills in parts of Ohio, Michigan, and even Illinois. The farther you move away from the Great Lakes, the higher the land gets. The plains slowly give way to hills, and by the time you get as far away from the Great Lakes as you can within the region, you are in the mountains.

Harney Peak, in the Black Hills mountains of South Dakota, is 7,242 feet above sea level. Underneath the Black Hills is Wind Cave. Wind Cave has more than 100 miles of winding passages. Alvin McDonald explored the cave in the 1890s. Read about his experience below.

Primary Sources

They are still finding new rooms at the Wind Cave and we have about come to the conclusion there is no end to it.

Alvin McDonald

Write About It What did Alvin McDonald conclude about Wind Cave?

(c)Wind Cave National Park/National Park Service, Wind Cave National Park (bkgd); Carol Wolfe, photographer

The Badlands

The Midwest has lakes, rivers, prairies, and mountains with caves. Is that all, you ask? No! There are also badlands in the Midwest. Badlands are very dry lands that have been chipped away by wind and water. The wind and water carved out canyons, ravines, gullies (narrow and deep holes that were created by water), and other such landforms. Badlands usually have a spectacular color that ranges from dark black or blue to bright red.

It just so happens that all of the badlands in the United States are in the Midwest. In North Dakota, there's Theodore Roosevelt National Park, while Badlands National Park is in South

PLACES

Wind Cave National Park is home to one of the world's longest caves and 28,295 acres of prairie, pine forest, and diverse wildlife.

Wind Cave

Dakota. There's also Toadstool Geologic Park in the Oglala National Grassland of Nebraska. Wind, water, and erosion have twisted the peaks and rocks of these badlands into unusual shapes.

Quick Check

Summarize **Describe the landforms of the Midwest region.**

Badlands National Park, South Dakota

D THE CLIMATE OF THE MIDWEST

Tornadoes whirl around at speeds of up to 200 miles per hour.

Temperatures in the Midwest can vary widely. The areas around the Great Lakes may also experience what is called the lake effect. Since water takes longer to heat and cool than land, the air over the water is often hotter or cooler than the air over the land. When winds blow across the lakes, they carry this hot or cool air over the land, affecting the temperature.

Storms occur in the Midwest, too. In winter, heavy snowstorms whip across the plains. In summer, strong winds can form dangerous, destructive tornadoes.

QUICK CHECK

Cause and Effect **How do the Great Lakes cause climate changes in the Midwest?**

Check Understanding

1. **VOCABULARY** Summarize this lesson in a paragraph using the vocabulary words below.

   fertile   prairie

2. **READING SKILL** Draw Conclusions Use the chart to write a paragraph about why the Mississippi River is so large.

Text Clues	Conclusion

3. **Write About It** Write a paragraph about how the geography of the Midwest drew people to settle there.

(t)crisserbug/Getty Images

Chart and Graph Skills

Compare Bar and Line Graphs

VOCABULARY
bar graph
line graph

A graph is a special kind of diagram that shows facts clearly. A **bar graph** uses bars to show information. A **line graph** shows how something has changed over time.

The bar graph below shows the value of Iowa's top five farm products in 2014. The line graph below shows how the population of the Midwest has changed.

Learn It

- Graph A is a bar graph. It shows the value of Iowa's top farm products in 2014. The height of the bars tells the value of each product in 2014.

- Graph B is a line graph. The numbers on the left of the line graph represent the population of the Midwest region. The labels at the bottom show the years that the graph covers.

Try It

- What was the population of the Midwest in 1910?

- What product had the most value in Iowa in 2014?

Apply It

- Find the number and kinds of pets your classmates have. Decide which kind of graph would be best to show the information. Make the graph.

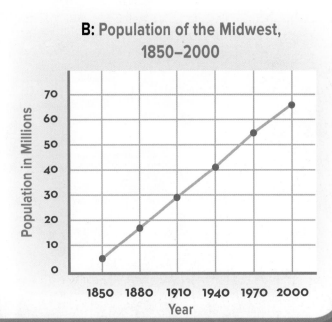

A: Iowa's Top Farm Products, 2014

B: Population of the Midwest, 1850–2000

199

Lesson 2

VOCABULARY

iron

ore

open-pit mining

agribusiness

mass production

assembly line

READING SKILL

Draw Conclusions

Copy the chart. Use it to draw conclusions about the future of the Midwest's economy.

Text Clues	Conclusion

STANDARDS FOCUS

SOCIAL STUDIES — Production, Distribution, and Consumption

GEOGRAPHY — Environment and Society

The Economy of the Midwest

Visual Preview

How have people made a living in the Midwest over time?

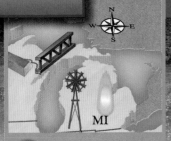

A Natural resources have always been an important part of the region's economy.

B By the 1900s, the Midwest had become a giant in steel production.

C Manufacturing and agriculture are important to the Midwest economy.

D Today the service and technology industries are important to the Midwest.

(bcl)Tupungato/Shutterstock.com, (bcr)Glow Images, (br)©Chris Sattlberger/Blend Images LLC, (bkgd)david hancock/Alamy

A A RICH LAND

The Midwest's economy starts with the land. The land provides energy sources, such as coal, oil, and natural gas, as well as metals, such as iron and copper.

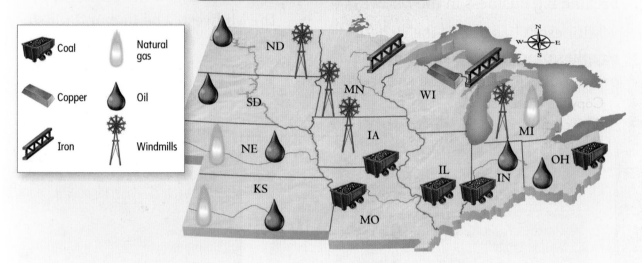

Resources of the Midwest

Coal
Natural gas
Copper
Oil
Iron
Windmills

Map Skill

LOCATION **Which states have both oil and coal as a natural resource?**

You already know that a region's economy depends heavily on the natural resources found in the region. The Midwest has many.

The region's water resources include the Great Lakes and rivers such as the Ohio, Mississippi, and Missouri. These waterways are used to ship goods across the country.

The rich soil of the Midwest provides ideal conditions for farming. When you go underground or in hills and mountains you find metals. Metals are a valuable resource.

That's not all the Midwest has. It also has wind! Strong winds that blow across the Midwest are an incredible energy source. They turn the blades of wind turbines that are used to create electricity.

QUICK CHECK

Summarize **What energy resources can be found in the Midwest?**

Ⓑ MINING FOR METAL

Iron is an important resource in the Midwest. Iron is valuable because it can be turned into steel—a strong metal used to make buildings, tools, and cars. In the 1800s, iron **ore** was found in Minnesota and Michigan. Ore is a rock with iron or another mineral inside. Iron mining became big business in the Midwest.

Minnesota has one of the richest supplies of iron ore in the world. The iron ore is found just below the surface of the ground so miners don't need to dig deep tunnels to reach it. Instead, miners dig a pit, remove the top layer of earth, and scoop up the ore beneath. This is called **open-pit mining**.

Steel and Skyscrapers

Steel changed the economy of the Midwest. The demand for steel across the United States soared in the 1800s and 1900s. Factories sprang up to turn the region's iron into steel.

Open-Pit Mine

surface

access road

pit bottom

ore

Open-pit copper mine

(bkgd)©Stephen Reynolds

By 1900 the Midwest had become a giant in steel production. Steel was used to make railroad cars, bridges, tall buildings, planes, and cars.

Willis Tower

QUICK CHECK

Main Idea and Details **How did steel change the economy of the Midwest?**

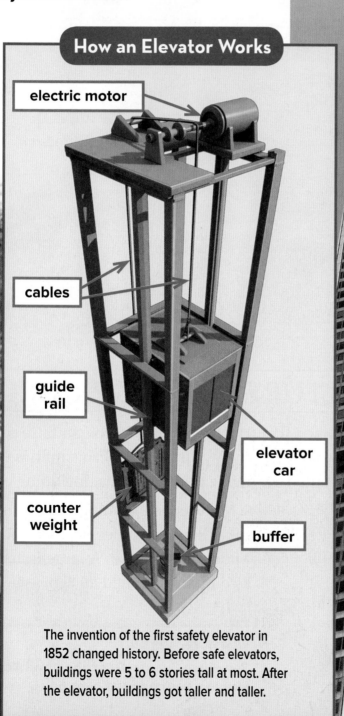

How an Elevator Works

electric motor

cables

guide rail

elevator car

counter weight

buffer

The invention of the first safety elevator in 1852 changed history. Before safe elevators, buildings were 5 to 6 stories tall at most. After the elevator, buildings got taller and taller.

Harvested soybeans being loaded onto a truck

© AGRICULTURE ON THE PRAIRIE

Early Midwestern farms were small. A farm family ate most of what they produced. After machines were invented to help farmers plant and harvest more crops faster, farmers could raise crops for money. The most important cash crops in the Midwest are corn, soybeans, and wheat. Iowa grows the most corn and soybeans in the United States, while Kansas raises the most wheat.

Dairy farming is also important to the Midwestern economy. Many farms in Wisconsin and Michigan raise cows for their milk. Some of this milk is used to make milk products, including cheese.

Midwestern farming has changed over time. Big companies now own some Midwest farmland. A large farm owned by a company is called an **agribusiness**.

QUICK CHECK

Sequence Events Describe how Midwestern farming has changed over time.

Kansas Wheat

Midwestern crops are used to feed people and animals across the United States. This is how the region earned its nickname "America's Breadbasket." These crops are also used to feed people around the world.

The Midwest does a huge business in farm exports, or the sale of crops to other nations. In 2003, Kansas farms earned $3 billion by selling their goods to other countries. The most important Kansas crop is wheat. More than half of Kansas's wheat is sold to other countries.

Japan, Mexico, Djibouti, and Nigeria are some of the countries that buy Kansas wheat. Japan is a nation with little land and many people. This means it must buy agricultural products from other countries. Although Mexico and Nigeria are nations with plenty of farmland, wheat does not grow well in their countries' hot climates.

Djibouti

▲ These bags of grain are sitting in a warehouse, ready to be shipped overseas.

A wheat field in Kansas

Kansas

Write About It Write a paragraph about why other countries may import agricultural products from the United States.

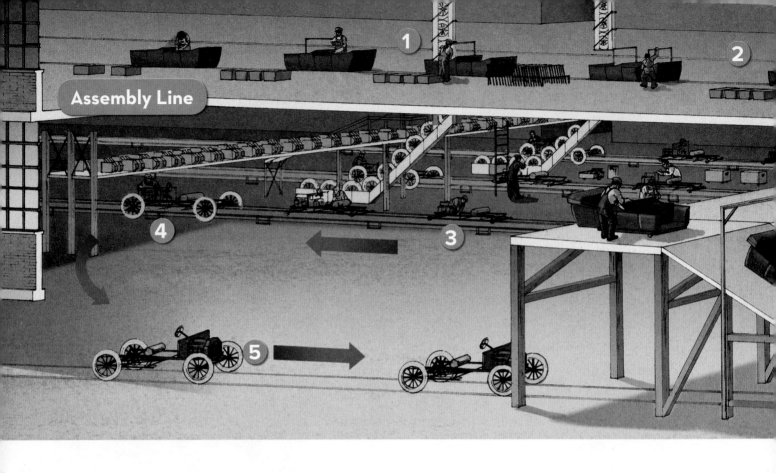

Assembly Line

Ⓓ CHANGING THE WORLD

In the early 1900s, many Midwestern cities became manufacturing centers. Detroit, Michigan, was famous for cars, Toledo, Ohio, for glass, and Minneapolis, Minnesota, for flour mills. As machines did more and more of the work on farms, people who lived in the countryside moved to Midwestern cities to find jobs in factories.

New Methods of Manufacturing

In Detroit, carmaker Henry Ford spent years researching ways to build cars quickly and cheaply. In 1913 Ford began creating cars through **mass production**. This is the manufacturing of many products at one time. Ford made thousands of cars on an **assembly line**, or a line of workers and machines that put together a product in steps. Each worker or machine does one task, again and again. The diagram above shows the steps from start to finish in Ford's early assembly line.

Working in the Midwest Today

(b)©Chris Sattlberger/Blend Images LLC

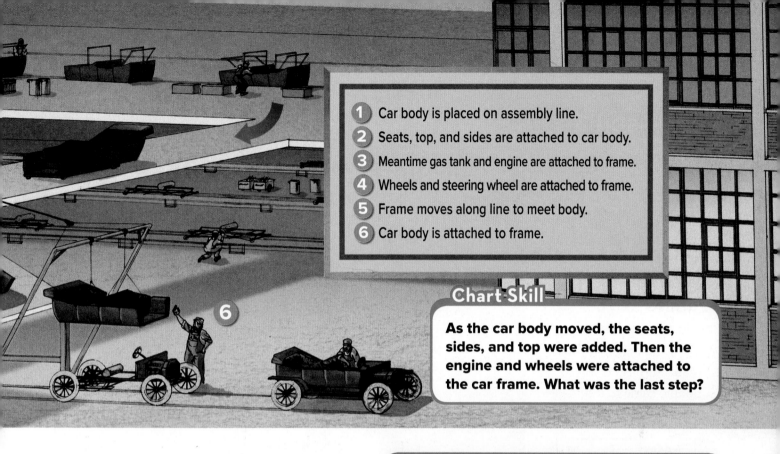

1. Car body is placed on assembly line.
2. Seats, top, and sides are attached to car body.
3. Meantime gas tank and engine are attached to frame.
4. Wheels and steering wheel are attached to frame.
5. Frame moves along line to meet body.
6. Car body is attached to frame.

Chart Skill

As the car body moved, the seats, sides, and top were added. Then the engine and wheels were attached to the car frame. What was the last step?

Jobs in the Midwest have continued to change. More people work in the service industry. Some service workers have jobs in hotels, banks, or insurance companies.

Many Midwesterners have jobs in technology. Illinois has one of the world's largest laboratories for studying atoms—Fermilab. Missouri is a leader in medical research, or looking for ways to cure diseases. Slowly, new industries will replace the factories that once led the Midwestern economy.

QUICK CHECK

Main Idea and Details **How did Henry Ford change the car industry?**

Check Understanding

1. **VOCABULARY** Write a sentence for each vocabulary word.

   iron   agribusiness   mass production

2. **READING SKILL Draw Conclusions** Use the chart to write about why the Midwest is a good place for both agriculture and industry.

Text Clues	Conclusion

3. **Write About It** Write a paragraph about iron ore in the Midwest.

Lesson 3

VOCABULARY

descendants

pioneer

migration

tradition

READING SKILL

Draw Conclusions

Copy the chart. As you read, list reasons why people came to the Midwest.

Text Clues	Conclusion

STANDARDS FOCUS

SOCIAL STUDIES   Culture

GEOGRAPHY   Human Systems

THE PEOPLE OF THE MIDWEST

Native American
Hoop Dancer

Visual Preview

How have the people of the Midwest adapted to change?

A   Native Americans were the first Midwesterners. Many of their mounds remain.

B   Many people from Europe made the Midwest their home.

C   Today immigrants to the Midwest come from all around the world.

D   The Midwest is home to many great artists, musicians, writers, and athletes.

(bl)Bear Dancer Studios/Mark Dierker, (bcl)image courtesy National Gallery of Art, (bcr)Ilene MacDonald/Alamy, (br)McGraw-Hill Education, ©Gunter Marx/Gunter Marx Photography/Corbis, (bkgd)Design Pics/Darren Greenwood

A THE FIRST MIDWESTERNERS

Native Americans were the first people of the Midwest. Today Midwesterners are the descendants, or the children and grandchildren, of Native Americans and immigrants who have come to the Midwest from around the world.

Hundreds of years ago, a group of people that were called mound builders lived in the Midwest. They were called mound builders because they built large hills. Mound builders farmed, traded, and built cities. At one time, one of the largest Mississippian cities, Cahokia, may have had up to 20,000 people living there. The mound cultures disappeared sometime around 1300. They were replaced by other cultures.

One of these cultures is the Ojibwa (sometimes called Chippewa). They lived in present-day Michigan and Ohio. The Ojibwa are part of a group of Native Americans called the Eastern Woodlands peoples. They hunted, fished, and sometimes farmed in the forests and waters of the Midwest before Europeans came to North America. Today there are many Ojibwa reservations in Wisconsin, Michigan, and Minnesota.

The Lakota live in the Midwest, too. They are part of a group known as the Plains peoples. In the past, they lived on the plains of Nebraska, North Dakota, South Dakota, and Minnesota. The Lakota depended on buffalo for food, clothing, and shelter. Today Lakota communities in the Midwest mix modern culture with traditional ways of life.

QUICK CHECK

Summarize What groups of people lived in the Midwest hundreds of years ago?

Indian Mounds Park ▶

Early settlers to the Midwest traveled by flatboat.

B PEOPLE OF THE MIDWEST

In the 1500s, European fur traders began exploring the Midwest for a new and inexpensive supply of furs. Around 1770, a fur trader named Jean Baptiste Pointe du Sable began a trading post near Lake Michigan. Du Sable was from the French colony of Haiti, an island in the Caribbean Sea. Du Sable's trading post grew into the city of Chicago.

Heading West

Fur traders shipped their goods to Europe from ports in the Northeast. Many people in these eastern cities learned about the fertile Midwestern soil. Fertile soil meant a chance for them to make a good living as a farmer. Many decided to move to the Midwest in search of this rich land with endless possibilities.

As more people traveled west, new trails opened. Later settlers traveled along these new trails in covered wagons. These wagons were pulled by horses, mules, or oxen. By 1850, more than five million people had settled in the Midwest.

image courtesy National Gallery of Art

Most of the Native Americans' land in Ohio, Indiana, and Illinois was taken by soldiers for the new settlers.

These first settlers to travel west were known as **pioneers**. The parents of Abraham Lincoln, our nation's sixteenth president, were pioneers.

New Immigrants

In the late 1800s and early 1900s, the population of the Midwest became more diverse. Norwegian farmers moved to Minnesota and people from Czechoslovakia worked the land in Nebraska. Polish immigrants found factory jobs in Illinois and thousands of Germans and Italians settled in Wisconsin, Missouri, and Ohio.

Thousands of African Americans traveled on the **Underground Railroad** to escape slavery in the South. By 1850 nearly 100,000 African Americans had fled to the Midwest and Canada. **Harriet Tubman** is one of the best known abolitionists who helped them escape.

Harriet Tubman

African Americans in the Midwest

African Americans headed to the Midwest from the South to escape slavery. They traveled on what is now known as the Underground Railroad—a network of people who helped enslaved people escape. William Wells Brown escaped slavery in 1833:

> **"**As we traveled towards a land of liberty, my heart would at times leap for joy.**"**

Later, African Americans moved from the South to the Midwest to find jobs and equality. Most settled in factory cities in Illinois, Ohio, and Michigan. Their move north between the years of 1914 and 1950 is called the Great **Migration**. A migration is a journey from one place to another.

QUICK CHECK

Summarize Describe the different people that have come to the Midwest.

◀ Midwesterners today come from around the world.

People from across the world continue to move to the Midwest. Many Mexicans have settled in Chicago. Immigrants from East Africa and Southeast Asia live in St. Paul and Minneapolis. Detroit has the largest population of Arab Americans in the United States. Today modern immigrants arrive by car, bus, or plane, not by flatboat or wagon.

Celebrating Cultures and Traditions

Different cultures make the Midwest fun and exciting. Many types of celebrations honor the region's ethnic heritage. People in Holland, Michigan, celebrate their Dutch roots with a tulip festival each spring. Milwaukee, Wisconsin, has a large German festival every summer, and St. Louis, Missouri, holds a Japanese festival every fall.

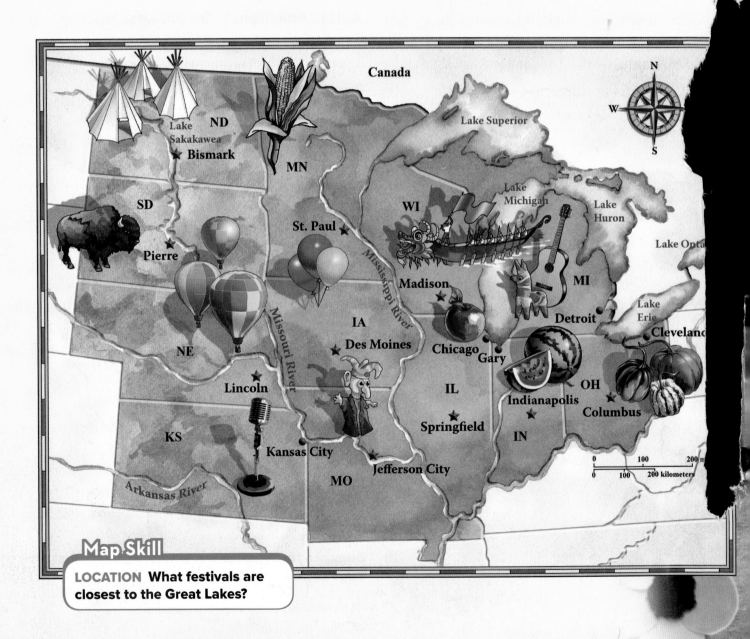

Map Skill

LOCATION What festivals are closest to the Great Lakes?

(bkgd)Ilene MacDonald/Alamy

Midwesterners also honor their region's history, weather, and **traditions**, or customs, that make the region a great place to live. St. Paul, Minnesota, holds a Winter Carnival to celebrate the region's cold weather. The Corn Palace in South Dakota is decorated with thousands of cornstalks to celebrate farming. St. Louis is proud of its history as the "Gateway to the West."

Dutch descendants celebrate their heritage during the Tulip Festival in Holland, Michigan. ▼

Legend

Great Mideast Dragon Boat Festival in Racine, WI

Apple Festival in Long Grove, IL

Brownstown Melonfest in Brownstown, IN

Circleville Pumpkin Show in Circleville, OH

PuppetFest Midwest in Trenton, MO

Iowa State Fair in Des Moines, IA

Tulipanes Latino Art & Film Festival in Holland, MI

Kansas City Kansas Street Blues Festival

Hot Air Balloon Festival in Wakefield, NE

Buffalo Roundup and Arts Festival in Custer State Park, SD

National boundary
State boundary
Major city
State capital

Northern Plains Indian Culture Fest Stanton, ND

Hinckley Corn & Clover Festival in Hinckly, MN

Citizenship

Express Your Opinion

Three friends learned that pollution was threatening the brook trout in streams near their township. In an effort to protect the fish, the girls formed a branch of a group called Save Our Streams (SOS). They wrote letters and talked with people and leaders in the area to work on a plan for keeping the streams clean.

Write About It Write a letter to your local newspaper expressing your opinion about an issue.

D MIDWEST ART, MUSIC, AND FUN

Throughout history, the states of the Midwest have been home to many great artists, musicians, writers, and athletes. Some of our nation's best-known writers, for example, are from the Midwest. Laura Ingalls Wilder wrote amazing stories about her life as a pioneer. The poet Thomas Stearns Eliot, known as T. S. Eliot, was born in St. Louis. Read what he had to say about it.

The Midwest is also known for its music. What kinds of music do you like? In the Midwest, the best answer is all of them! Cleveland disc jockey Alan Freed helped develop rock and roll in the 1950s. Today, Cleveland is home to the Rock and Roll Hall of Fame. Detroit is famous for soul music. Kansas City is known for jazz. Bluegrass star Alison Krauss grew up in Illinois.

Mount Rushmore National Memorial, South Dakota

(bl)Photodisc/Punchstock, (bkgd)McGraw-Hill Education

The 500 Mile Race

The largest sport facility in the world is in Indianapolis, Indiana, and is called the Indianapolis Motor Speedway. Every year, it holds the Indy 500 race over Memorial weekend. In 2006, the Indy 500 race celebrated its 90th anniversary. But that's not all that happens at the Speedway. Famous races such as the Allstate 400 and the United States Grand Prix are also held there. These races attract thousands of visitors from around the world.

▲ The Indianapolis 500 is held every year in Indianapolis, Indiana.

QUICK CHECK

Summarize **What are some of the things people in the Midwest do for fun?**

Check Understanding

1. **VOCABULARY** Use each vocabulary word to describe the people of the Midwest.

    pioneer   migration   tradition

2. **READING SKILL** Draw Conclusions Use the chart from page 208 to write about why you think the Midwest inspires so many writers and artists.

Text Clues	Conclusion

3. **Write About It** Write a short essay about what the Great Migration might have been like for the people who migrated.

◄ The Rock and Roll Hall of Fame

Vocabulary

Copy the sentences below. Use the list of vocabulary words to fill in the blanks.

mass production **iron**
fertile   **pioneer**

1. Wheat and corn are grown in the ____ soil of the Midwest.

2. Henry Ford was one of the first to use ____ in manufacturing.

3. Steel is made in part from a metal known as ____.

4. An early settler of the Midwest is called a ____.

Comprehension and Critical Thinking

5. How were the Great Lakes formed?

6. Who was Jean Baptiste Pointe du Sable?

7. **Reading Skill** Why is the Midwest home to so many musical styles? Draw conclusions.

8. **Critical Thinking** What do you think it was like to be a pioneer?

Skill

Use Line and Bar Graphs

Write a complete sentence to answer each question.

9. Which state has the largest population?

10. Which state has the smallest population?

Population of Great Lakes States, 2014

People in Millions (y-axis: 0, 2, 4, 6, 8, 10, 12, 14)

States (x-axis): Ohio, Michigan, Indiana, Illinois, Wisconsin, Minnesota

Test Preparation

Read the paragraphs. Then answer the questions.

Without warm ocean breezes, much of the Midwest is extremely cold in the winter. Icy winds travel across the plains, chilling everything in their path. Blizzards, or winter storms with strong winds and snow, can form and become dangerous.

Cities near the Great Lakes receive the heaviest snowfall. This lake effect snow occurs when cold, dry air from Canada meets warmer, damp air over the Great Lakes. Moisture in the air cools and becomes snow. Some areas can receive more than 200 inches of lake effect snow each year.

1. What conclusions can you draw about winters in the Midwest?

   A. It is warmer inland in winter.

   B. Most people leave the Midwest during the winter.

   C. The weather in Canada affects winters in the Midwest.

   D. The weather in Canada is cold.

2. What causes lake effect snow?

   A. temperatures fall below freezing

   B. dry air from Canada meets damp air over the Great Lakes

   C. winds travel across the plains

   D. cold air comes from Canada

3. What cities receive the heaviest snowfall?

   A. Most of the cities in the Midwest receive heavy snowfall.

   B. Cities near the Great Lakes

   C. Cities in Canada

   D. None of the cities in the Midwest experience heavy snowfall.

4. How do you think the lake effect snow affects the people of the Midwest?

5. What might it be like to live in a part of the Midwest that has an extreme climate, such as the Badlands or a desert?

Activities

How do natural resources affect a region's growth?

Write About the Big Idea

FOLDABLES™
Study Organizer

Expository Essay

Use the Unit 5 foldable to help you write an essay that answers the Big Idea question, "How do natural resources affect a region's growth?" Be sure to begin your essay with an introduction. Use the notes you wrote under each tab in the foldable for details to support each main idea. End with a concluding paragraph that answers the question.

Geography | Economy | People

Create a Diorama

Work in a small group to create a diorama showing a pioneer family coming to the Midwest on a flatboat or covered wagon.
Here's how you can get started:

1. Research the pioneers who headed west.

2. Choose the structures you would like to represent in your diorama.

3. Choose the materials you will use to build your diorama.

4. Build the pieces and assemble the diorama.

5. Write a paragraph telling what is happening in your diorama.

Unit 6

EXPLORE The Big Idea

Essential Question

How do people adapt to their environments?

FOLDABLES Study Organizer

Cause and Effect
Use a layered book foldable to take notes as you read Unit 6. Write **The Southwest** across the bottom of the foldable. Label the layers **Geography**, **Economy**, and **People**. Use the foldable to organize information as you read.

People
Economy
Geography
The Southwest

LOG ON For more about Unit 6 go to connectED.mcgraw-hill.com

The Southwest

PEOPLE, PLACES, AND EVENTS

Francisco Vasquez de Coronado

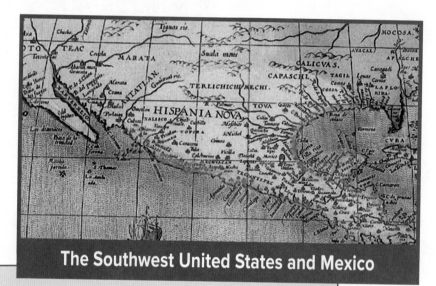
The Southwest United States and Mexico

Between 1540 and 1542, a Spanish explorer named **Francisco Vasquez de Coronado** led a group of people in a search for cities of gold. Although he did not find any gold, Coronado explored **the Southwest United States and Mexico.**

Today you can visit the Coronado National Memorial in Arizona.

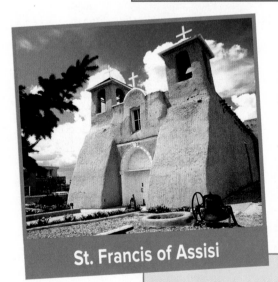
St. Francis of Assisi

Traditional Mexican Dancers

Before the Southwest became part of the United States, most of it belonged to Mexico. Mexican culture can be seen in buildings such as the **St. Francis of Assisi** church.

Today you can watch **traditional Mexican dancers** at festivals throughout the region.

(tr)Digital Vision/Getty Images, (bl)Jack Hollingsworth/Photodisc/Getty Images, (br)Glow Images

Bill Pickett

By the mid-1800s, ranching and cattle herding were important to the economy of the Southwest. Nat Love, Addison Jones, and **Bill Pickett** were famous African American cowboys.

Today you can visit the **National Cowboys of Color Museum and Hall of Fame** in Fort Worth, Texas.

The Grand Canyon

John Wesley Powell

The Grand Canyon is a beautiful natural landform in our country. **John Wesley Powell** was one of the first explorers to see its deep ravines and the rushing Colorado River.

Today you can visit Grand Canyon National Park in Arizona and explore its many trails.

Southwest Region

The hot, dry climate of the Southwest hosts plants, animals, and landforms.

1 Chili peppers are often used in southwestern cooking.

5 The Alamo, a Spanish mission, was the site of an 1836 battle between Texas and Mexico. Today it is a museum devoted to Texas history.

Lake Mead

Colorado River

AZ

Phoenix

SONORAN DESERT

Gulf of California

2 The Grand Canyon is one mile deep and 277 miles long.

COLORADO PLATEAU

PAINTED DESERT

Gila River

1

Santa Fe ★

Albuquerque

NM

ROCKY MOUNTAINS

Pecos River

Rio Grande

MEXICO

Great Salt Plains State Park

Oklahoma City ★

OK

4

Amarillo

Red River

Dallas

Abilene

TX

EDWARDS PLATEAU

Austin ★

Colorado River

Brazos River

San Antonio **5**
THE ALAMO

GULF COASTAL PLAIN

Houston

3

Gulf of Mexico

0   100   200 miles
0   100   200 kilometers

N
W   E
S

3 Oil is an important natural resource. Machines called oil derricks help pump oil from underground.

4 The armadillo is found throughout the Southwest. *Armadillo* means "little armored one" in Spanish.

Lesson 1

VOCABULARY

mesa

butte

canyon

drought

aquifer

READING SKILL

Cause and Effect

Copy the chart. As you read, fill it in with information about how the geography of the Southwest formed.

Cause	→	Effect
	→	
	→	
	→	

STANDARDS FOCUS

SOCIAL STUDIES — People, Places, and Environments

GEOGRAPHY — Physical Systems

Visual Preview

How have the people of the Southwest adapted to their environment?

A The Southwest has coastline, plains, prairies, deserts, and mountains.

B Erosion has caused some strange landforms in the Southwest.

C The Southwest has long rivers.

D The Southwest has a dry climate with little rainfall.

FROM COAST TO PLAINS

There are only four states in the Southwest region, but the area it covers is huge. It's no surprise that this region has many different landforms and environments.

There's only one state in the Southwest that has a coastline— Texas. This coastline runs along the Gulf of Mexico. A gulf is a body of water that is partly surrounded by land. The flat lowland next to the coast is called the Gulf Coastal Plain.

As you move inland from the Texas coastline, the land rises. You soon come to broad, rolling plains which continue into Oklahoma. The plains are dry, but grass grows well there. This area is a vast prairie, or grassland. Once, Native American groups and European settlers hunted buffalo on these plains. Today cattle graze here instead.

Other Landforms

The Southwest isn't just coast and plains. In parts of Texas, there are swamps. There are also many deserts in the Southwest. All the Southwestern states have mountains. The plants and animals in each of these environments have adapted to their surroundings.

Plants and Animals of the Southwest

Prickly-pear Cactus

Roadrunner

Joshua Tree

Kangaroo Rat

Saguaro Cactus

Jackrabbit

QUICK CHECK

Cause and Effect **How has the use of the prairie in the Southwest changed?**

225

Picture a tower of rock 1,000 feet tall that looks like a ship. Another rock has a hole through it. Still others look like mittens sticking out of the ground. Why are the rocks such unusual shapes?

Eroded Rock

The strange forms were made by erosion. Over millions of years, wind wore away the softer rock, leaving the remaining harder rock in unusual shapes. Some of the strangest formations are in an area of Arizona and Utah called Monument Valley.

Plateaus, Mesas, and Buttes

Look at the map of the Southwest Region at the beginning of this unit. Find the place where Utah, Colorado, Arizona, and New Mexico meet. Do you see why this spot is known as the Four Corners? This is where you find a huge area called the Colorado Plateau that extends into four states. A plateau is an area that

butte

In Monument Valley, Arizona, the softer rocks have worn away and the harder rocks remain.

rises steeply from the land around it. At 130,000 square miles, the Colorado Plateau is larger than the entire state of New Mexico!

Erosion has created other unusual landforms, too. Land that looks like high hills with flat tops are called **mesas** from the Spanish word for table. The region also has **buttes**. A butte is a hill with a flat top and its width is smaller than the width of a mesa.

PLACES

One special place on the Colorado Plateau is **the Painted Desert** in Arizona. Here the sides of the mesas and buttes look like an artist has used a giant brush to paint stripes of blue, purple, orange, red, pink, and gold.

The Painted Desert

QUICK CHECK

Summarize **What caused the strange rock formations seen in the Southwest?**

plateau

According to a famous legend, a giant named Paul Bunyan dragged his pick behind him as he walked across Arizona. The pick left a gash in the ground a mile deep and almost 300 miles long!

Today we call this area the Grand Canyon. A **canyon** is a deep valley with steep rocky walls. Of course, we know the Grand Canyon was really formed by the Colorado River.

The Colorado River starts in the Rocky Mountains. From there, it flows through five states and empties into the Gulf of Mexico. On its way, the river carries along dirt and pebbles. As the dirt and pebbles flow downriver, they rub against the river banks. Over millions of years, the dirt and pebbles carried in the running water wore away softer rocks and carved out the Grand Canyon.

The Grand Canyon is deeper than 22 football fields are long.

(bkgd)Michael Russelle/Digital Vision/SuperStock

How grand is the Grand Canyon? At places it is a mile deep. If there was a bridge across the Grand Canyon at its widest point (18 miles), it would take you about six hours to walk across it. Read what President Roosevelt said about the Grand Canyon.

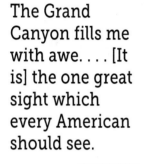

The Grand Canyon fills me with awe. . . . [It is] the one great sight which every American should see.

PRESIDENT
THEODORE ROOSEVELT

The Rio Grande

The Rio Grande is another important river in the Southwest. Rio Grande means "big river" in Spanish. The Rio Grande flows almost 1,900 miles from the Rocky Mountains, across New Mexico, and forms the border between Texas and Mexico. Much of its water is used by farms along the way.

QUICK CHECK

Cause and Effect **How did the Grand Canyon form?**

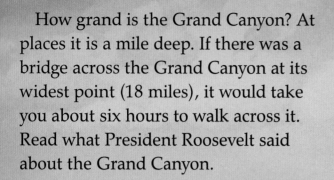

Natalie wanted to learn more about water resources. She watched a television program about Sandia Laboratory in New Mexico. Scientists there are finding ways to desalinate ocean water, or to turn ocean water into freshwater by taking the salt out of it. Natalie decided to write to Sandia Laboratory to find out more about how this process worked.

Write About It Research how desalination works. Write a report explaining why freshwater is an important resource.

The Southwest is the driest region of the United States. In some places, such as in the Sonoran Desert in Arizona, it rains as little as three inches a year. Because there is so little rain, having enough water is always a big concern.

The grasslands of Oklahoma and Texas normally get enough rain for prairie grasses to grow, but in some years there can be a **drought**. A drought is a long period of time with little or no rain. There was a drought during the 1930s. The crops died and the soil was so dry it turned to dust. The winds whipped up the dust and blew it in great drifts. The area became known as the Dust Bowl. Thousands of farmers had to sell their farms and leave the area.

Underground Water

Much of the water used for drinking and for watering crops in the Midwest and Southwest now comes from the Ogallala **Aquifer**. An aquifer is an underground area of rock, sand, or gravel that contains water. Aquifers formed thousands of years ago from streams, rivers, and melting glaciers. They are a renewable resource. Sometimes, however, people use a lot of water, and there is not enough rainfall to refill the aquifers. Then we have a shortage of water.

QUICK CHECK

Summarize **What are the problems with water in the Southwest?**

Rain in the Southwest usually comes in the form of afternoon thunderstorms.

Check Understanding

1. **VOCABULARY** Draw a picture of each vocabulary word.

   mesa   butte   canyon

2. **READING SKILL Cause and Effect** Use the chart to write about what would happen to the water supply if the aquifers in the Southwest were emptied.

Cause	→	Effect
	→	
	→	
	→	

3. **Write About It** Write a paragraph about challenges that the geography and climate of the Southwest cause for people living there.

Map and Globe Skills

Use Special Purpose Maps: Population Maps

VOCABULARY

population density

population distribution

When you need to know the number of people who live in a place, you can look at a population map. Most population maps show population density. **Population density** measures how many people live in a certain area. The populations might be shown by state, county, or smaller areas.

Another kind of population map shows **population distribution**. This kind of map shows you where in an area people live. Look at the maps on the next page.

Learn It

- Map A is a population density map. On this map, the different colors stand for different population densities per county.

- The map key in Map A shows the number of people that each color represents. The color orange shows that between 100,000 and 199,999 people live in the counties that are shaded orange. Which color stands for the most people?

- Map B is a population distribution map.

- The map key in Map B shows where people are distributed within an area. Each color represents the number of people per square mile. For example, areas that are dark purple contain between 7,000 and 23,000 per square mile. By looking at the distribution of color, you can see where the most people live.

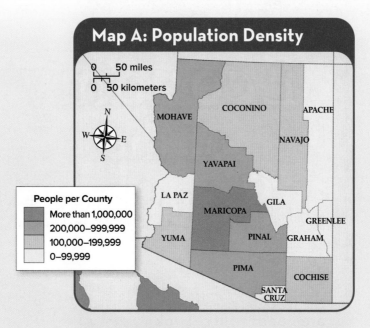

Map A: Population Density

0 50 miles
0 50 kilometers

People per County
- More than 1,000,000
- 200,000–999,999
- 100,000–199,999
- 0–99,999

MOHAVE, COCONINO, APACHE, NAVAJO, YAVAPAI, LA PAZ, GILA, MARICOPA, GREENLEE, YUMA, PINAL, GRAHAM, PIMA, COCHISE, SANTA CRUZ

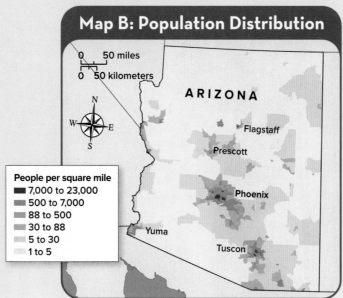

Map B: Population Distribution

0 50 miles
0 50 kilometers

ARIZONA

People per square mile
- 7,000 to 23,000
- 500 to 7,000
- 88 to 500
- 30 to 88
- 5 to 30
- 1 to 5

Flagstaff, Prescott, Phoenix, Yuma, Tuscon

Try It

Look at the maps. Then answer the questions.

- What does the color yellow mean in the key for Map A?

- Which county has more than 1,000,000 people?

Apply It

Look at the maps. Then answer the questions.

- What does Map B tell you that Map A does not?

- Which metropolitan area is larger, Tuscon or Flagstaff?

Lesson 2

VOCABULARY

kerosene

irrigation

silicon

solar energy

READING SKILL

Cause and Effect
Copy the chart. As
you read, fill it in with
information about the
economy of the
Southwest.

Cause	→	Effect
	→	
	→	
	→	

STANDARDS FOCUS

SOCIAL STUDIES — Science, Technology, and Society

GEOGRAPHY — Environment and Society

The Economy of the Southwest

Visual Preview

How do people in the Southwest use natural resources?

A Oil, minerals and cattle are natural resources of the Southwest.

B Growing crops and grazing animals are important in the Southwest.

C Many people in the Southwest work in technology.

(bc)David Hughes/iStock/Getty Images, (br)NASA, (bkgd)Comstock Images/Alamy

A UNDERGROUND RESOURCES

If you flew over Oklahoma and Texas, you would see hundreds of oil wells. Every day, these wells pump up the Southwest's most valuable resource—petroleum.

Most petroleum is found deep underground. In the 1850s, petroleum was hard to get. People used it to make **kerosene**, a fuel oil burned in lamps and heaters. Then someone discovered that oil could be pumped to the surface through wells drilled in the ground.

Almost overnight, land that contained petroleum became extremely valuable. People throughout the region began to drill oil wells. Today the oil industry provides many jobs in the Southwest. Petroleum is used to make heating oil, gasoline, paints, and plastics.

EVENT

In 1901, **oil was found** in Spindletop, Texas. The new oil well produced over 75,000 barrels a day.

Spindletop

Mines and Metals

Gold, silver, and copper are all metals found in the Southwest. Use the map below to learn where to find other resources of the Southwest.

QUICK CHECK

Cause and Effect **What happened after underground petroleum was discovered?**

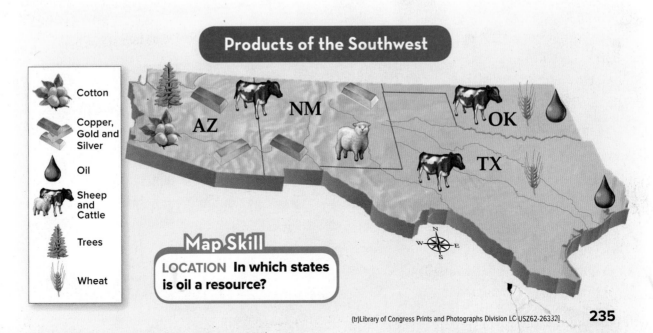

Products of the Southwest

- Cotton
- Copper, Gold and Silver
- Oil
- Sheep and Cattle
- Trees
- Wheat

Map Skill

LOCATION **In which states is oil a resource?**

Not every resource in the Southwest is underground. If you drove through the Southwest, you would see mile after mile of farmland. The crops you see growing will vary depending on where you are.

Sugar cane and rice grow along the Gulf Coast in Texas where there is plenty of rain. In Oklahoma and Texas, farmers grow wheat and barley. Vegetables such as potatoes, cauliflower, broccoli, and lettuce are also grown in the Southwest.

In the 1830s and 1840s, many farmers moved from the Southeast to the Southwest to grow cotton. Today cotton is grown in all four southwestern states.

Because the Southwest is a dry region, farmers sometimes have a problem getting enough water. Some farmers use **irrigation** to grow crops. Irrigation is using pipes or ditches to bring water to fields. Many residents worry that the region's limited resources cannot provide enough water for everyone to use. Using water for irrigation has caused conflicts between farmers, Native Americans, and city residents.

Sheep graze in the desert in Navajo Nation, Arizona.

Cotton grows in all four states in the Southwest.

cotton

Grazing Fields

The plains of Oklahoma and Texas are dry. They do not have enough water for trees, but grass grows well there. Buffalo once roamed over this land and ate the grass. Today the grassy plains feed sheep and cattle.

chili peppers

Chili peppers grow in this irrigated field in Phoenix, AZ

Cattle came to the Southwest with Spanish settlers who started the region's first ranches. Later many African Americans, Native Americans, and whites worked together as cowboys in the Southwest.

You can still find cattle and sheep ranches across the Southwest. Texas leads the nation in producing beef cattle. Think of Southwest cattle next time you eat a hamburger!

QUICK CHECK

Make Generalizations **Why is the Southwest a good place for cattle ranches?**

Cowboys work on cattle ranches across the Southwest.

(tl)chengyuzheng/iStock/Getty Images, (cl)Photo by Tim McCabe, USDA Natural Resources Conservation Service, (b)Design Pics/Carson Ganci

C TECHNOLOGY

Have you used a computer or cell phone lately? The chip in your computer or cell phone may have come from the Southwest. Texas, Arizona, and Oklahoma are all known for their computer technology industries.

New Mexico has worked hard to get technology companies to move there. New Mexico governor Bill Richardson said:

"Technology-based economic development builds on some of New Mexico's greatest strengths in science, research and technology. . . ."

Today, central New Mexico is home to a large computer industry. The nickname for this area is "**silicon** mesa." Silicon is a natural material that is found in rocks and sand. It is used to make computer chips. Did you notice a landform of the Southwest in the nickname?

Another important technology is the development of new sources of energy. One of these is **solar energy**, or energy that comes from the Sun. Solar energy is collected when sunlight hits solar panels. The Sun shines a lot in New Mexico, which makes it the perfect place for research into solar energy.

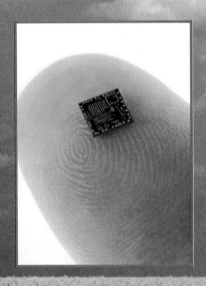

◀ Many computer chips are made in the Southwest.

Solar panels absorb energy from the sun to use for electricity or heating. ▼

(t)Photographer's Choice RF/Getty Images, (b)allou/Getty Images

Ships and Spaceships

Texas has a long coast on the Gulf of Mexico. The Gulf ports of Houston, Texas, and Galveston, Texas, are major centers for shipping oil and other goods.

Another kind of ship is important in Houston, too—the space ship! Houston is the location of the Johnson Space Center, where part of our country's space program is located.

Because of its clear skies and dry climate, the Southwest is a good place for telescopes. Scientists use these telescopes to gather data about the stars and learn more about outer space.

QUICK CHECK

Summarize **What different technology industries exist in the Southwest?**

Check Understanding

1. **VOCABULARY** Write a sentence for each vocabulary word.

   kerosene   irrigation   silicon

2. **READING SKILL Cause and Effect** Use the chart to write about how the climate affects agriculture in the Southwest.

Cause	→	Effect
	→	
	→	
	→	

3. **Write About It** Write a paragraph about how new technologies have helped the Southwest grow.

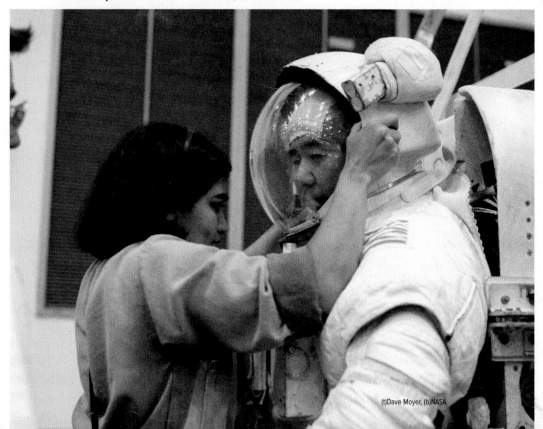

Astronaut Takao Doi prepares for training at NASA's Johnson Space Center in Houston, Texas. ▼

(t)Dave Moyer, (b)NASA

THE PEOPLE OF THE SOUTHWEST

VOCABULARY

pueblo

adobe

powwow

READING SKILL

Cause and Effect
Copy the chart. As you read, fill it in with information about why different people have moved to the Southwest.

Cause	→	Effect
	→	
	→	
	→	

STANDARDS FOCUS

SOCIAL STUDIES   Culture

GEOGRAPHY   The Uses of Geography

Taos Pueblo in New Mexico

Visual Preview

How does the culture of a people affect their region?

A Native American groups include the Navajo, Hopi, and Pueblo people.

B Many people in the Southwest have Spanish or Mexican heritage.

C Immigrants and older Americans are moving to the Southwest today.

D People in the Southwest celebrate their culture in festivals.

A MYSTERY

Although Chaco Canyon is quiet now, many people lived there over 1,000 years ago. Who were these people? Where did they go?

Long ago, the people called the Ancestral Pueblo lived in Chaco Canyon. **Pueblo** is the Spanish word for village, and the Spanish use it to describe both the people and their homes. The Ancestral Pueblo built their homes along the steep sides of cliffs. They were built of **adobe**, a sun-baked clay brick. The pueblo in Chaco Canyon was once the center of trade and culture for the Ancestral Pueblo. It was home to about 1,000 people.

About 700 years ago, the Ancestral Pueblo left behind their cliff buildings, pueblos, and the beautiful pottery that they made. They settled in other parts of the Southwest. Today's Zuni, Hopi, and other Pueblo people are the descendents of the Ancestral Pueblo.

Some Pueblo people still live in pueblos today. The people of Acoma Pueblo in northwest New Mexico say that people have lived there for more than 700 years. That makes it the oldest continuously lived-in community in North America.

PEOPLE

After the Spanish introduced sheep to the Southwest, **Navajo weavers** used the sheep's wool to make beautiful blankets and rugs. The Navajo are still famous for their weaving.

Navajo weaver

The Navajo

Between 500 and 1,000 years ago, the Navajo (or Diné) came to the Southwest from farther north. At first the Navajo lived by hunting and growing corn.

The Spanish arrived in the 1500s and brought sheep to the region. The Navajo soon learned how to raise large herds of sheep.

Today many Native Americans of the Southwest live on reservations. In fact the Navajo reservation is the largest reservation in the United States. It covers parts of three states.

QUICK CHECK

Cause and Effect **How did Navajo life change after the Spanish brought sheep?**

B EUROPEANS IN THE SOUTHWEST

The first Europeans to explore the Southwest were the Spanish. Some, like Francisco de Coronado, came looking for gold. He came in 1540 with nearly 300 soldiers. The Spanish had heard stories of seven cities of gold and were eager to claim such a prize.

Coronado trekked as far as Kansas before he gave up. He found no gold, but he claimed many lands for Spain.

Some European explorers brought people from Africa to be scouts or guides in the Southwest. One of these men was Estevanico, a man from the country of Morocco in North Africa.

Spanish Settlements

Before the Pilgrims landed on Plymouth Rock, the Spanish had already built several settlements in the Southwest. One of their earliest settlements, Santa Fe, was founded in 1607 in the area that would become New Mexico. It was one of the first European settlements in the United States. The Spanish would build many more settlements in the Southwest.

Signs of Spanish and Mexican heritage can still be seen in the Southwest. In some locations, such as San Antonio, Texas, and Santa Fe, New Mexico, the city names are Spanish. Many buildings in the Southwest

(bkgd)Library of Congress, Prints and Photographs Division [LC-USZ62-37993]

This church in Sorroco, New Mexico, was built between 1615 and 1626 in a Spanish style.

Francisco de Coronado and his soldiers explored the Southwest

were built using Spanish styles. Today more than one out of every four people in the Southwest has either Spanish or Mexican heritage.

Other Settlers

Once the area became part of the United States, other settlers hurried to get there. Some came looking for silver, copper, and gold. Others came to farm or to raise cattle and sheep.

QUICK CHECK

Sequence **What happened to the lands that Coronado began to explore in 1540?**

Primary Sources

The first Spanish explorer of the Southwest was Cabeza de Vaca. In 1537, he wrote in his journal about a statement made by local Native American people:

"[T]hey gave us to understand that, very far from there, was a province called Apalachen in which there was much gold."

Write About It Write a journal entry describing what Cabeza de Vaca saw as he explored the Southwest.

For many years, the Southwest had the fewest people of any region. In the early 1900s, artists began coming to Arizona and New Mexico. They came because of the region's natural beauty. Today the cities of Santa Fe and Taos in New Mexico are famous as centers for art. Artists there are often inspired by the art of the region's Native Americans.

The development of the automobile and the highways and roads that followed made it easier for people to travel across the Southwest. Roads also made it easier to ship goods. By 1911 Phoenix, Arizona, had its first paved street.

Another reason people moved to the Southwest was air conditioning. In 1911 Willis Carrier built the first air conditioner. Within 20 years, many buildings in the Southwest were cooled by air conditioning. This invention made

Sandia Mountains ▲

it possible for more people to live year-round in the warm Southwestern climate.

Population Increases

People are still moving to the Southwest. Phoenix, Arizona, is the fastest growing city in the nation. Many newcomers to the region are immigrants from other countries, such as Mexico and Honduras.

Tourists gather under a hoodoo at Lees Ferry, Arizona.

(tr)Sergio Salvador/Getty Images, (b)©Dave Moyer

Other newcomers come from different regions of the United States. Many older Americans retire to the Southwest. Tourists visit the Southwest, too. They are attracted by the natural beauty, the area's history and culture, and the mild winter climate.

QUICK CHECK

Summarize **What things attract people to the Southwest today?**

DataGraphic
Population Growth

Study the graph and map. Then answer the questions that follow.

Population Growth in the Southwest

People in Millions / Year
1900 1920 1940 1960 1980 2000

Phoenix, Arizona

New River — Maricopa County — Salt River — Gila River — Pinal County

0 5 10 miles
0 5 10 kilometers

Urban area, 1955
Urban area, 1975
Urban area, 2000
County boundary

Think About Changes in Population

1. How has the size of the urban area of Phoenix, Arizona, changed since 1955?

2. What is the difference in the population in the Southwest between 1900 and 2014?

3. How are the data shown in the chart and in the map similar?

245

▲ The buffalo dance is one of many types of dances that can be seen at Native American celebrations.

Ⓓ CELEBRATING CULTURE

Like the people of other regions, Southwesterners like to celebrate their heritage. Some attend **powwows**. A powwow is a Native American festival. What can you do at a powwow? You can see Native American dancing, listen to drummers, and taste fry bread, a delicious treat. One of the largest powwows in North America is held in Albuquerque, New Mexico, every spring.

Rain is important to Native Americans. Without enough rain, it is difficult to raise crops. The Hopi people pray to kachinas, or spirits, for rain. Every two years in August, dancers perform the Snake Dance to ask these spirits for rain. This

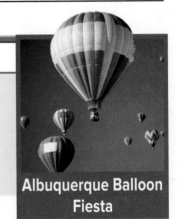

EVENT

Every October, hot air balloons fill the skies at the **Albuquerque Balloon Fiesta** in Albuquerque, New Mexico.

Albuquerque Balloon Fiesta

ceremony attracts thousands of visitors to Arizona.

Some festivals are held to celebrate local foods. In Crystal Beach, Texas, a Crab Festival is held every year. At the Hatch Chile Festival in Hatch, New Mexico, people can taste the chili peppers in many different recipes.

Still other festivals are just for fun. Albuquerque, New Mexico, has a hot-air balloon fiesta every October.

Historical Celebrations

Many people in the Southwest celebrate Cinco de Mayo, which means the "fifth of May" in Spanish. This Mexican holiday honors the Mexican army's victory over French soldiers at the Battle of Puebla in 1862.

March 2 is a state holiday in Texas. This holiday is called Texas Independence Day. On this day, people in Texas remember March 2, 1836. This was the day the settlers in Texas declared their independence from Mexico.

QUICK CHECK

Compare and Contrast **Describe the different celebrations in the Southwest.**

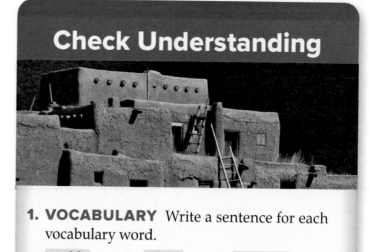

Check Understanding

1. **VOCABULARY** Write a sentence for each vocabulary word.

   pueblo   adobe   powwow

2. **READING SKILL** **Cause and Effect** Use the chart to write about why the population of the Southwest has grown.

Cause	→	Effect
	→	
	→	
	→	

3. **Write About It** Write a paragraph about how Spanish settlers influenced the culture of the Southwest.

Cinco de Mayo is a Mexican holiday that is celebrated throughout the Southwest.

Vocabulary

Copy the sentences below. Use the vocabulary words to fill in the blanks.

adobe   **irrigation**

solar energy   **drought**

1. A farmer's entire crop could die if there is a ___ .

2. Many farmers in the Southwest depend on ___ for water.

3. Since New Mexico is sunny, it is a good place to study ___.

4. People in the Southwest use ___ bricks for building.

Comprehension and Critical Thinking

5. What natural resources are found in the Southwest?

6. To which countries did the states of the Southwest once belong?

7. **Critical Thinking** What makes grass important to the economy of the Southwest?

8. **Reading Skill** What is one cause of population growth in the Southwest?

Skill

Use Special Purpose Maps

Use the map to answer the questions.

9. Which county on the map has a population density of more than 1,000,000 people?

10. Which counties on the map have the second greatest population density?

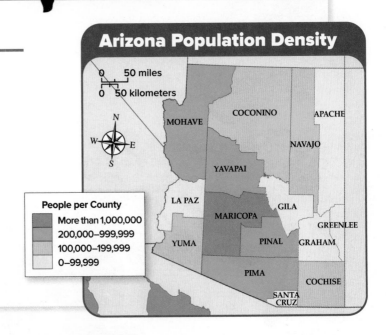

Arizona Population Density

0   50 miles

0   50 kilometers

N W E S

COCONINO   APACHE

MOHAVE

NAVAJO

YAVAPAI

LA PAZ   GILA

MARICOPA

GREENLEE

YUMA   PINAL   GRAHAM

PIMA

COCHISE

SANTA CRUZ

People per County

More than 1,000,000
200,000–999,999
100,000–199,999
0–99,999

Digital image courtesy of the Getty's Open Content Program

Test Preparation

Read the paragraph. Then answer the questions.

> The artist Georgia O'Keeffe especially loved the Southwest. Although she was not born there, she loved the landscape and the light in the region. She said it inspired her to do some of her best work. When asked why she liked Texas, for instance, she replied: "The openness. The dry landscape. The beauty of that wild world."

1. What is the main idea of this passage?

   A. Georgia O'Keeffe was a great artist.

   B. Texas has a very dry landscape.

   C. Georgia O'Keeffe loved the Southwest and thought it inspired some of her best work.

   D. Georgia O'Keeffe was not born in the Southwest.

2. Which statement best explains why the writer of the passage included a quote from Georgia O'Keeffe?

   A. The writer liked the sound of the quote.

   B. The writer liked New Mexico.

   C. The quote explains how O'Keeffe painted her pictures.

   D. The quote explains what O'Keeffe loved about the Southwest.

3. What inspired O'Keefe to do her best work?

   A. the landscape

   B. the landscape and the light

   C. the fact that she was born there

   D. the openness

4. Why might open, beautiful landscapes inspire an artist?

5. What else do you think might inspire an artist?

The Big Idea Activities

How do people adapt to their environment?

Write About the Big Idea

Expository Essay
In Unit 6, you read about the geography, economy, and people of the Southwest. Review the notes in the completed foldable. Begin with an introductory paragraph describing the environment in the Southwest. Then write a paragraph describing how the geography, economy, and people of the Southwest adapt to the environment. The final paragraph should summarize the main ideas of the essay.

FOLDABLES™
Study Organizer

People
Economy
Geography
The Southwest

Planning a Garden

Work independently to plan a xeriscape garden. A xeriscape garden contains plants that need very little water. Here's how to design your garden:

1. Do research to learn what xeriscape plants look like. Consider the height and color of the plants. Think about how much sunlight and water the plants need.

2. Choose several plants to use in your garden.

3. Draw a garden design that uses these plants.

4. Write an explanation of your plant selection and garden design.

5. Present your garden design to the class.

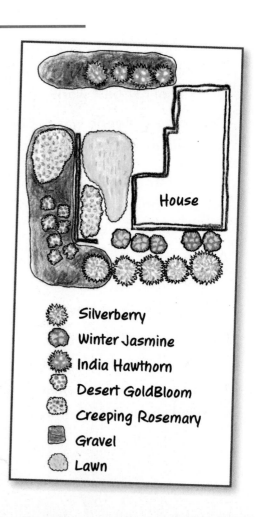

House

- Silverberry
- Winter Jasmine
- India Hawthorn
- Desert GoldBloom
- Creeping Rosemary
- Gravel
- Lawn

(tl)McGraw-Hill Education

The West

Unit 7

EXPLORE The Big Idea

Essential Question
How does technology change people's lives?

FOLDABLES Study Organizer

Make Generalizations
Use a three-tab book foldable to take notes as you read Unit 7. Label the three tabs **Geography**, **Economy**, and **People**.

Geography Economy People

LOG ON For more about Unit 7 go to
connectED.mcgraw-hill.com

PEOPLE, PLACES, AND EVENTS

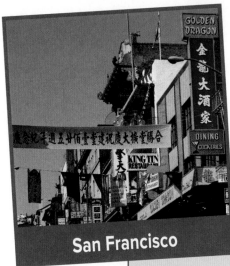

San Francisco

Chinatown–International District Summer Festival

New immigrants come to the United States each day. The Chinatown area of **San Francisco**, California, is home to many recent immigrants from Asia.

Today you can watch the **Chinatown–International District Summer Festival** in Seattle, Washington.

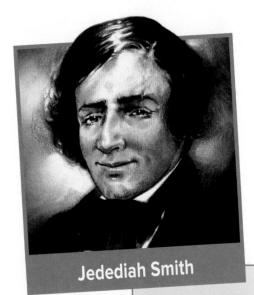

Jedediah Smith

The Rocky Mountains

In the early 1800s, trappers known as "mountain men" lived in **the Rocky Mountains** and hunted beavers for trade. Sometimes mountain men such as **Jedediah Smith** led pioneers across the mountains.

Today you can travel through Rocky Mountain National Park.

 (tl)Photographs in the Carol M. Highsmith Archive, Library of Congress, Prints and Photographs Division [LC-DIG-highsm-11907], (tr)©David R. Frazier Photolibrary, Inc./Alamy, (br)Getty Images/iStockphoto

Sutter's Mill in Sacramento, California

Miners

Gold was found at **Sutter's Mill in Sacramento, California**, in 1848. Between the late 1840s and the early 1860s, **miners** traveled throughout the West in search of gold.

Today you can visit Sutter's Mill in the Marshall Gold Discovery State Historic Park in California.

Volcanologists study Kilauea

Kilauea

Hawaii was formed by volcanoes. **Kilauea**, one of these volcanoes, is still erupting! **Volcanologists study Kilauea** to learn more about what causes volcanoes to erupt.

Today you can visit Kilauea and learn more about volcanoes.

(tl)The Jon B. Lovelace Collection of California Photographs in Carol M. Highsmith's America Project, LOC [LC-DIG-highsm-23836], (tr)Library of Congress Prints and Photographs Division [LC-DIG-ppmsc-01699], (bl)Photo by J.B. Judd/U.S. Geological Survey, (br)J.D. Griggs/USGS

West Region

People visit the cities, national parks, and ski resorts of the West.

1 The 605-foot Space Needle was built for the 1962 Seattle World's Fair.

Kauai

Niihau

Oahu

HI

5

Honolulu

Molokai

Lanai

Maui

PACIFIC
OCEAN

Kahoolawe

Hawaii

0   100   200 miles

0   100   200 kilometers

N
W   E
S

0   100   200 miles

0   100   200 kilometers

N
W   E
S

5 Hawaiians wear different lei for different reasons. The most popular is the lei made of flowers.

6 Sequoia National Park is home to sequoias, the largest trees in the world.

(tr)Jeremy Edwards/Getty Images, (bl)©Pgiam/Getty Images, (br)Comstock Images/Alamy

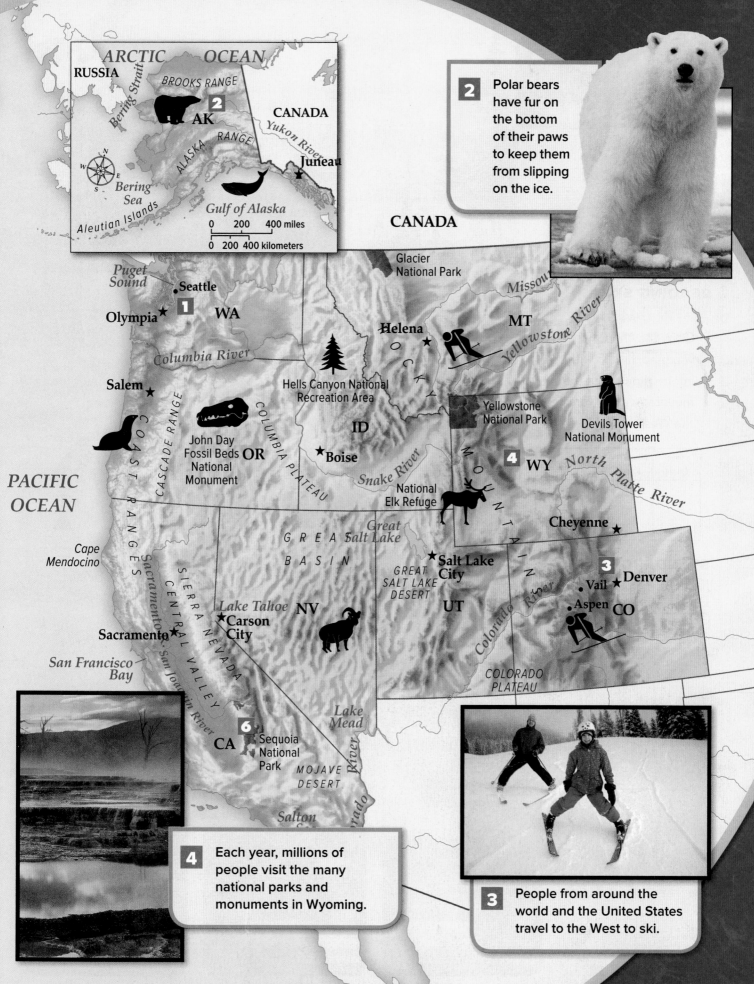

ARCTIC OCEAN

RUSSIA

BROOKS RANGE

2

AK

ALASKA RANGE

Juneau

CANADA

Yukon River

Bering Sea

Aleutian Islands

Gulf of Alaska

0   200   400 miles
0 200 400 kilometers

CANADA

2 Polar bears have fur on the bottom of their paws to keep them from slipping on the ice.

Glacier National Park

Missou

Puget Sound

Seattle

Olympia ★ 1   WA

Helena ★   MT

Yellowstone River

Columbia River

Salem ★

Hells Canyon National Recreation Area

COAST RANGES

CASCADE RANGE

John Day Fossil Beds National Monument OR

COLUMBIA PLATEAU

ID

Boise

Snake River

Yellowstone National Park

Devils Tower National Monument

4 WY

North Platte River

PACIFIC OCEAN

National Elk Refuge

MOUNTAIN

Cheyenne ★

Cape Mendocino

Great Salt Lake

GREAT BASIN

Salt Lake City ★

3

Sacramento River

SIERRA NEVADA

Lake Tahoe

★ Carson City

NV

GREAT SALT LAKE DESERT

UT

Colorado River

Vail · ★ Denver

· Aspen CO

Sacramento ★

San Francisco Bay

San Joaquin River

CENTRAL VALLEY

COLORADO PLATEAU

Lake Mead

6

CA

Sequoia National Park

MOJAVE DESERT

Salton

Colorado River

4 Each year, millions of people visit the many national parks and monuments in Wyoming.

3 People from around the world and the United States travel to the West to ski.

(tr)Dawn Wilson Photography/Getty Images, (bl)Kevin McNeal/Getty Images, (br)Design Pics/Don Hammond   255

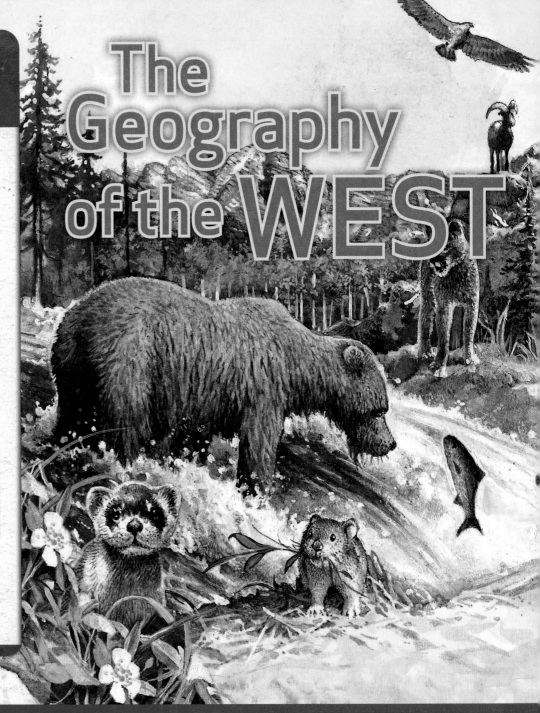

The Geography of the WEST

VOCABULARY

earthquake p. 260

magma p. 260

geyser p. 261

timberline p. 262

READING SKILL

Make Generalizations
Copy the chart. As you read, fill it in with information about the mountains and rivers in the West.

Text Clues	What You Know	Generalizations

STANDARDS FOCUS

SOCIAL STUDIES — People, Places, and Environments

GEOGRAPHY — Physical Systems

Visual Preview

How has the geography of the West affected the way people live?

A The West is a land of extreme environments.

B The West has tall mountains and the Great Salt Lake.

C The West has earthquakes, volcanoes, and geysers.

D Elevation and latitude affect climate in the West.

A VAST REGION

Volcanoes, a tropical rain forest, hot deserts, bubbling mud flats, glaciers, and the country's tallest mountains make the West a land of extreme environments.

The West is the largest region of the United States. It contains eleven states. This region includes Hawaii, our only island state, and Alaska, our largest state. The West is a vast area, and as you might guess, the landforms and climates vary greatly.

Many Environments

The West has almost every landform and type of environment you can name. It includes landforms from snow-capped mountains to fiery volcanoes. The environments range from sun-baked deserts to thick forests that receive a huge amount of rain.

The many plants and animals of the region have adapted to the different environments. Animals such as bears and golden eagles live in forests and along the coast. Plants such as the blue columbine live in the Rocky Mountains, while the frangipani is native to Hawaii.

Plants and Animals of the West

Ponderosa Pine

Salmon

Quaking Aspen

Grizzly Bear

Rocky Mountain Blue Columbine

Golden Eagle

frangipani

bea

QUICK CHECK

Make Generalizations **How do plants and animals survive in different environments?**

The Rocky Mountains are North America's largest mountain range. They stretch more than 3,000 miles from Alaska to New Mexico. At 14,433 feet high, Colorado's Mount Elbert is the highest mountain in the range.

How did the Rocky Mountains form? Earth's surface is made up of huge plates. The plates float on an underground layer of warm, soft rock. The floating plates often bump together or grind into each other. Sometimes one plate slides under another plate and pushes the top plate up. The Rocky Mountains formed when two plates collided.

Rivers

The Rockies get a lot of snow. In some places, the winter snows start in August and don't melt until the following June. As this snow melts, rivers form. The Rio Grande, the Missouri, and the Colorado, as well as many tributaries, all have their sources in the Rocky Mountains.

◄ Melting snow runs downhill into this stream in the Colorado mountains.

The Great Salt Lake

The rivers and streams that flow into Utah's Great Salt Lake bring freshwater and about a million tons of salt each year. The hot summer sun evaporates the water, and salt is left behind. Since more and more water evaporates each year, the Great Salt Lake is shrinking.

Today the Great Salt Lake is saltier than the ocean. With all of that salt, swimmers can float easily.

The Great Salt Lake is too salty for fish, but plenty of shrimp live there. These shrimp attract many birds. Pelicans, ibis, and other birds visit the marshes along the lake's shores to feed on the shrimp.

QUICK CHECK

Cause and Effect What forces formed the Rocky Mountains?

This ibis looks for food in the Great Salt Lake. ▶

The Grand Tetons are a part of the Rocky Mountain range.

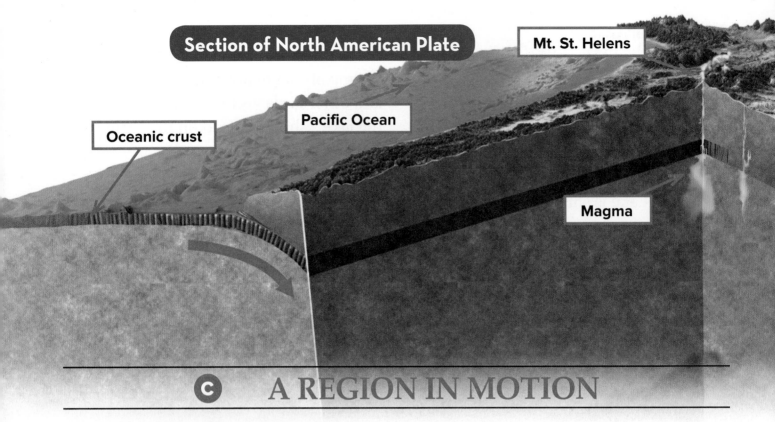

Section of North American Plate

Mt. St. Helens

Pacific Ocean

Oceanic crust

Magma

C   A REGION IN MOTION

Have you ever felt your house or the ground shake from an **earthquake**? In a mild earthquake, the ground trembles and dishes rattle on shelves. During a powerful earthquake, buildings can fall down and large cracks appear in roads.

A powerful earthquake damaged property in Northridge, California. ▼

As you know, Earth's surface is made up of plates. The movement of one plate against another can cause earthquakes. The Pacific coast, the region's border, is one place where plates push together. Earthquakes occur frequently along the coast.

Volcanoes

Magma, or underground melted rock, may push through openings that are made as plates move. When magma reaches Earth's surface, it is called lava. Sometimes volcanoes erupt violently and throw lava, hot ash, or gases into the air. Mount St. Helens, in Washington, erupted with a huge explosion in 1980. Other volcanoes, such as Kilauea, in Hawaii, allow lava and gases to flow quietly out of cracks in the ground.

(bl)USGS

Cascades

Continental Divide

Yellowstone

Continental Crust

Magma

Diagram Skill

Where does magma reach the surface?

Hot Spots

Some volcanoes form from hot spots, or places in the middle of a plate where magma reaches Earth's surface. Yellowstone National Park is a giant collapsed volcano that formed from a hot spot. Although the volcano last erupted many years ago, the heat from the magma still causes mud to bubble. It warms water in springs and shoots steam and water into the air.

Hot springs are bodies of water that are heated by magma. Sometimes, the underground water gets so hot it turns to steam. The pressure from the steam builds up until a **geyser** occurs. A geyser is a hot spring that occasionally shoots hot water or steam into the air.

PLACES

Old Faithful is the most famous geyser in Yellowstone. It sends up 100-foot sprays of water about every hour.

Old Faithful

The Hawaiian islands formed because of a hot spot underneath the Pacific Ocean. Lava from this hot spot formed volcanoes on the ocean floor. Over time, these volcanoes grew larger and reached the surface. Since some of the volcanoes still erupt, the islands continue to grow.

QUICK CHECK

Cause and Effect **What causes an earthquake?**

You can see the timberline on these mountains in the John Muir Wilderness Area in California.

... I have walked ... up in the higher piney ... scented forests of the cool mountains.

–JOHN MUIR

D CLIMATE IN THE WEST

You already know that the higher up a mountain you go, the colder it gets. Another way to say this is to say that elevation affects climate.

If you hike in the Rockies, you can see and feel the change in temperature. The valleys are covered with forest, but as you climb higher, the trees are shorter and there are fewer of them. Finally, you reach an elevation where it is too cold for trees to grow. This is called the **timberline**, or tree line. Instead of trees, there are stretches of grass and low-growing plants.

Did you know that Hawaii has mountains? Many of the mountains are volcanos. A few of them are so high that it is cold enough for snow to fall on the mountaintops.

Latitude and Climate

If you have ever heard someone say, "This place feels like the North Pole!" you know that means it's really cold. The closer a location is to either the North Pole or the South Pole, the colder the temperature. The latitude of a place, or how close or far a place is to the equator, affects climate.

 (t)Jacobs Stock Photography/BananaStock/PunchStock, (cl)Library of Congress Prints and Photographs Division [LC-USZ62-107697]

For example, Alaska is the most northern state in the United States. It is far away from the equator. Alaska has cool summers and very cold winters. During the summer, temperatures may reach 80 degrees Fahrenheit. In the winter, the temperature can become colder than 60 degrees below zero.

Latitudes nearer the equator are warmer. Hawaii's latitude is closer to the equator. Although Hawaii's mountain-tops get snow, most of Hawaii has a warm, tropical climate.

Precipitation

The Olympic Peninsula in Washington is the wettest area in the United States, not counting Hawaii. This area receives as much as 160 inches of rain every year. Some plants and animals that live in this area are found nowhere else in the world. They grow well in the heavy precipitation and mild climate.

What effect does a mountain range have on precipitation? The areas on the western side of the Rocky Mountains receive a lot of rain. The eastern areas are in the rain shadow of the Rocky Mountains and receive very little rain.

QUICK CHECK

Compare and Contrast How are the climates of Alaska and Hawaii different?

The plants that grow on the Olympic Peninsula in Washington are similar to plants that grow near the equator. ▼

Check Understanding

1. **VOCABULARY** Draw a picture of each vocabulary word.

   earthquake   magma
   geyser   timberline

2. **READING SKILL Make Generalizations** Use the chart to write about the climate in the Rocky Mountains.

Text Clues	What You Know	Generalization

3. **Write About It** Write a paragraph about how the geography of the West may cause challenges to people who live there.

Map and Globe Skills

Use Road Maps

VOCABULARY

interstate highway

road map

There are thousands of roads in our country. Some roads follow the paths that Native Americans or early settlers used. Other roads, such as interstate highways, were planned. An **interstate highway** has two or more lanes and goes across two or more states.

A **road map** shows where the roads go in a certain area. By reading a road map, you can figure out how to travel from one place to another.

Learn It

- The map of Montana's highways shows several different types of highways. Each highway is known by a number and a symbol.

- In most cases, odd-numbered highways run north and south, and even-numbered highways run east and west. This numbering system helps drivers figure out which road to take.

- The symbol with double red lines behind a red and blue shield represents interstate highways. Interstate highways are usually fast roads that have on- and off-ramps and do not have traffic lights.

- The symbol for U.S. highways is one red line behind a white shield. These highways often pass through town centers.

- A black line behind a white oval is the symbol for a state highway. State highways run only within a state.

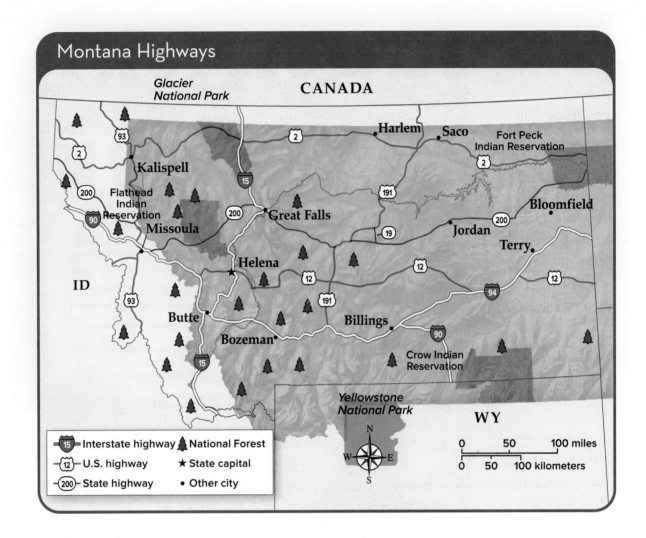

Montana Highways

Glacier National Park

CANADA

Harlem · Saco
Fort Peck Indian Reservation

Kalispell
Flathead Indian Reservation
Missoula
Great Falls
Bloomfield
Jordan
Terry

ID
Helena

Butte
Bozeman
Billings
Crow Indian Reservation

Yellowstone National Park
WY

Legend:

- 🛣 **15** Interstate highway
- 🛡 **12** U.S. highway
- ⬭ **200** State highway
- 🌲 National Forest
- ★ State capital
- • Other city

0   50   100 miles
0   50   100 kilometers

N W E S

Try It

- How is the direction of Interstate 15 different from Interstate 94?

- Which road would you take to get from Billings to Terry?

Apply It

- Which cities can you reach by traveling on state highway 2?

- Find a road map that shows your state. What roads are near where you live?

Lesson 2

VOCABULARY

telecommunications

conservationist

READING SKILL

Make Generalizations
Copy the chart. As you read, fill it in with information about natural resources and farming in the West.

Text Clues	What You Know	Generalization

STANDARDS FOCUS

SOCIAL STUDIES   Production, Distribution, and Consumption

GEOGRAPHY   The World in Spatial Terms

The ECONOMY of the WEST

The Trans Alaska Pipeline.

Visual Preview

How does technology change the economy of a region?

A Oil, lumber, and minerals are resources that provide many jobs in the West.

B Ranching and farming are important to the economy of the West.

C Movies and high-tech manufacturing are growing industries.

D Tourism is an important part of the economy of the West.

266 Lesson 2   (bl)Dave Moyer, (bcr)©Ingram Publishing/SuperStock, (br)Blend Images/Alamy, (bkgd) Photo by Tim Dawson, USGS Earthquakes Hazards Program

A NATURAL RESOURCES

Many settlers came to the West because of the rich natural resources.
These natural resources are still providing jobs today.

When gold was discovered in California in 1848, word spread quickly. Thousands of people caught "gold fever" and rushed west to strike it rich. The same thing happened with silver in Nevada in 1859 and with gold in Alaska in 1898. Mining minerals is still an important part of the economy of many western states.

Energy resources are important, too. Wyoming's most important industry is the production of oil and natural gas. Wyoming is also the leading producer of uranium in the United States. Uranium is used to produce nuclear energy.

Alaskan Oil

What is made of metal, 800 miles long, and filled with oil? The Alaska pipeline, of course! When oil was discovered in northern Alaska in 1968, experts decided the best

way to transport the oil was by pipe. The pipeline was built to carry the oil from the Arctic to the ice-free port of Valdez. From there, ships carry the oil to refineries, where the oil is broken down into products suchas gasoline.

QUICK CHECK

Make Generalizations Why would it be useful to have oil in Alaska piped to an ice-free port?

Logging is an important industry in western Montana, Idaho, Washington, and Oregon. ▶

Montana has huge deposits of copper ore. ▶

BY LAND AND SEA

As you have learned, the landforms in the West vary greatly. How does this affect the economy of the West? Some places are good for farming and for raising animals. In other places, people make a living by fishing. The products and industries in the West are as varied as the landscape itself.

QUICK CHECK

Summarize **How do the landforms in the West affect the economy?**

Have you ever seen a one-hundred-pound cabbage? Since Alaska is so far north, summer days can be 20 hours long. With all that sunlight, farmers in Alaska have grown cabbages that large!

Alaska has a coast more than 6,000 miles long, and leads the country in commercial fishing. Catching, harvesting, and canning seafood make food-processing Alaska's biggest industry.

Sugarcane and pineapples are grown in large fields in Hawaii. Cattle ranching is also important to the state's economy.

California has a valley running down the middle of the state called the Central Valley. This one valley produces more fruits, nuts, and vegetables than almost any place on Earth!

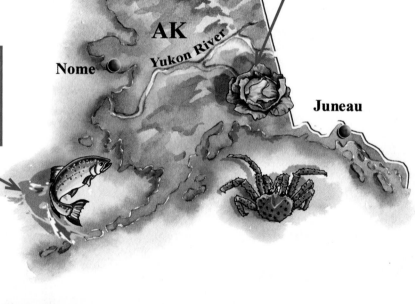

Honolulu

HI   Hilo

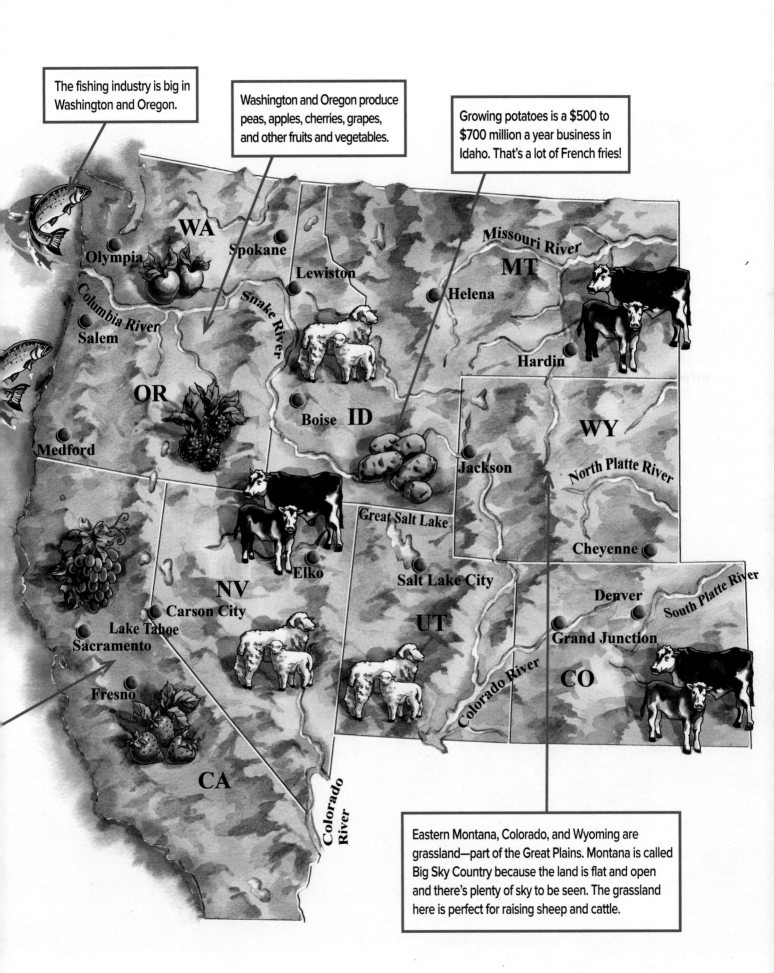

The fishing industry is big in Washington and Oregon.

Washington and Oregon produce peas, apples, cherries, grapes, and other fruits and vegetables.

Growing potatoes is a $500 to $700 million a year business in Idaho. That's a lot of French fries!

Eastern Montana, Colorado, and Wyoming are grassland—part of the Great Plains. Montana is called Big Sky Country because the land is flat and open and there's plenty of sky to be seen. The grassland here is perfect for raising sheep and cattle.

WA
Olympia
Spokane
Columbia River
Salem
OR
Medford
Lewiston
Snake River
Boise
ID
Missouri River
MT
Helena
Hardin
WY
North Platte River
Jackson
Great Salt Lake
Cheyenne
Salt Lake City
Denver
South Platte River
Carson City
UT
Grand Junction
Lake Tahoe
Sacramento
NV
Elko
CO
Colorado River
Fresno
CA
Colorado River

269

The economy of the West depends on natural resources and farming. It also depends on industries that make technology and on the federal government.

Some of the West's natural resources are used to make goods. Pencils, baseball bats, lumber for houses, and a thousand other things are manufactured from trees that grow in Western forests.

Hollywood, California, is famous for a special industry. Can you guess what it is? The movie business, of course! The movie industry employs hundreds of other people besides the stars you see on the screen. These people write the stories, create scenery and costumes, style hair, and put on make-up. They also work cameras, create computerized special effects, and do many other jobs that need to be done in order for a movie to be finished.

Technology

The area around San Jose and Santa Clara in California is famous for another big industry—computers. The area's nickname is Silicon Valley, named for the natural material used to make computer chips. Companies in Washington and Utah are leaders in the manufacturing of computers and other high-tech equipment.

Today many people use cell phones. Cell phones depend on **telecommunications**, or the technology that lets people send messages and images over long distances. Many people in the West work in the telecommunications industry.

The famous Hollywood sign in Hollywood, California.

Ingram Publishing/SuperStock

◄ A Space Exploration Vehicle (SEV) scales rocky terrain.

Federal Government

The federal government is a big employer in the West. In Hawaii, for example, one in ten people are either members of the army or navy or family members of someone in the military.

Almost two-thirds of the land in Utah and more than three-quarters of the land in Nevada is owned by our federal government. The flat deserts are perfect places for testing fast cars, planes, and missiles. Military pilots learn to fly at military bases located throughout the West.

The federal government is the top customer of companies in Utah that manufacture rocket engines. The government also supports scientific research in the West, including monitoring earthquakes and volcanoes and sending robot exploration devices into space.

QUICK CHECK

Make Inferences **What makes a flat desert a perfect place to test cars or rockets?**

Citizenship
Volunteering

In 1989 an oil tanker spilled 11 million gallons of oil into the ocean off the coast of Alaska. The oil stuck to the feathers and fur of thousands of animals and contaminated miles of Alaska shoreline. Volunteers caught and cleaned the dirty animals and washed the shoreline.

Write About It Write a paragraph explaining ways students can help protect the environment.

Global Connections

International Trade

International trade happens when countries buy and sell each other's goods. Why would people buy goods made in another country? Sometimes the goods may be natural resources or products that people in that country don't have. Sometimes goods can be made more cheaply in one country.

Bicycles can be made more cheaply in China than in the United States, for example. In 1990 about six times more bicycles were made in China than in the United States. More stores wanted to buy bicycles from China because they were less expensive. By 2000, companies in China made fifty-two times more bicycles than companies in the United States.

China

United States

▲ Workers in China make bicycles.

▲ Families in the United States buy bicycles.

(bl)©Image Source/Alamy, (br)Stewart Cohen/Pam Ostrow/Blend Images/Getty Images

Ⓓ SERVICE JOBS

Remember all that awesome scenery you read about? It brings lots of visitors to the West. In winter, people grab skis and snowboards and hit the snowy slopes of the mountains. In summer, tourists explore the wilderness on foot or on horseback. Tourists also enjoy the beaches in California and Hawaii.

What do all of these vacationing people have to do with jobs? Think of all the things tourists need or want, from hotel rooms to restaurants to tour guides. Tourism provides lots of jobs. In some places, entire towns have sprung up to serve the needs of tourists.

National Parks

Many of the most beautiful places in the West have been set aside forever as national parks. These parks were the work of **conservationists**, or people who want to protect wilderness and wildlife. Each year, thousands of people visit the many National Parks in the West.

QUICK CHECK

Main Idea and Details Why is tourism important to the economy of the West?

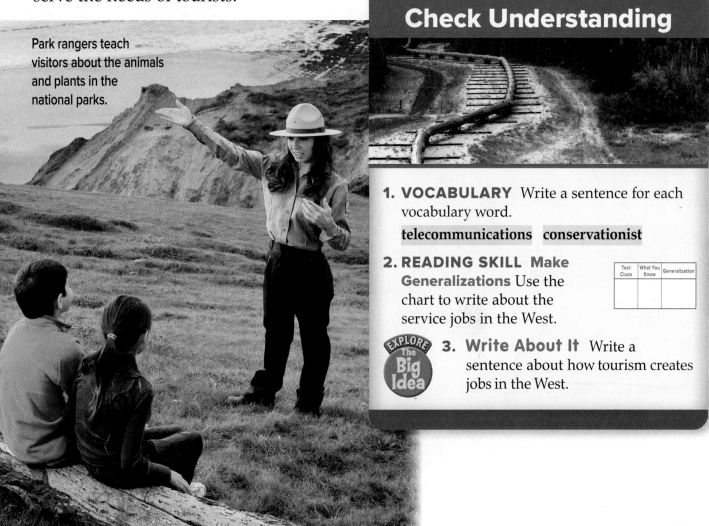

Park rangers teach visitors about the animals and plants in the national parks.

Check Understanding

1. **VOCABULARY** Write a sentence for each vocabulary word.

   telecommunications   conservationist

2. **READING SKILL** Make Generalizations Use the chart to write about the service jobs in the West.

Text Clues	What You Know	Generalization

3. **EXPLORE The Big Idea Write About It** Write a sentence about how tourism creates jobs in the West.

Lesson 3

VOCABULARY

bison

rodeo

READING SKILL

Make Generalizations
Copy the chart. As
you read, fill it in with
information about the
people who have lived in
the West.

Text Clues	What You Know	Generalizations

STANDARDS FOCUS

SOCIAL STUDIES — Individuals, Groups, and Institutions

GEOGRAPHY — The Uses of Geography

THE PEOPLE *of the* WEST

Visual Preview

How has the culture of the West changed over time?

A The West is home to many Native Americans.

B People from around the world have come to the West.

C The West has interesting cities, events, and festivals.

LIVING IN THE WEST

Today there are people from every continent living in the eleven states of the West. First, though, there were the Native Americans.

You have learned that the West has many different environments, from forests to grasslands to deserts. The Native Americans who lived in these different environments had different ways of life.

Some Native Americans hunted, fished, and gathered food in the mountains and moved with the seasons. They often joined the Plains Indians to hunt antelope or **bison**. Most people call the bison a buffalo. A bison is a large, shaggy animal.

Along the Pacific coast, the people lived in villages near the ocean. They fished for salmon in the ocean and in rivers, and built sturdy homes of cedarwood. Further north, the Inuit survived in the icy Arctic by hunting and fishing. The people who first settled Hawaii came from the South Pacific islands about 1,000 years ago.

Native Americans Today

Many Native Americans still live in the West. Some live on reservations and others live in towns and cities. Native American groups such as the Lakota continue to teach their art and language to children and adults.

QUICK CHECK

Make Generalizations **How did Native American foods depend on their location?**

Kevin Red Star is a Native American artist who paints images of historical and modern Crow culture. ▼

B WESTWARD HO!

People have been heading to the West for many years. The Spanish settled throughout California and the Southwest. Later, fur trappers known as "mountain men" led people heading west through the dangerous Rocky Mountains.

In the 1830s and 1840s, settlers who wanted rich farmlands in Oregon began traveling west by wagon train. In the late 1840s, Asian immigrants came to mine for gold. Around 1879 many African Americans called Exodusters moved west to find freedom from unfair treatment.

When the first railroad to cross the continent was finished in 1869, more and more people began moving west. In the early 1900s, the invention of the automobile made travel to the West even easier.

PEOPLE

Dorothea Lange became famous when she photographed Dust Bowl farmers who migrated to California in the 1930s.

Dorothea Lange

Spanish settlers built missions and raised cattle.

Chinese workers came to mine for gold. Many stayed to work on the railroads.

(tr)Library of Congress Prints & Photographs Division (LC-DIG-fsa-8b27245), (bkgd)Robert Schwemmer, CINMS, NOAA

The West Today

The West is one of our nation's fastest-growing regions. The population of Nevada alone doubled between 1990 and 2004. Immigrants have come from all over, but especially from Asian countries such as Japan, China, India, and Vietnam.

Seema Handu, a scientist who moved to California from India, said,

"... I always wanted to come to the United States to study and do research .... There are so many opportunities here."

QUICK CHECK

Summarize **What events caused people to move to the West?**

Primary Sources

[This country] has assuredly the most healthy climate in the world ... Any [one] ... would be satisfied.

From a letter written by Oregon settler Isaac Statt, 1847

Write About It Write about how the climate of your area affects the crops grown there.

In the 1930s, many families traveled from the Midwest to the West to escape the Dust Bowl.

Many Asian immigrants now work in the West.

(tr)Library of Congress Prints and Photographs Division [LC-USZC4-2634]

277

Giant floating balloons are part of many parades throughout the west.

C SIGHTS AND CELEBRATIONS

Many people come to the West to see its wide-open spaces and breathtaking scenery. The West also has big cities and celebrations that attract visitors.

People from around the world visit the hotels and shows in Las Vegas, Nevada. Seattle, Washington, has a tower called the Space Needle. You can ride an elevator to its restaurant, which is 520 feet, or about 43 stories, above the city.

In California, travelers visit San Francisco's Chinatown and the Golden Gate Bridge. Theme parks and Hollywood bring visitors to Los Angeles.

Portland, Oregon, is another beautiful Western city. Each year, more than half a million people visit Portland for the Rose Festival. They watch a parade and enjoy the floats, carnivals, boat races, music, and, of course, roses!

EVENT

In Alaska's **Iditarod** race, dogsled drivers take an average of 10 days to drive teams of dogs over a thousand miles of snow!

Iditarod

(t)©Cal Vornberger/Alamy, (b)U.S. Air Force photo by Tech. Sgt. Keith Brown

Ride 'em Cowboy!

What's the West without a **rodeo**? Rodeos are shows that have contests in horseback riding, roping, and other similar skills. Rodeos were started as a way to celebrate cowboy skills. One favorite event is bull riding. Cowboys climb onto the back of a 2,000-pound bull, hold on with just one hand, and try to stay on for eight seconds. Another event is steer wrestling, in which a cowboy on horseback chases and ropes a steer, then jumps off the horse and wrestles the steer to the ground. Finally he ties its legs together. Whoever does all this in the fastest time wins!

Crow Festival

One of the largest Native American festivals in the nation is held each year in Crow Agency, Montana. Native Americans and visitors come from all over the West. They set up more than 1,500 teepees along the banks of the Little Bighorn River. You can listen to drum groups and watch dances.

QUICK CHECK

Summarize **Why do visitors come to the West?**

Rodeos and bull riding are very popular in the west. ▼

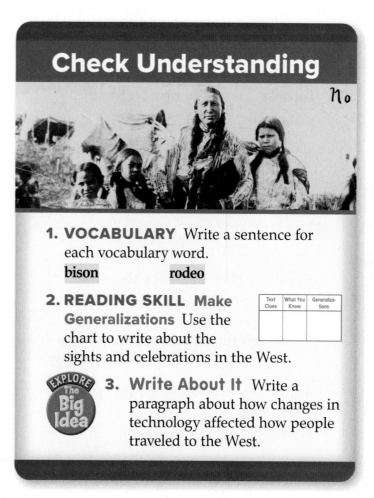

Check Understanding

no

1. **VOCABULARY** Write a sentence for each vocabulary word.
   bison   **rodeo**

2. **READING SKILL Make Generalizations** Use the chart to write about the sights and celebrations in the West.

Text Clues	What You Know	Generalizations

3. **EXPLORE The Big Idea** **Write About It** Write a paragraph about how changes in technology affected how people traveled to the West.

Unit 7 Review and Assess

Vocabulary

Copy the sentences below. Use the vocabulary words to fill in the blanks.

magma   **timberline**
conservationist   **rodeo**

1. Contests in riding and roping happen at a ___.

2. When liquid rock is underground, it is called ___.

3. The elevation where the temperature is too cold for trees to grow is called the ___.

4. A ___ works to preserve and protect the wilderness.

Comprehension and Critical Thinking

5. What nonrenewable resources are found in the West?

6. What are some of the crops grown in the West?

7. **Reading Skill** Which area of the West would you prefer to live in? Make generalizations to tell why.

8. **Critical Thinking** How do the different landforms of the West affect the kinds of jobs that people in those areas have?

Skill

Use Road Maps

Write a complete sentence to answer each question.

9. Which road would you take to travel from Salt Lake City to Cedar City?

10. Which interstate highways run near Fishlake National Forest?

Utah Road Map

15 Interstate highway ★ State capital
40 U.S. highway • Other city

ID   Wasatch-Cache National Forest

0   50   100 miles
0   50   100 kilometers

Great Salt Lake

N
W   E
S

84
15
84
WY

80
80

Salt Lake City
Provo
Vernal

40
191

Nephi
6
Price

NV

6
6

6
15

70
CO

Fishlake National Forest

Cedar City
15

191

Bryce Canyon National Park

AZ   NM

Test Preparation

Read the paragraphs. Then answer the questions.

> In 1869 Wyoming's government decided to let women vote in local elections. Wyoming was not yet a state, only a territory. At that time, no other part of the United States allowed women to vote.
>
> Soon Colorado and Idaho let women vote in some elections, too. Other states did the same. Finally, in 1920, voters amended the Constitution to allow women to vote in all elections. Wyoming had led the way.

1. What would be a good title for this passage?

A. All About Voting

B. Women's Right to Vote

C. The Constitution Changes

D. Women in the Mountain States

2. According to the passage, which statement is true?

A. Today, women are not permitted to vote in some states.

B. The Constitution allowed women to vote as early as 1867.

C. Idaho was the first territory in the United States to allow women to vote.

D. After 1920, women could vote in all elections.

3. Which territory was the first to allow women to vote?

A. Idaho

B. Colorado

C. Washington, D.C.

D. Wyoming

4. Why do you think women were not allowed to vote before 1869?

5. Why do you think it took 51 years from the time women in Wyoming were allowed to vote for the Constitution to be changed to allow all women to vote?

The Big Idea **Activities**

How does technology change people's lives?

Write About the Big Idea

Expository Essay

In Unit 7, you read about the geography, economy, and people of the West. Review your notes in the completed foldable. Write a paragraph describing how the geography, economy, and people of the West use technology to change their lives. Begin with an introductory paragraph describing the environment in the Southeast. The final paragraph should summarize the main ideas of the essay.

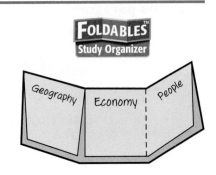

FOLDABLES™
Study Organizer

Geography Economy People

Living and Working in the West

Work in a small group to make a collage. The subject is living and working in the West. Here's how to make your collage:

1. Research how people in the West live and work.

2. Come up with ideas about what you want to show in your collage. Be sure to include examples of the landforms of the region.

3. Look through magazines for photos that show your ideas. Ask for permission before you cut out the photos.

4. Arrange your photos on a background so they tell a story about living and working in the West. Write a paragraph that describes the work your group has done.

5. Present your collage to the class.

(tl)©Fancy/Veer, (br)Ken Karp/McGraw-Hill Education

Reference Section

The Reference Section has many parts, each with a different type of information. Use this section to look up people, places, and events as you study.

Reading Skills R2

Unit 1 Sequence Events. R2

Unit 2 Compare and Contrast R4

Unit 3 Main Idea and Details R6

Unit 4 Summarize. R8

Unit 5 Draw Conclusions. R10

Unit 6 Cause and Effect. R12

Unit 7 Make Generalizations R14

Geography Handbook. GH1

Atlas GH12

United States: Political GH12

United States: Physical. GH14

World: Political GH16

North America GH18

Glossary. REF1

Index. REF9

Credits REF16

Unit 1 • Reading Skills
Sequence Events

In this unit you will read about important events in United States history. When you read, think about the order in which events happen. This order is called the sequence of events. The sequence of events will help you understand and remember what you read.

Learn It

- Look for words such as *first, next, then, after, finally,* and *last.* These words show the order of events.
- Look for dates that tell you exactly when things happened. They are also clue words.
- Read the paragraph below. Look for the sequence of events.

Clue Words
These words show the sequence of events.

Events
These words describe each event.

About 20,000 years ago, during the last Ice Age, people traveled thousands of miles to get to North America looking for a better life. They became the first Native Americans. Much later, about 3,000 years ago, a culture, or way of life, began in the Ohio River Valley. These people traded and made crafts. Native Americans who lived along the coast depended on the ocean or rivers for food. While those who lived inland hunted and gathered berries and nuts from the forest. Today, Native Americans live throughout the United States.

Copy and complete the chart below. Then, fill in the chart by recording the events on page 8 in the correct sequence.
How did you figure out the sequence of events?

First

↓

Next

↓

Last

Apply It

- Review the sequencing steps in Learn It.
- Read the paragraph below. Then, create a sequence of events chart using the information.

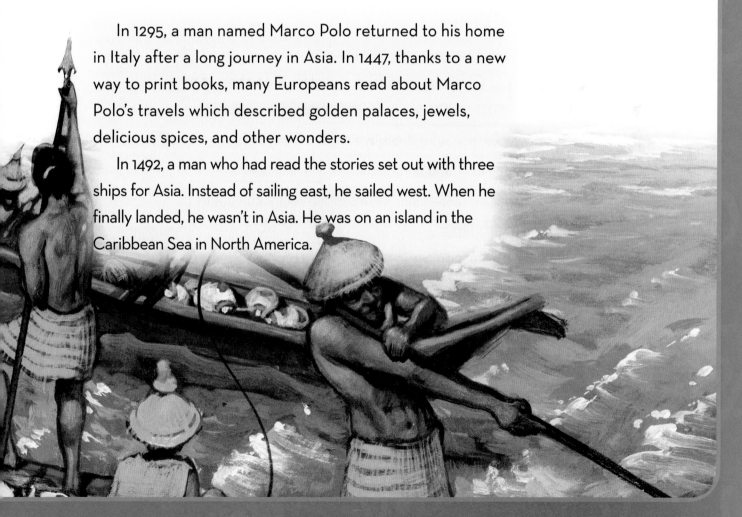

In 1295, a man named Marco Polo returned to his home in Italy after a long journey in Asia. In 1447, thanks to a new way to print books, many Europeans read about Marco Polo's travels which described golden palaces, jewels, delicious spices, and other wonders.

In 1492, a man who had read the stories set out with three ships for Asia. Instead of sailing east, he sailed west. When he finally landed, he wasn't in Asia. He was on an island in the Caribbean Sea in North America.

Unit 2 • Reading Skills
Compare and Contrast

In this unit you will learn how geography affects how people live and work in the United States. Learning to compare and contrast will help you understand what you read about in social studies.

Learn It

- To compare two or more things, note how they are similar, or alike.
- To contrast two or more things, note how they are different.
- Read the passage. Think about how living in Gloucester, Massachusetts, and Tarpon Springs, Florida, are alike and different.

Similarities
People in both towns earn a living from the sea.

Differences
People earn a living by fishing in Gloucester.
In Tarpon Springs, they dive for sponges.

Gloucester, Massachusetts, is on the Atlantic Ocean. People there have always made a living from the sea. They fish for cod and trap lobsters. In summer, tourists visit the area's beaches or go whale watching.

Tarpon Springs, Florida, is on the Anconte River, near Florida's Gulf Coast. People in Tarpon Springs make a living from the sea, too, but instead of fishing, they dive for sponges. Tourists visit the docks to buy sponges and other souvenirs.

Similarities
Tourists visit both towns.

Try It

Copy and complete the Venn diagram to help you compare and contrast the information. Fill in the chart with details from the paragraphs on page R4.

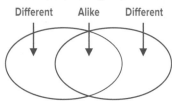

Different   Alike   Different

What information did you look for to compare and contrast?

Apply It

- Review the steps for comparing and contrasting in Learn It.

- Read the passage below. Then create a Venn diagram using the information.

Our changing economy has affected how and where people live. At one time, most people moved to rural areas. They needed lots of land because they worked in agriculture. Later people moved from rural areas to urban areas in order to find jobs in the manufacturing industry. Today many people live in urban areas.

Unit 3 • Reading Skills
Main Idea and Details

In this unit you will learn about the land, economy, and culture of the Northeast. Thinking about the main idea and details will help you understand how and why the region has changed over time.

The main idea is what a paragraph is all about. Often it is the first sentence in a paragraph. The supporting details tell about, or support, the main idea.

Learn It

- Think about what a paragraph is all about.

- Decide whether the first sentence states the main idea.

- Look for details. Think about what these details tell about.

- Now read the paragraph below. Look for the main ideas and details.

Main Idea
The first sentence states the main idea.

Details
These details tell where most of the energy comes from.

The Northeast's energy comes from different sources. Oil and gas supply much of the region's power. The Northeast also uses water power to produce energy. Hot water and steam from deep underground also provide energy in parts of the region.

(bkgd)©Ocean/Corbis

Try It

Copy the chart below. Then fill in the chart with the main idea and details from the paragraph on page R6.

Main Idea	Details

How did you find the main idea and supporting details?

Apply It

- Review the steps for finding the main idea and details in Learn It.

- Now read the paragraph below. Make a chart to show the main idea and supporting details.

   In the late 1700s, some people in England learned how to build machines that wove lots of cloth all at once. These machines ran on water power. As you learned in the last lesson, the Northeast has plenty of water power.
By the middle 1700s, many settlers were using the region's rivers and falls to run mills that turned grain into flour.

Unit 4 • Reading Skills
Summarize

In this unit you will learn about the Southeast. Learning how to summarize, or stating the important ideas in a reading passage, will help you remember what you learned. A summary gives the main ideas, but leaves out minor details. Summarizing will help you understand and remember what you read.

Learn It

- Find the main ideas in a passage. Restate these important points briefly.

- Find important details and combine them in your summary.

- Leave out details that are not important.

- Now read the passage below and think about how you would summarize it.

Main Topic
This is the main topic of the paragraph.

Supporting Facts
These facts support the main topic.

There are many rivers in the Southeast, but the Mississippi River is one of the largest. The writer Mark Twain called it "the majestic, the magnificent Mississippi." The river flows 2,350 miles from Minnesota to the Gulf of Mexico in Louisiana. As it flows south, it carries 400 million tons of silt and mud. All this silt and mud gets dumped at the river's mouth to make a landform known as the Mississippi Delta.

(bkgd)Aaron Roeth Photography

Try It

Copy the chart below. Then fill in the chart with your conclusions from the paragraph on page R8.

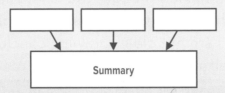

What did you look for to summarize the paragraph?

Apply It

- Review the steps for summarizing in Learn It.
- Read the passage below. Then summarize the passage using a summary chart.

The Southeast has hundreds of islands. Some were formed by ocean waves that dropped tons of sand along the coast. Others were made from the bones of millions and millions of coral, a tiny sea animal.

The largest island of the Southeast is Puerto Rico, in the Caribbean Sea. It was formed millions of years ago by the action of volcanoes on the ocean floor. Much of Puerto Rico is mountainous, but it has beautiful beaches, too.

Unit 5 • Reading Skills
Draw Conclusions

In this unit you will learn about the land, economy, and culture of the Midwest. Sometimes meanings and connections are not clear. Drawing conclusions is one way to better understand what you read. A conclusion is based on several pieces of information and explains what those facts mean.

Learn It

- As you read, ask yourself what the topic is about.
- Gather facts about the topic.
- Make a conclusion or a statement. It connects the facts you have gathered.
- Now read the paragraph below. Draw conclusions as you read.

Topic
Iowa grows much of the nation's corn.

Facts
Corn is fed to farm animals.

Facts
Corn is used in many everyday items.

Farmers in Iowa grow more than a million bushels of corn each year. Iowa leads the nation in corn production. Much of that corn is fed to farm animals such as hogs and cattle. Corn is also used to make crayons, paper, peanut butter, pet food, toothpaste, and margarine.

(bkgd)Andy Stanton/Moment/Getty Images

Try It

Copy the chart below. Then fill in the chart with your conclusions from the paragraph on page R10.

Text Clues	Conclusion

What did you use to help you draw conclusions?

Apply It

- Review the steps for drawing conclusions in Learn It.
- Read the passage below. Then draw conclusions using the information from the passage.
- Name some occasions when drawing conclusions can help you study.

In the last 20 years, many American fast food restaurants have opened in China. China also buys many food products from the United States. One of these products is soybeans. The United States sells more than $1 billion in soybeans to China each year. Some soybeans are used to produce cooking oil. Others are made into soybean meal to feed poultry and beef cattle.

Unit 6 • Reading Skills
Cause and Effect

In this unit you will learn about the land, economy, and culture of the Southwest. Thinking about causes and effects will help you understand how and why the Southwest has changed over time.

A cause is an event that makes something happen. An effect is what happens. When one thing causes another thing to happen, they have a cause-and-effect relationship.

Learn It

- As you read, ask yourself what happened. This will help you find an effect.

- Ask yourself why something happened. This will help you find a cause.

- Look for the words *because, therefore, so,* and *as a result.* These clue words point to causes and effects.

- Now read the paragraphs below. Look for causes and effects as you read.

Cause Much of the Southwest belonged to Spain.

In the early 1600s, much of the Southwest belonged to Spain. The Spanish made settlements, including the city of Santa Fe, built in 1610. Spanish priests came because they wanted to teach the Native Americans Christianity. Later the lands of the Southwest became part of Mexico.

Effect Many cities have Spanish names.

As a result of years under Spanish and Mexican rule, many places still have Spanish names. Spanish and Mexican foods are popular. People from Mexico and other Spanish-speaking countries still move to this part of our country, and many people speak Spanish.

Try It

Copy the chart below. Then fill in the chart with causes and effects from the paragraph on page R12.

Cause	→	Effect
	→	
	→	
	→	

What questions helped you identify cause and effect?

Apply It

- Review the steps for understanding cause and effect in Learn It.
- Read the passage below. Then create a cause and effect chart using the information.

Early settlers of the Southwest came to farm or start ranches. After World War II, many people moved to the region to get jobs in the oil and technology industries. Today people also move there to retire to a warmer climate. Therefore, the Southwest is one of the fastest growing regions in the United States.

Make Generalizations

As you read you sometimes come across information about things that seem to have nothing in common. On a closer look, however, you may see similarities. You might be able to make a generalization. A generalization is a broad statement that shows how different facts, people, or events have something in common.

Learn It

- As you read, ask yourself what the topic is about.
- Gather text clues about the topic.
- Look for similarities in the clues.
- Now read the paragraph below. Make generalizations as you read.

Text Clue
Montana has mountains rich in copper and silver.

Text Clue
Colorado has mountains rich in gold.

Text Clue
Wyoming has mountains that produce coal, oil, and uranium.

More than two-thirds of Montana is mountains. The mountains are rich in mineral deposits, such as copper and silver. Colorado has mountains, too. When gold was discovered in Colorado's mountains, thousands of people rushed there. Wyoming is a mountainous state, as well. Its mountains produce coal, oil, and uranium.

(b)Getty Images/iStockphoto

Try It

Copy the chart below. Then fill in the chart with your conclusions from the paragraph on page R14.

Text Clues	What You Know	Inferences

What steps did you take to make your generalization?

Apply It

- Review the steps for Make Generalizations in Learn It.

- Read the passage below. Then make generalizations using the information from the passage.

- Name some occasions when making generalizations may help you study.

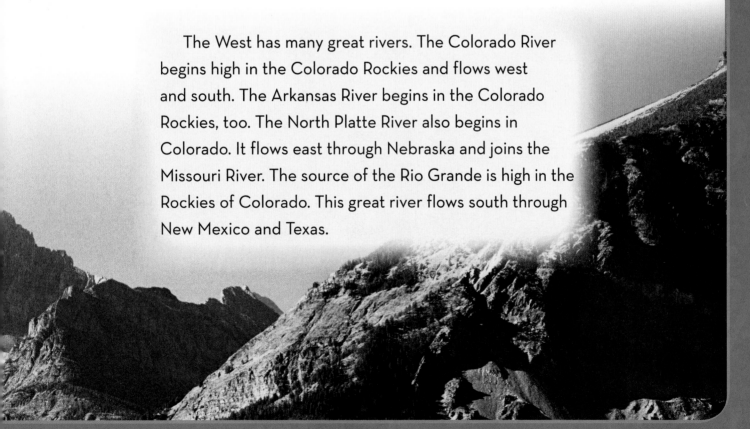

The West has many great rivers. The Colorado River begins high in the Colorado Rockies and flows west and south. The Arkansas River begins in the Colorado Rockies, too. The North Platte River also begins in Colorado. It flows east through Nebraska and joins the Missouri River. The source of the Rio Grande is high in the Rockies of Colorado. This great river flows south through New Mexico and Texas.

Geography Handbook

Geography and You GH1

Six Essential Elements GH1

Five Themes of Geography GH2

Dictionary of Geographic Terms GH4

Reviewing Geography Skills GH6

Read a Physical Map GH6

Read a Route Map GH8

Hemispheres GH10

Latitude and Longitude GH11

Atlas

United States Political GH12

United States Physical GH14

World Political GH16

North America: Political/Physical GH18

Photo by Gene Alexander, USDA Natural Resources Conservation Service

Geography and You

Geography is the study of our Earth and the people who live here. Most people think of geography as learning about cities, states, and countries, but geography is more than that. Geography includes learning about land, such as plains and mountains. Geography also helps us learn how to use land and water wisely.

Did you know that people are part of geography? Geography includes the study of how people adapt to live in a new place. How people move around, how they move goods, and how ideas travel from place to place are also parts of geography.

In fact, geography includes so many things that geographers have divided this information into six elements, or ideas, so you can better understand them.

Six Essential Elements

The World in Spatial Terms: Where is a place located, and what land or water features does this place have?

Places and Regions: What is special about a place, and what makes it different from other places?

Physical Systems: What has shaped the land and climate of a place, and how does this affect the plants, animals, and people there?

Human Systems: How do people, ideas, and goods move from place to place?

Environment and Society: How have people changed the land and water of a place, and how have the land and water affected the people of a place?

Uses of Geography: How does geography influence events in the past, present, and the future?

Five Themes of Geography

You have read about the six elements of geography. The five themes of geography are another way of dividing the ideas of geography. The themes, or topics, are **location**, **place**, **region**, **movement**, and **human interaction**. Using these five themes is another way to understand events you read about in this book.

1. Location

Washington, D. C.

In geography, *location* means an exact spot on the planet. A location is usually a street name and number. You write a location when you address a letter.

2. Place

Seattle, Washington

A *place* is described by its physical features, such as rivers, mountains, or valleys. You would also include the human features, such as cities, language, and traditions, in the description of a place.

3. Region

Florida Everglades National Park

A *region* is a larger area than a place or location. The people in a region are affected by landforms. Their region has typical jobs and customs. For example, the fertile soil of the Mississippi Lowlands helps farmers in the region grow crops.

4. Movement

Los Angeles, California

Throughout history, people have *moved* to find better land or a better life. Geographers study why these movements occurred. They also study how people's movements have changed a region.

5. Human Interaction

Columbus, Ohio

Geographers are interested in how people adapt to their environment. Geographers also study how people change their environment. This *interaction* between people and their environments determines how land is used for cities, farms, or parks.

Dictionary of Geographic Terms

1 **BASIN** A bowl-shaped landform surrounded by higher land

2 **BAY** Part of an ocean or lake that extends deeply into the land

3 **CANAL** A channel built to carry water for irrigation or transportation

4 **CANYON** A deep, narrow valley with steep sides

5 **COAST** The land along an ocean

6 **DAM** A wall built across a river, creating a lake that stores water

7 **DELTA** Land made of soil left behind as a river drains into a larger body of water

8 **DESERT** A dry environment with few plants and animals

9 **FAULT** The border between two of the plates that make up Earth's crust

10 **GLACIER** A huge sheet of ice that moves slowly across the land

11 **GULF** Part of an ocean that extends into the land; larger than a bay

12 **HARBOR** A sheltered place along a coast where boats dock safely

13 **HILL** A rounded, raised landform; not as high as a mountain

14 **ISLAND** A body of land completely surrounded by water

15 **LAKE** A body of water completely surrounded by land

16 **MESA** A hill with a flat top; smaller than a plateau

17 **MOUNTAIN** A high landform with steep sides; higher than a hill	**22** **PLAIN** A large area of nearly flat land	**27** **SOURCE** The starting point of a river
18 **MOUNTAIN PASS** A narrow gap through a mountain range	**23** **PLATEAU** A high, flat area that rises steeply above the surrounding land	**28** **VALLEY** An area of low land between hills or mountains
19 **MOUTH** The place where a river empties into a larger body of water	**24** **PORT** A place where ships load and unload their goods	**29** **VOLCANO** An opening in Earth's surface through which hot rock and ash are forced out
20 **OCEAN** A large body of salt water; oceans cover much of Earth's surface	**25** **RESERVOIR** A natural or artificial lake used to store water	**30** **WATERFALL** A flow of water falling vertically
21 **PENINSULA** A body of land nearly surrounded by water	**26** **RIVER** A stream of water that flows across the land and empties into another body of water	

GH5

Reviewing Geography Skills

Read a Physical Map

Maps are drawings of places on Earth. Most maps use colors and symbols to show information. Physical maps show and label landforms, such as mountains and deserts, and water features, such as lakes and rivers. Map makers use shading and color to show different physical features, such as blue to show water or dark shading to show mountains.

Map Title Map titles tell you what information is on the map.

Inset Map An inset map is a small map set into the main map. It shows an area that is too large, too small, or too far away to be included on the main map. Inset maps usually use a different scale than the main map.

Map Key The map key, or legend, gives the meaning of the colors and symbols on a map.

Map Scale The map scale is a line that shows the relationship between distances on a map and distances on Earth. Here, the length of the line on the map represents 400 miles on Earth.

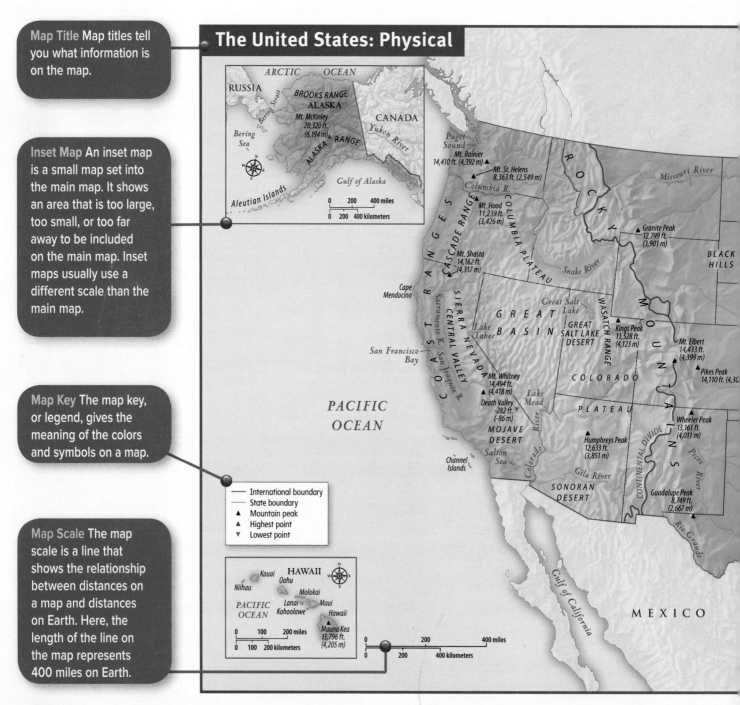

The United States: Physical

ARCTIC OCEAN
RUSSIA
Bering Strait
BROOKS RANGE
ALASKA
Mt. McKinley 20,320 ft. (6,194 m)
CANADA
Yukon River
Bering Sea
ALASKA RANGE
Gulf of Alaska
Aleutian Islands

0   200   400 miles
0   200   400 kilometers

Puget Sound
Mt. Rainier 14,410 ft. (4,392 m)
Mt. St. Helens 8,363 ft. (2,549 m)
Columbia R.
Mt. Hood 11,239 ft. (3,426 m)
ROCKY
Missouri River
CASCADE RANGE
COLUMBIA PLATEAU
Mt. Shasta 14,162 ft. (4,317 m)
Snake River
Granite Peak 12,799 ft. (3,901 m)
BLACK HILLS
Cape Mendocino
COAST RANGES
SIERRA NEVADA
CENTRAL VALLEY
Sacramento R. San Joaquin R.
Great Salt Lake
GREAT BASIN
GREAT SALT LAKE DESERT
WASATCH RANGE
Kings Peak 13,528 ft. (4,123 m)
MOUNTAINS
Mt. Elbert 14,433 ft. (4,399 m)
Pikes Peak 14,110 ft. (4,30
Lake Tahoe
San Francisco Bay
Mt. Whitney 14,494 ft. (4,418 m)
Death Valley -282 ft. (-86 m)
Lake Mead
COLORADO
PLATEAU
Wheeler Peak 13,161 ft. (4,011 m)
MOJAVE DESERT
Colorado River
Humphreys Peak 12,633 ft. (3,851 m)
CONTINENTAL DIVIDE
PACIFIC OCEAN
Channel Islands
Salton Sea
Gila River
SONORAN DESERT
Guadalupe Peak 8,749 ft. (2,667 m)
Pecos River
Rio Grande

International boundary
State boundary
▲ Mountain peak
▲ Highest point
▼ Lowest point

Kauai
HAWAII
Niihau
Oahu
Molokai
PACIFIC OCEAN
Lanai
Kahoolawe
Maui
Hawaii
Mauna Kea 13,796 ft. (4,205 m)

0   100   200 miles
0   100   200 kilometers

Gulf of California
MEXICO

0   200   400 miles
0   200   400 kilometers

Think About It About how far is it from Mt. Hood to Mt. Shasta in the Cascade Range?

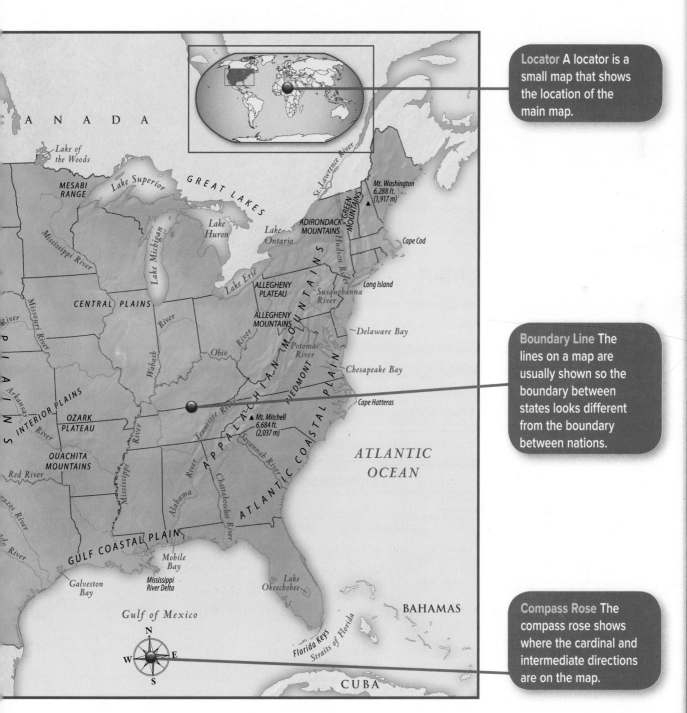

Locator A locator is a small map that shows the location of the main map.

Boundary Line The lines on a map are usually shown so the boundary between states looks different from the boundary between nations.

Compass Rose The compass rose shows where the cardinal and intermediate directions are on the map.

Read a Route Map

You know that many route maps show distances as shorter than they are on Earth. How can you find out how much shorter the distances are? Maps are drawn using map scales. A map scale shows a unit of measurement that stands for a real distance on Earth. Not all maps have the same scale. You can see on page GH9 that a distance of one inch on the map equals 50 miles on Earth.

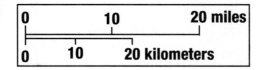

Look at the map. How far is Sandusky from Fremont? Place a slip of paper just below both cities. Make one mark where Fremont is and another where Sandusky is. Then place your slip of paper just under the map scale, with your first mark at zero. Where is the second mark? You can see that Sandusky is about 25 miles from Fremont.

Think About It How far is Mansfield from Oberlin?

NASA image by Jeff Schmaltz, MODIS Rapid Response Team, Goddard Space Flight Center

Route Maps

Suppose you want to go somewhere you have never been before. How would you know which roads to take? You would use a route map. Route maps show the roads in a certain area. By reading a route map, you can figure out how to get from one place to another. Many route maps are also grid maps, like this one.

Grid Maps

A grid map has a special grid to help you locate things. Each box can be named with a number and a letter. For example, you might want to find Akron, Ohio, but you don't know where to look. You can see from the index that Akron is located in square B-3. Put one finger on the letter B along the side of the map. Put another finger on the number 3 at the top. Then move your fingers across and down the map until they meet. You have found B-3 on the grid, and now that you only have to search one square instead of the whole map, it's easy to find Akron.

Think About It Find Lima on the map. What grid box is it in?

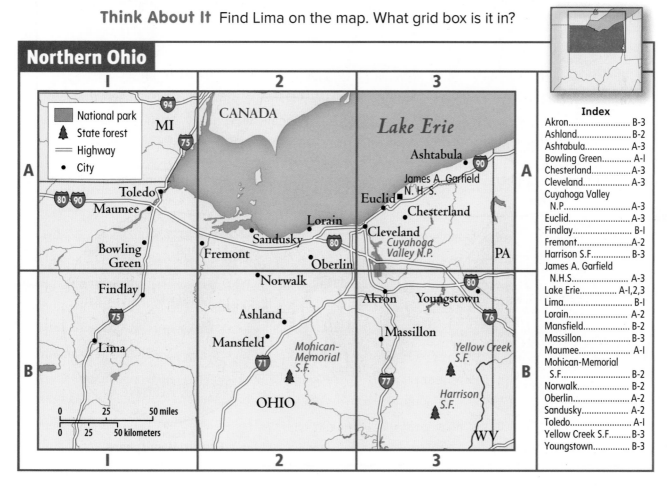

Northern Ohio

Index

Akron........................ B-3
Ashland..................... B-2
Ashtabula.................. A-3
Bowling Green........... A-1
Chesterland............... A-3
Cleveland.................. A-3
Cuyahoga Valley
   N.P........................ A-3
Euclid....................... A-3
Findlay...................... B-1
Fremont.................... A-2
Harrison S.F.............. B-3
James A. Garfield
   N.H.S.................... A-3
Lake Erie............. A-1,2,3
Lima.......................... B-1
Lorain....................... A-2
Mansfield.................. B-2
Massillon................... B-3
Maumee..................... A-1
Mohican-Memorial
   S.F......................... B-2
Norwalk..................... B-2
Oberlin...................... A-2
Sandusky................... A-2
Toledo....................... A-1
Yellow Creek S.F......... B-3
Youngstown............... B-3

Hemispheres

You can think of Earth as a sphere, like a ball or a globe. A hemisphere is half of a sphere. Geographers have divided Earth into the Northern Hemisphere and the Southern Hemisphere at the equator, an imaginary line that circles Earth halfway between the North Pole and the South Pole. Another important imaginary line is the prime meridian. It divides Earth from east to west. The area west of the prime meridian is called the Western Hemisphere, and the area east of the prime meridian is called the Eastern Hemisphere.

Think About It In which two hemispheres is North America?

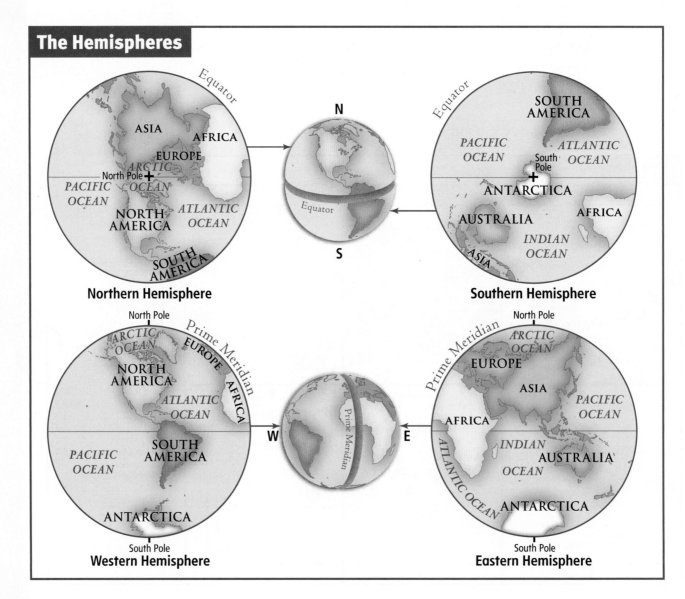

Latitude and Longitude

Earth can be divided into a grid of lines called latitude and longitude. Lines of latitude measure how far north or south a place is from the equator. Lines of longitude measure distance east or west from the prime meridian. Both the equator and the prime meridian represent 0 degrees. The symbol for degrees is °. Latitude lines measure the distance in degrees from the equator, and longitude lines measure the distance in degrees from the prime meridian. Look at the map. You can see that Los Angeles is located very near the longitude line labeled 120°W at the top of the map. That means that Los Angeles is about 120° west of the prime meridian.

Think About It Is Lagos north or south of the equator?

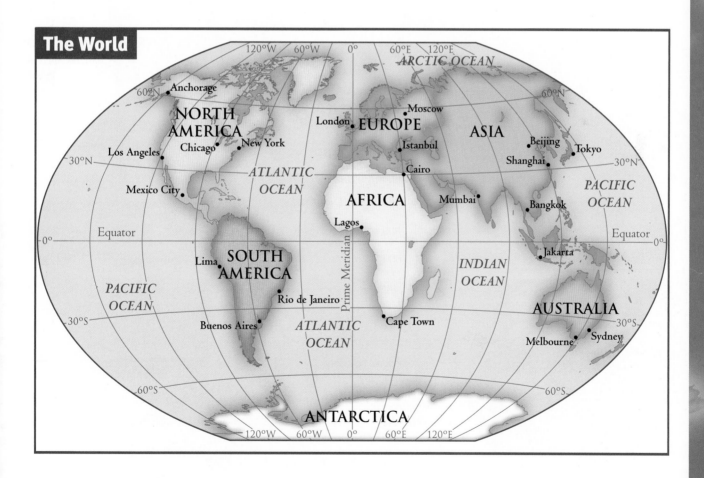

ARCTIC OCEAN

RUSSIA

CANADA

180°W   70°N   120°W

Arctic Circle

Nome   Yukon R.   Fairbanks

ALASKA

60°N

Anchorage

Juneau

N
W   E
S

130°W

0   200   400 miles
0   200   400 kilometers

170°W   160°W   150°W   140°W

40°N   130°W

Seattle

Olympia   Spokane

River

WASHINGTON

Columbia

Great Falls   Missouri River

Helena   MONTANA

Portland
Salem

Billings

Eugene

OREGON   IDAHO

Boise   WYOMING

Snake River   Casper

Pocatello

Eureka   Great Salt Lake   Ogden

Redding   Salt Lake City   Cheyenne

Reno   Provo

Sacramento   Carson City   UTAH   Denver

San Francisco   Oakland   NEVADA   COLORADO

San Jose   Colorado River   Colorado Springs

Fresno   Pueblo

CALIFORNIA   Las Vegas

PACIFIC
OCEAN   Bakersfield

Santa Fe

Los Angeles   Albuquerque

Long Beach   ARIZONA   NEW MEXICO

Phoenix

San Diego

30°N   Tucson

El Paso

Rio Grande

130°W   Gulf of California

0   200   400 miles
0   200   400 kilometers

MEXICO

160°W   155°W

Kauai   HAWAII

Oahu   N
W   E
S

Niihau   Molokai

Honolulu

PACIFIC   Lanai   Maui
OCEAN   Kahoolawe

20°N

Hilo

Hawaii

	International boundary
	State boundary
⊛	National capital
★	State capital
•	Other city

0   100   200 miles
0   100   200 kilometers

Tropic of Cancer

20°N

120°W   110°W

CANADA

NORTH DAKOTA
Grand Forks
Fargo
Bismarck

SOUTH DAKOTA
Pierre
Sioux Falls

NEBRASKA
Omaha
Lincoln
Platte River

Duluth
MINNESOTA
St. Paul
Minneapolis

Lake Superior

Marquette

MICHIGAN

Lake Huron

Green Bay
WISCONSIN
Milwaukee
Madison

Grand Rapids
Lansing

Lake Michigan

Cedar Rapids
IOWA
Des Moines

Chicago
Gary
Davenport

ILLINOIS
Indianapolis
INDIANA

Detroit
Lake Erie
Toledo Cleveland
OHIO
Columbus
Cincinnati

Lake Ontario

Buffalo

NEW YORK

NEW HAMPSHIRE
VERMONT
Montpelier

MAINE
Augusta
Portland
Concord

Boston
MASSACHUSETTS

Albany

Hartford
Providence
RHODE ISLAND
CONNECTICUT
Newark
New York
Trenton
NEW JERSEY
Philadelphia
Dover
DELAWARE

PENNSYLVANIA
Harrisburg

Pittsburgh
Baltimore

Washington, D.C.
WEST VIRGINIA
Charleston

Annapolis
MARYLAND

70°W

Missouri River

Kansas City
Topeka
KANSAS
Kansas City
Wichita

St. Louis
Springfield
Jefferson City
MISSOURI

Evansville
Ohio River
Frankfort
Louisville
KENTUCKY

Richmond
Norfolk
VIRGINIA

Raleigh
NORTH CAROLINA
Charlotte

Nashville
Tennessee River
Knoxville

Arkansas River

Tulsa
Oklahoma City
OKLAHOMA

Fort Smith
ARKANSAS
Little Rock

Memphis

Mississippi River

Birmingham
ALABAMA
Montgomery

Columbia
SOUTH CAROLINA

Atlanta
GEORGIA
Columbus

Charleston

Savannah

ATLANTIC OCEAN

Red River

Fort Worth
Dallas

TEXAS

Brazos River
Colorado River
Austin
San Antonio
Corpus Christi
Laredo

Shreveport
LOUISIANA
Baton Rouge
New Orleans

Jackson
MISSISSIPPI

Mobile
Biloxi

Tallahassee

Jacksonville

30°N

Houston

Gulf of Mexico

Lake Okeechobee

Orlando
FLORIDA
Tampa

Miami

BAHAMAS

N
W E
S

CUBA

100°W

90°W

80°W

GH13

ARCTIC OCEAN

RUSSIA

BROOKS RANGE
ALASKA
Mt. McKinley
20,320 ft.
(6,194 m)

CANADA
Yukon River

ALASKA RANGE

Bering Sea

Gulf of Alaska

Aleutian Islands

N
W E
S

0   200   400 miles
0   200   400 kilometers

Puget Sound

Mt. Rainier
14,410 ft. (4,392 m)

Mt. St. Helens
8,363 ft. (2,549 m)

Columbia R.

Mt. Hood
11,239 ft.
(3,426 m)

CASCADE RANGE

Mt. Shasta
14,162 ft.
(4,317 m)

Cape Mendocino

COAST RANGES

Sacramento R.

SIERRA NEVADA

CENTRAL VALLEY

Lake Tahoe

San Joaquin R.

San Francisco Bay

Mt. Whitney
14,494 ft.
(4,418 m)

Death Valley
-282 ft.
(-86 m)

MOJAVE DESERT

PACIFIC OCEAN

Channel Islands

Salton Sea

COLUMBIA PLATEAU

Snake River

ROCKY

Missouri River

Granite Peak
12,799 ft.
(3,901 m)

BLACK HILLS

GREAT BASIN

Great Salt Lake

GREAT SALT LAKE DESERT

WASATCH RANGE

Kings Peak
13,528 ft.
(4,123 m)

Mt. Elbert
14,433 ft.
(4,399 m)

Pikes Peak
14,110 ft. (4,301

COLORADO

MOUNTAINS

Lake Mead

Colorado River

PLATEAU

Humphreys Peak
12,633 ft.
(3,851 m)

Wheeler Peak
13,161 ft.
(4,011 m)

CONTINENTAL DIVIDE

Pecos River

SONORAN DESERT

Gila River

Guadalupe Peak
8,749 ft.
(2,667 m)

Rio Grande

Gulf of California

MEXICO

International boundary
State boundary
▲ Mountain peak
▲ Highest point
▼ Lowest point

Kauai   HAWAII

Niihau   Oahu

Molokai

PACIFIC OCEAN   Lanai   Maui

Kahoolawe

Hawaii

Mauna Kea
13,796 ft.
(4,205 m)

N
W E
S

0   100   200 miles
0   100   200 kilometers

0   200   400 miles
0   200   400 kilometers

CANADA

Lake of
the Woods

MESABI
RANGE

Lake Superior

GREAT LAKES

St. Lawrence River

Mt. Washington
6,288 ft.
(1,917 m)

GREEN MOUNTAINS

ADIRONDACK
MOUNTAINS

Lake
Ontario

Lake
Huron

Lake Michigan

Cape Cod

Hudson River

Lake Erie

ALLEGHENY
PLATEAU

Long Island

Susquehanna
River

CENTRAL PLAINS

Mississippi River

GREAT PLAINS

Missouri River

Platte River

ALLEGHENY
MOUNTAINS

APPALACHIAN MOUNTAINS

Delaware Bay

Wabash River

River

Ohio River

Potomac
River

PIEDMONT

Chesapeake Bay

Cape Hatteras

Arkansas River

INTERIOR PLAINS

OZARK
PLATEAU

Tennessee River

Mt. Mitchell
6,684 ft.
(2,037 m)

ATLANTIC COASTAL PLAIN

Savannah River

ATLANTIC
OCEAN

OUACHITA
MOUNTAINS

Red River

Mississippi River

Alabama River

Chattahoochee River

Brazos River

Colorado River

DWARDS
LATEAU

GULF COASTAL PLAIN

Mobile
Bay

Galveston
Bay

Mississippi
River Delta

Lake
Okeechobee

BAHAMAS

Gulf of Mexico

N
W E
S

Florida Keys

Straits of Florida

CUBA

GH15

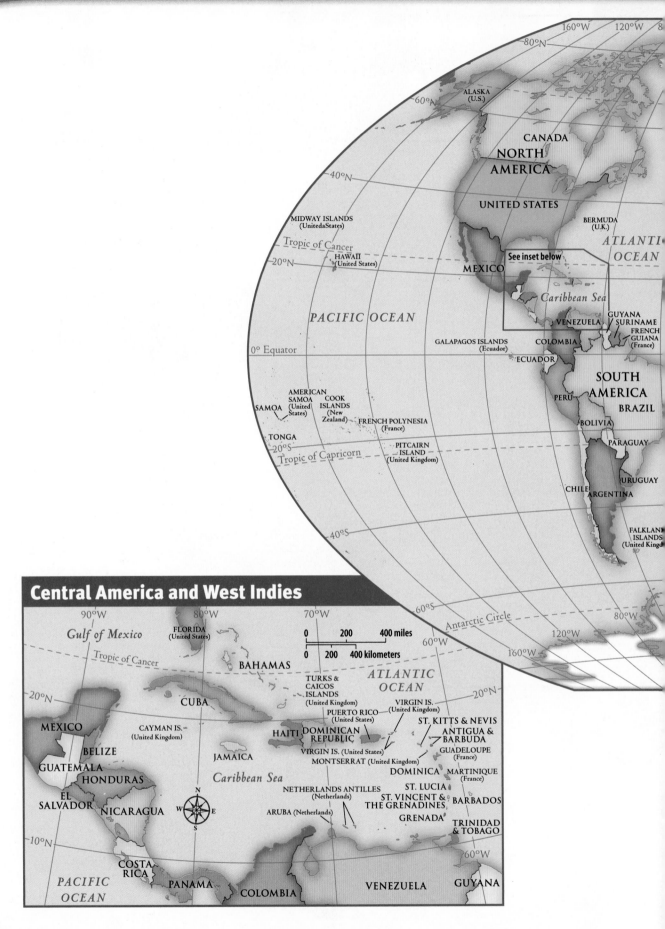

Central America and West Indies

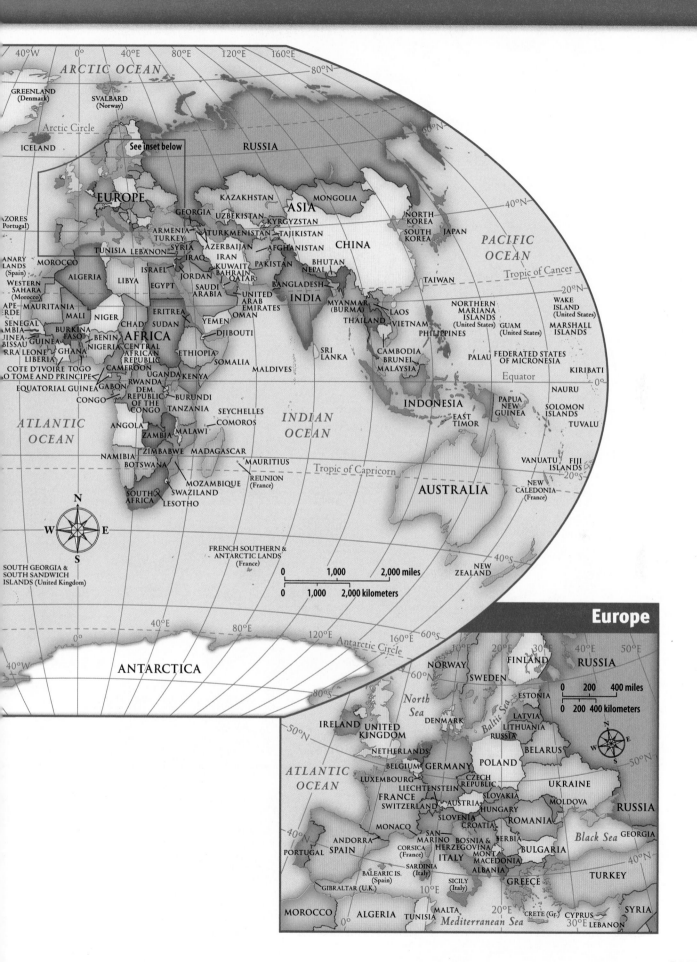

40°W · 0° · 40°E · 80°E · 120°E · 160°E

ARCTIC OCEAN

80°N

GREENLAND
(Denmark)

SVALBARD
(Norway)

Arctic Circle

ICELAND

See inset below

RUSSIA

EUROPE

AZORES
(Portugal)

KAZAKHSTAN · MONGOLIA

GEORGIA · UZBEKISTAN

ASIA

40°N

NORTH
KOREA

JAPAN

KYRGYZSTAN

ARMENIA · TURKMENISTAN · TAJIKISTAN

SOUTH
KOREA

PACIFIC
OCEAN

TURKEY · AZERBAIJAN · AFGHANISTAN

CHINA

ANARY
LANDS
(Spain)

MOROCCO

TUNISIA · LEBANON · SYRIA · IRAN

IRAQ · PAKISTAN

BHUTAN
NEPAL

Tropic of Cancer

WESTERN
SAHARA
(Morocco)

ALGERIA

LIBYA

ISRAEL

JORDAN · KUWAIT
BAHRAIN
QATAR

BANGLADESH

TAIWAN

20°N

APE
RDE

MAURITANIA

MALI

NIGER

EGYPT

SAUDI
ARABIA

UNITED
ARAB
EMIRATES

INDIA

MYANMAR
(BURMA)

LAOS

NORTHERN
MARIANA
ISLANDS
(United States)

WAKE
ISLAND
(United States)

SENEGAL

CHAD

ERITREA

SUDAN

OMAN

YEMEN

THAILAND

VIETNAM

GUAM
(United States)

MARSHALL
ISLANDS

JINEA
AMBIA

BURKINA
FASO

BENIN

AFRICA

DJIBOUTI

PHILIPPINES

RRA LEONE
BISSAU · GUINEA

NIGERIA

CENTRAL
AFRICAN
REPUBLIC

ETHIOPIA

SRI
LANKA

CAMBODIA

BRUNEI

PALAU

FEDERATED STATES
OF MICRONESIA

KIRIBATI

GHANA
LIBERIA

COTE D'IVOIRE · TOGO
O TOME AND PRINCIPE

CAMEROON

UGANDA

SOMALIA

KENYA

MALDIVES

MALAYSIA

Equator

0°

NAURU

EQUATORIAL GUINEA

GABON

CONGO

RWANDA
DEM.
REPUBLIC
OF THE
CONGO

BURUNDI

TANZANIA

SEYCHELLES

INDONESIA

PAPUA
NEW
GUINEA

SOLOMON
ISLANDS

TUVALU

ATLANTIC
OCEAN

ANGOLA

ZAMBIA

MALAWI

COMOROS

INDIAN
OCEAN

EAST
TIMOR

NAMIBIA

ZIMBABWE

MADAGASCAR

BOTSWANA

MAURITIUS

Tropic of Capricorn

AUSTRALIA

VANUATU · FIJI
ISLANDS

20°S

MOZAMBIQUE

REUNION
(France)

NEW
CALEDONIA
(France)

N

W · E

S

SOUTH
AFRICA

SWAZILAND

LESOTHO

FRENCH SOUTHERN &
ANTARCTIC LANDS
(France)

NEW
ZEALAND

40°S

SOUTH GEORGIA &
SOUTH SANDWICH
ISLANDS (United Kingdom)

0 · 1,000 · 2,000 miles

0 · 1,000 · 2,000 kilometers

40°E · 80°E · 120°E · 160°E · 60°S

Antarctic Circle

40°W

0°

80°S

ANTARCTICA

Europe

NORWAY · FINLAND · RUSSIA

60°N

SWEDEN

North
Sea

ESTONIA

0 · 200 · 400 miles

0 · 200 · 400 kilometers

IRELAND · UNITED
KINGDOM

DENMARK

Baltic Sea

LATVIA

LITHUANIA

RUSSIA

50°N

N

W · E

S

NETHERLANDS

BELARUS

50°N

ATLANTIC
OCEAN

BELGIUM · GERMANY

POLAND

LUXEMBOURG · LIECHTENSTEIN

CZECH
REPUBLIC

UKRAINE

FRANCE

SLOVAKIA

SWITZERLAND

AUSTRIA

HUNGARY

MOLDOVA

RUSSIA

40°N

SLOVENIA

ROMANIA

MONACO

SAN
MARINO

CROATIA

SERBIA

Black Sea

GEORGIA

ANDORRA

CORSICA
(France)

BOSNIA &
HERZEGOVINA

MONT.

BULGARIA

PORTUGAL · SPAIN

ITALY

MACEDONIA

TURKEY

40°N

BALEARIC IS.
(Spain)

SARDINIA
(Italy)

ALBANIA

GREECE

GIBRALTAR (U.K.)

SICILY
(Italy)

CRETE (Gr.)

CYPRUS

SYRIA

MOROCCO · ALGERIA · TUNISIA · MALTA

10°E · 20°E

Mediterranean Sea

30°E · LEBANON

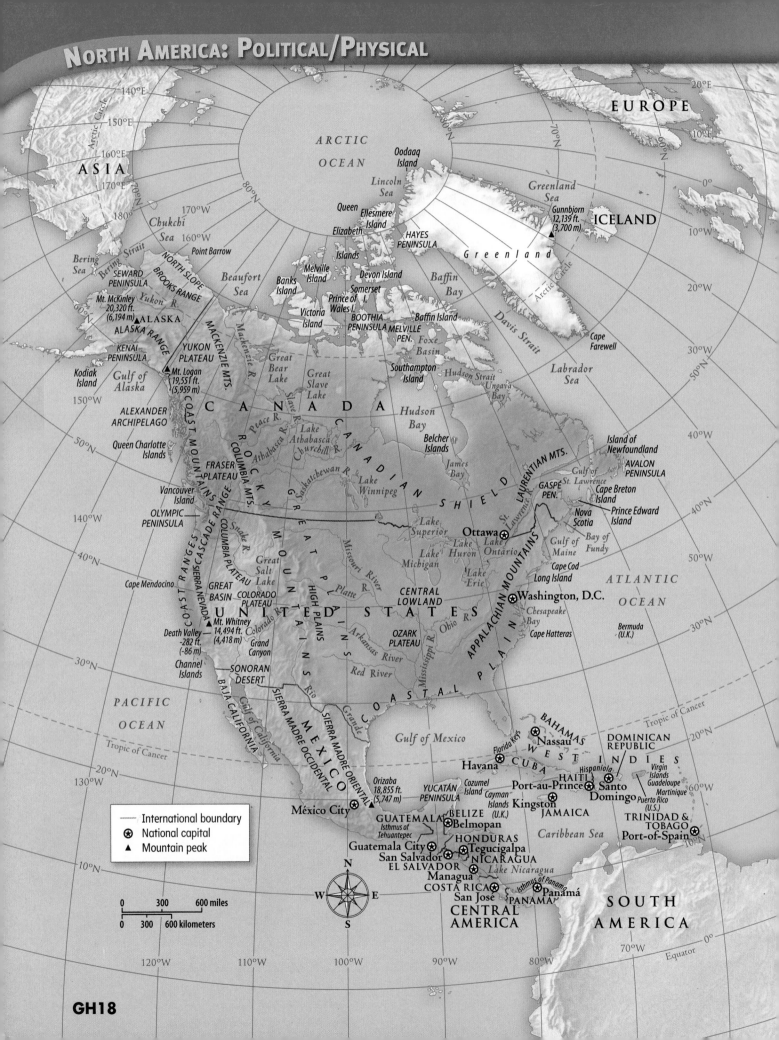

EUROPE

ASIA

Arctic Circle

140°E
150°E
160°E
170°E
180°
170°W
160°W
150°W
130°W
120°W

ARCTIC OCEAN

Oodaaq Island

Lincoln Sea

Queen Elizabeth Islands

Ellesmere Island

HAYES PENINSULA

Greenland Sea

Gunnbjorn 12,139 ft. (3,700 m)

ICELAND

Chukchi Sea

Point Barrow

Beaufort Sea

Melville Island

Banks Island

Devon Island

Somerset Prince of Wales I.

Baffin Bay

Greenland

Arctic Circle

Bering Strait

SEWARD PENINSULA

NORTH SLOPE

BROOKS RANGE

Yukon R.

Victoria Island

BOOTHIA PENINSULA MELVILLE PEN.

Baffin Island

Davis Strait

Cape Farewell

Bering Sea

Mt. McKinley 20,320 ft. (6,194 m)

ALASKA

ALASKA RANGE

Foxe Basin

Labrador Sea

KENAI PENINSULA

YUKON PLATEAU

MACKENZIE MTS.

Southampton Island

Hudson Strait

Ungava Bay

Kodiak Island

Gulf of Alaska

Mt. Logan 19,551 ft. (5,959 m)

Great Bear Lake

Hudson Bay

Island of Newfoundland

ALEXANDER ARCHIPELAGO

C A N A D A

Great Slave Lake

Belcher Islands

AVALON PENINSULA

Queen Charlotte Islands

Peace R.

Slave R.

Lake Athabasca

Churchill R.

C A N A D I A N   S H I E L D

James Bay

LAURENTIAN MTS.

Gulf of St. Lawrence

Cape Breton Island

FRASER PLATEAU

ROCKY MTS.

Athabasca R.

Saskatchewan R.

Lake Winnipeg

GASPÉ PEN.

Prince Edward Island

Vancouver Island

COAST MOUNTAINS

COLUMBIA MTS.

Lake Superior

St. Lawrence R.

Nova Scotia

OLYMPIC PENINSULA

CASCADE RANGE

COLUMBIA PLATEAU

Snake R.

Missouri River

Lake Michigan

Lake Huron

Lake Ontario

Ottawa

Gulf of Maine

Bay of Fundy

Cape Mendocino

COAST RANGES

SIERRA NEVADA

GREAT BASIN

Great Salt Lake

COLORADO PLATEAU

R O C K Y   M O U N T A I N S

Platte R.

CENTRAL LOWLAND

Lake Erie

APPALACHIAN MOUNTAINS

Cape Cod

Long Island

ATLANTIC OCEAN

Mt. Whitney 14,494 ft. (4,418 m)

Death Valley -282 ft. (-86 m)

U N I T E D   S T A T E S

Colorado R.

HIGH PLAINS

Arkansas River

OZARK PLATEAU

Ohio R.

Mississippi R.

Washington, D.C.

Chesapeake Bay

Cape Hatteras

Bermuda (U.K.)

Channel Islands

Grand Canyon

Red River

C O A S T A L   P L A I N

SONORAN DESERT

BAJA CALIFORNIA

Rio Grande

SIERRA MADRE OCCIDENTAL

Gulf of California

M E X I C O

SIERRA MADRE ORIENTAL

Gulf of Mexico

Tropic of Cancer

BAHAMAS

Nassau

Florida Keys

W E S T

DOMINICAN REPUBLIC

PACIFIC OCEAN

Tropic of Cancer

Havana

CUBA

I N D I E S

Virgin Islands

Orizaba 18,855 ft. (5,747 m)

YUCATÁN PENINSULA

Cozumel Island

Cayman Islands (U.K.)

Hispaniola

Port-au-Prince

HAITI

Santo Domingo

Guadeloupe

Martinique

Puerto Rico (U.S.)

México City

GUATEMALA

Isthmus of Tehuantepec

BELIZE

Belmopan

Kingston

JAMAICA

TRINIDAD & TOBAGO

Port-of-Spain

Guatemala City

HONDURAS

Tegucigalpa

Caribbean Sea

San Salvador

EL SALVADOR

NICARAGUA

COSTA RICA

Managua

Lake Nicaragua

San José

CENTRAL AMERICA

PANAMA

Isthmus of Panama

Panamá

SOUTH AMERICA

Equator

130°W
20°N
10°N
120°W
110°W
100°W
90°W
80°W
70°W
60°W
50°W
40°W
30°W
20°W
10°W
0°
10°E
20°E
20°N
30°N
40°N
50°N
60°N
70°N
80°N

— International boundary

⊛ National capital

▲ Mountain peak

0   300   600 miles

0   300   600 kilometers

N
S
E
W

Glossary

This glossary will help you to pronounce and understand the meanings of the vocabulary in this book. The page number at the end of the definition tells you where the word first appears.

Pronunciation Key									
a	at	ē	me	ô	fork	ü	rule	th	thin
ā	ape	i	in	oi	oil	u̇	pull	th	this
ä	far	ī	ice	ou	out	ûr	turn	zh	measure
âr	care	o	hot	u	up	hw	white	ə	about, taken, pencil,
e	end	ō	old	ū	use	ng	song		lemon, circus

A

adobe (ə dō′bē) A brick made of clay that is sometimes mixed with straw and then dried in the sun.

agribusiness (ag′ri biz nis) A large farm owned by a company.

agriculture (ag′ri kul chər) The science and business of growing crops and raising animals.

Allies (al′īz) The countries that fought against the Axis Powers in World War II —Great Britain, France, United States, and the Soviet Union among many others.

aquifer (ak′wə fər) A layer of rock or gravel that traps water underground and supplies wells and springs.

article (är′ti kəl) A story in a newspaper describing an important event that has taken place recently.

artifact (är′tə fakt) An object such as a tool or weapon made by people in the past.

assembly line (ə sem′blē līn) A line of workers and machines used for putting together a product step by step in a factory.

Axis (ak′səs) The countries that fought against the Allied Powers in World War II —Germany, Italy, and Japan among many others.

B

bar graph (bär graf) A graph that can be used to show changes over time or changes among different types of information.

basin (bā′sin) A low landform, shaped like a bowl and surrounded by higher land.

bay (bā) A body of water surrounded by land on three sides.

bison (bis ən) A large, shaggy animal with short horns and a hump on its back.

blizzard (bliz′ərd) A heavy snowstorm with very strong winds.

bluegrass (blü'gras) A kind of folk music played on fiddles, banjos, and guitars popular in the Appalachian Mountains.

butte (būt) A flat-topped mountain or hill that stands alone in an area of flat land.

byline (bī'līn) The part of a newspaper article that tells the reader who wrote the story.

canal (kə nal') A human-made waterway built for boats and ships to travel through, and for carrying water to places that need it.

canyon (kan'yən) A deep valley with very high, steep sides.

capital resources (kap'i təl rē'sôr sez) The tools, machines, and factories businesses use to produce goods.

checks and balances (cheks and bal'an s əz) A system in which the power of each branch of government is balanced by the powers of the other branches.

circle graph (sûr'kəl graf) A graph in the shape of a circle that shows how the different parts of something fit into a whole; also called a pie graph.

citizen (sit'ə zən) A person who was born in a country or who has earned the right to become a member of a country by law.

civil rights (siv'əl rīts) The rights of every citizen to be treated equally under the law.

Civil War (siv'əl wôr) The war between the Union states of the North and the Confederate states of the South, 1861–1865.

climate (klī'mət) The pattern of weather of a certain place over many years.

colony (kol'ə nē) A place that is ruled by another country.

communism (kom'yə niz əm) A system in which business, property, and goods are owned by the government.

conservationist (kon sər vā'shə nist) A person who supports the wise use and protection of natural resources.

constitution (kon sti tu'shən) A plan of government.

consumer (kən sü'mər) A person who buys goods and uses services.

county (koun'tē) One of the sections into which a state or country is divided.

credit (kred'it) A way to purchase something, in which a person borrows money that must be repaid, usually with interest.

culture (kul'chər) The arts, beliefs, and customs that make up a way of life for a group of people.

Declaration of Independence (dek lə rā'sh ən uv in də pen'dəns) A document written in 1776 by colonists telling the world why the colonies wanted independence.

degree (di grē') A unit for measuring distance on Earth's surface.

democracy (di mok'rə sē) A system of government in which people elect their leaders.

descendant (di send'ənt) A person who is related to a particular person or group of people who lived long ago.

dialect (dī'ə lekt) A form of a language spoken in a certain place by a certain group of people.

dictator (dik tā'tər) A person who rules a country without sharing power or consulting anyone else.

discrimination (di skrim' ə nā shən) An unfair difference in the way people are treated.

diverse (dī vûrs') Great difference; variety.

drought (drout) A long period of time when there is very little rain or no rain at all.

earthquake (ûrth'kwāk) A shaking of the earth.

economy (i kon'ə mē) The way a country or other place uses or produces natural resources, goods, and services.

editorial (ed' i tôr'ē əl) A newspaper article that offers a personal opinion about a topic.

elevation (el ə vā'shən) The height of land above sea level.

Emancipation Proclamation (i man sə pā'sh ən prok lə mā'shən) An announcement by President Lincoln in 1863 that all enslaved people living in Confederate states were free.

erosion (i rō'zhən) A wearing away of Earth's surface.

executive branch (eg zek'yə tiv branch) The branch of government that signs bills into laws.

expedition (ek spi dish'ən) A journey of exploration.

fall line (fôl līn) A line joining the waterfalls on numerous rivers where an upland meets a lowland.

federal (fed'ər əl) A system of government that shares power between state, local, and national governments.

fertile (fûr'təl) Land that is able to produce crops and plants easily and plentifully.

frontier (frun tîr') The far edge of a settled area.

fuel (fū'əl) Something used to produce energy.

geyser (gī'zər) A hot, underground spring from which steam and hot water shoot into the air.

glacier (glā'shər) A large mass of ice that moves slowly.

graph (graf) A diagram that represents information.

grid (grid) A set of squares formed by crisscrossing lines that can help you determine locations, such as on a map or globe.

headline (hed'līn) Words printed at the top of an article or story which tell the reader what the story is about.

historian (his tôr'ē ən) A person who studies the past.

human resources (hyü mən rē'sôr sez) All the people employed at a business or organization.

hunter-gatherer (hun'tər gath'ər ər) A person who found food by both hunting animals and gathering plants, fruit, and nuts.

hurricane (hûr'i kān) A storm with very strong winds and heavy rain.

immigrant (im'i grənt) A person who comes to a new country to live.

independent (in di pen'dənt) Free from the control of others.

industry (in'də strē) All the businesses that make one kind of product or provide one kind of service.

interdependent (in'tər di pen'dənt) Relying on one another to meet needs and wants.

interest (in'tər ist) Money that is paid for the use of borrowed or deposited money.

interstate highway (in'tər stāt hī'wā) A road with at least two lanes of traffic in each direction that connects two or more states.

invention (in ven'shən) A product that is made for the first time.

iron (ī'ərn) A hard metal mainly used to make steel.

irrigation (ir i gā'shən) The use of ditches or pipes to bring water to dry land.

jazz (jaz) The form of popular music that grew out of African American culture in the 1920s.

judicial branch (jü dish'əl branch) The branch of government that interprets the laws.

jury (jür'ē) A group of citizens in a court of law who decide if someone accused of a crime is innocent or guilty.

justice (ju'stis) Fair treatment.

kerosene (kar'ə sēn) A fuel made from petroleum.

lake effect (lāk i fekt') The effect water has in changing the weather nearby.

large-scale map (lärj skāl map) A map that shows many details in a small area.

latitude (lat'i tüd) A measure of the distance north or south of the equator on Earth.

legislative branch (lej'is lā tiv branch) The branch of government that makes laws.

levee (le'vē) A wall of earth built along a river to keep the river from overflowing onto land.

line graph (līn graf) A graph that shows patterns and amounts of change over time.

longitude (lon'ji tüd) A measure of distance east or west of the prime meridian on Earth.

Louisiana Purchase (lü ē zē an'ə pûr'chəs) The territory purchased by the United States from France in 1803.

magma (mag'ə) Melted rock.

map scale (map scāl) The measurement a map uses to represent real distance on Earth.

mass production (mas prə duk'shən) The process of making large numbers of one product quickly.

megalopolis (meg ə lop'ə lis) A large urban area formed by several cities.

meridian (mə rid'ē ən) A line of longitude; see longitude.

mesa (mā'sə) A hill or mountain with a flat top and steep sides; a high plateau.

migration (mī grā'shən) A large movement of people or animals from one place to another.

mineral (min'ər əl) A nonrenewable resource found in nature that is not an animal or plant.

mission (mish'ən) A Spanish settlement in the Americas where priests talked about the Christian religion.

mouth (mouth') The place where a river empties into a larger body of water.

municipal (mū nis'ə pəl) Having to do with local or city government.

Natural resources (nach'ər əl rē'sôr sez) Materials found in nature that people use.

newspaper (nüz'pā pər) A paper that is usually printed daily or weekly and contains news, opinions, and advertising.

nonrenewable resource (non ri nü'ə bəl rē'sôrs) A thing found in nature that cannot be replaced such as coal.

Northwest Passage (nôrth' west' pas'ij) A water route from Europe to Asia through North America.

official document (ə fish'əl dok'yə mənt) A document that contains information that has been agreed upon by one or more people or institutions.

open-pit mining (ō'pən pit mī'ning) A method of removing ore deposits close to the surface of the ground using power shovels.

ore (ôr) A mineral or rock that is mined for the metal or other substance it contains.

P

parallel (par'ə lel) A line of latitude.

patriotism (pā'trē ə tiz'əm) A love for and loyal support of one's country.

peninsula (pə nin'sə lə) Land that has water on three sides.

petroleum (pə trō'lē əm) A fuel, commonly called oil, that forms underground from dead plants.

pioneer (pī ə nîr') A person who leads the way or one who settles a new part of the country.

plateau (pla tō') An area of flat land, higher than the surrounding country.

population density (pop ū lā'shən den'sə tē) A measurement of how many people live in a particular area; a type of map that shows the same.

population distribution (pop ū lā'shən dis trə bū'shən) A measurement of where in an area people live; a type of map that shows the same.

powwow (pou'wou) A Native American festival.

prairie (prâr'ē) Flat or rolling land covered with grass.

precipitation (pri sip i tā'shən) The moisture that falls to the ground in the form of rain, sleet, hail, or snow.

prehistory (prē his'tōr ē) The time before written records.

primary source (prī'mer ē sôrs) An artifact, photograph, or eyewitness account of an event in the past.

prime meridian (prīm mə rid'ē ən) The line of longitude, marked 0°, from which other meridians are numbered.

producer (prə dū'sər) A person or company that makes or creates something.

pueblo (pweb' lō) Native American town or village with adobe and stone houses; any Native American group or people who live or whose ancestors lived in adobe or stone houses usually in the Southwest United States.

R

rain shadow (rān shad'ō) The side of the mountain that is usually dry because precipitation falls on the other side.

Reconstruction (rē kvn struk'shən) The period after the Civil War in which Congress passed laws designed to rebuild the country and bring the Southern states back into the Union.

refinery (ri fī'nə rē) A factory which turns crude oil into useful products such as heating oil, gasoline, plastics, and paint.

region (rē'jen) An area, or group of states, with common features that set it apart from other areas.

renewable resource (ri nü' ə bəl rē'sôrs) A natural resource that can be replaced, such as trees or water.

reservation (rez ûr vā'shən) Land set aside by the government as settlements for Native Americans.

resource (rē' sôrs') A person, thing, or material that can be used for help or support.

revolution (rev ə lü'shən) The overthrow of a government.

road map (rōd map) A map that shows roads.

rodeo (rōd ē ō) A rodeo is a show that has contests in horseback riding, roping, and other similar skills.

rule of law (rool əv lô) The belief that a country's laws apply to all of its people equally.

S

sea level (sē lev'vl) The level of the surface of the sea.

secondary source (sek'ən der e sôrs) An account of an event from a person who did not see or experience it.

segregation (seg ri gā'shən) The practice of keeping racial groups separate.

service (sûr'vis) Something that is done to help another person.

silicon (sil i kän) A material used in the manufacture of computer chips.

small-scale map (smôl skāl map) A map that shows few details of a large area.

solar energy (sō'lər en'ər jē) Energy that comes from the sun.

source (sôrs) The starting point of a river.

sovereign (sov'ər in) A nation or group of people not controlled by others; independent.

suburban (sə bûr'ben) Describes a community near a city.

suffrage (suf'rij) The right to vote.

T

tax (taks) Money people and businesses must pay to the government so that it can provide public services.

technology (tek nol'ə jē) The use of skills, tools, and machines to meet people's needs; new method of doing something.

telecommunications (tel'i kə mū ni kā' sh ənz) The technology that allows people to send messages and images long distances quickly.

territory (ter'i tôr'ē) Land owned by a country either within or outside the country's borders.

terrorism (ter'ə riz əm) The use of violence and threats to acheive a political goal.

timberline (tim'bər līn) A tree line.

tornado (tôr nā'dō) A powerful wind storm with a funnel-shaped cloud that moves quickly over land.

tourist (tur'ist) A person who is traveling for pleasure.

tradition (trə dish'ən) A custom that is passed down from parents to their children. This includes festivals, songs, and dances.

tributary (trib'yə ter ē) A river or stream that flows into a larger river.

urban (ûr'bən) A city and its surrounding areas.

veto (vē'tō) The power of the executive branch to reject a bill passed by the legislature.

wetland (wet'land) A low flat area covered with water.

Index

This index lists many topics that appear in the book, along with the pages on which they are found. Page numbers after a *c* refer you to a chart or diagram, after a *g*, to a graph, after an *m*, to a map, after a *p*, to a photograph or picture, and after a *q*, to a quotation.

A

Abernathy, Ralph, *p180*, 180–181
Acadia, 176
Addams, Jane, 49
Adirondack Mountains, 132
Adirondack State Park, 131, *p131*
Adobe, 241
African Americans
  Civil Rights Movement and, *p180*, 180–181
  as cowboys, 237
  discrimination against, 58
  freedom for, 44
  Great Migration of, 125, *p125*, 211
  Jim Crow laws and, 44
  music and, *p182*, 182–183, *p183*
  in Northeast, 146, *p147*
  in Southeast, 178
  Underground Railroad and, 211, *p211*
  voting rights for, 181
  in World War II, 58
Agribusiness, 204
Agriculture, 82. See also Farming
  cash crops in, 204
  Dust Bowl and, 52, *p52*, 53
  fertile soil in, 194, 210
  irrigation and, 236
  in Midwest, 201, *p204*, 204–205, *p205*
  in Southeast, *p168*, 169, m169
  in Southwest, *p234*, 236–237, *p236–237*
  in West, *p268*, 268–269
Airplanes, 276
Air pollution, reducing, 61
Alabama, space research in, 173
Alamo, 38, *p38*, 222, *p222*
Alaska, 75, 257, 268, *p268*
  climate in, 263
  Iditarod dogsled races in, 278, *p278*
  oil in, 267
Alaska Range, 75
Allies in World War II, 55, 57

Allstate 394, 215
American Alligators, 69, *p69*
American Bison, 190, *p190*
American Revolution, 26–27, *p26–27*
  American soldiers in, *p29*
  British soldiers in, *p28*
  Concord in, 27
  Lexington in, 27
  Native Americans in, 29
  redcoats in, 27, *p27*
  strengths and weaknesses in, 28
  surrender of British in, 30
  Valley Forge in, 29, *p29*
  women in, 28, *p28*
Americans, first, 8–9, *p8–9*
Amish, 147, *p147*
Anacostia Community Museum (Washington, DC), 125
Anasazi people, 13, 241
Animals
  in Midwest, *p190*, *p192*, 193, *p193*
  in Northeast, 129, *p129*
  in Southeast, 159, *p159*, *p160*, 161, *p161*, *p165*
  in Southwest, 223, *p223*, *p224*, 225, *p225*
  in West, *p256*, 257, *p257*, 259, *p259*
Apache, 13
Appalachian Mountains, *p70*, 73, 74, 129, 132, *p162–163*, 163, 165
  animals in, 76
  coal mining in, 82, *p83*
  farming in, 72, *p72*
Aquifers, 231
Arapaho, 46
Arctic Ocean, 75
Arizona, computer industry in, 238
Armadillo, 223, *p223*
Arms race, 57
Armstrong, Louis, 182, *p183*
Armstrong, Neil, 3, *p3*
Artifacts, 9
Art in West, *p214*
Asian immigrants, 276, *p277*
Assateague Island, 157, *p157*

Assembly, 102, *p102*
Assembly line, 206
Atlanta, King Center in, 2
Atlantic Ocean, 71, 90, 133
Automated teller machines (ATMs), 97, *p97*
Automobiles, 276
  development of, 244
Axis in World War II, 55

B

Badlands, 197, *p197*
Badlands National Park, 197, *p197*
Baltimore, Maryland, growth of, 130
Banks, 89, 96–97
Bar graphs, 199, *p199*
Barley, 236
Barrier Islands, 157, *p157*
Barter, 94
Basins, 74
Bays, 130
Bell, Alexander Graham, 47
Big Sky Country, 269, *p269*
Bill, becoming law, *c103*
Bill of Rights, 31
Bison, 275
Black bears, 131, *p131*
Black Hills, 196
Bluegrass, 182, *p182*
Blue Ridge Mountains, *p72*
Bonneville Salt Flats, *p271*
Boothbay Harbor, Maine, 125, *p125*
Boston, 25
Boston Tea Party, *p24*, 26
Broadleaf trees, 131, *p131*
Brown, William Wells, 211
Brown pelicans, *p165*
Buffalo, 12, *p13*, 237
Bunyan, Paul, 191, *p191*, 228
Bush, George W., 60
Business, *p86*
  advertising in, 90
  getting organized, 88
  key to success, 90
  need for money, 89
  production in, 90
  resources for, 95, *c95*
  starting, 87, 96
Buttes, 227, *p227*

C

Cactus, 76
Cahokia, 9, *p9*, 209
Cajuns, 178, 182
California, discovery of gold in, 39, *p39*, 253, *p253*, 267
California Gold Rush, 39, *p39*
Canals, 36, *p36–37*
Canyons, 228–229, *p228–229*
Cape Canaveral, Florida, *p172*
Cape Cod, Massachusetts, 126, *p126*
Capital resources, *c95*, 96
Carbon dioxide, 171
Carnegie, Andrew, 48, 49
Carrier, Willis, 244
Cascade Mountains, 75, 87
Cash crops, 204
Cattle in Southwest, 237, *p237*
Cavelier, René-Robert (Sieur de La Salle), 19, *p19*
Central Valley, 268, *p269*
Chaco Canyon, 241
Charbonneau, 35
Chart and Graph Skills
  Compare Bar and Line Graphs, 199, *g199*
  Reading Circle Graphs, 167, *g167*
  Read Line Graphs, 99, *g99*
Checks and balances, 102, 110
Cheese, 191, *p191*
Cherokee, 11, *p176*, 177, *p177*
  and Trail of Tears, 177
Cherrystone clams, *p133*
Cheyenne, 46
Chiao, Leroy, *p239*
Chicago, 73
  settlement houses in, 49
  immigrants in, 212
Child labor, 139
Chile peppers, 222, *p222*
China
  communism in, 57
  international trade and, 272, *p272*
Chinatown, 278
Chinese workers, *p276*
Chinook, 14
Chippewa, 209
Chumash, 15
Cinco de Mayo, 246–247, *p247*

Circle graphs, 167, p167
Circular flow, 98, c98
Citizens, 109
  being responsible, 115
  working together, 116–117
Citizenship
  Be Informed, 230, p230
  Being Informed, 181, p191
  Express Your Opinion, 213, p213
  Volunteering, 271, p271
  Working for the Common Good, 150, p150
Civil Rights Act (1964), 59, 181
Civil rights movement, 58–59, p58–59, p176, p180, 180–181
  African Americans and, p180, 180–181
  King, Martin Luther, Jr. in, 2, p2, 58–59, p58–59, p116, p119, p180, 180–181
  school desegregation in, 157, p157, 180, p180
  sit-ins in, 181, p181
Civil War (1861-1865), 41, 180
  drummer boys in, 3, p3
  enslaved people in, 40, p40–41
  Gettysburg, battle of, 3, p3, 42–43
  Monitor versus Virginia in, 42, p42
  North in, 41, 43
  South in, 41, 42
  strengths and weaknesses in, 42–43
Clark, William, 34–35, p34–35
Clemens, Samuel. See also Twain, Mark, 195, p195
Cleveland, 73
  Rock and Roll Hall of Fame in, 214, p214–215
Climate, 80, 85, p86, 86 water and. See also Weather
  lake effect and, 88, p88
  latitude and, 262–263
  in Midwest, 198, p198
  in Northeast, 129, 134, p134
  in Southeast, d164, 164–165
  in Southwest, 222, 224, 230, p231, 244
  storms and, 91
  temperature in, 85, g89, m89
  in West, p256, 262–263
Coal
  burning, 171
  mining, 72, 82, p83, 170, p170, 171

Coastal plain, 72
Cold War, 57–59
Colonists, conflict with Native Americans, 22, p22
Colorado Plateau, 226–227
Colorado River, 228, 259
Columbian Exchange, 17
Columbus, Christopher, p16–17, 17
Comanche people, 12
Communism, 57
Computer industry, 238
Computers, 60
Conch, 159, p159
Concord, Battle of, 27
Confederate States of America, 41
Congress, U.S., 109, 111
Conservationists, 273
Constitution, U.S., 31, 109, 180
Constitutional Convention (Philadelphia), p30–31
Consumers, 94, 98
Continental Divide, 74, p261
Coolidge, Calvin, 117, q117
Copper, 235, p235, p267
Corn, 204
Corn Palace, 212
Coronado, Francisco Vasquez de, 18, p18, 220, p220, 242, p243
Cotton, 169, p236
Counties, 104
Country music, 158
Country Music Hall of Fame, 158, p158
Courthouse, p105
Covered wagons, 210–211
Cowboy boots, 68, p68
Cowboys, 221, p221, p237, 279, p279
  African Americans as, 237
Crater Lake, Oregon, c71
Crazy Horse monument, 214, p214
Credit, 96
Credit cards, 96
Crockett, Davy, 38
Crow Agency, Montana, 279
Cultural regions, 79
Culture, 145
  celebrating, in Southwest, p79, p221, p246, 246–247, p247

Dairy farming, 137, 204
DataGraphic
  Jobs in Southeast, 173

Population Growth, 245, m245, g245
  United States: Average January Temperatures, 89, g89
Davis, Jefferson, 41
Death Valley, California, c71
Declaration of Independence, 27, 114, p114, 115, 119
Deer, 76
Degrees, 106
Democracy, 108, 109
Denali (Mount McKinley), 75
Desalination, 230
Descendants, 209
Desegregation, school, 157, p157
Detroit, 73
  immigrants in, 212
  manufacturing in, 206
  music in, 214
De Vaca, Cabeza, 243, q243, p243
Dialect, 179
Diné, 241
Discrimination, 58, 119
Djibouti, p205
Dogsleds, p266, 278, p278
Drought, 230
Drummer boys, 3, p3
Durham, NC, 173
Dust Bowl, 52, 53, 230, 277

Earth Day, 61, p61
Earthquakes, 260, p260
East, p72, 72–73
Eastern Woodlands, 10–11, p10–11
  Native Americans in, 10–11, 124, 209
Economy, 82
  basics of, 94–95
  circular flow of, 98, c98
  free-enterprise, p86, 87
  in Midwest, p200, m201, 201–204, p202, p203, p204
  needs and wants in, 93
  in Northeast, 137–141
  opportunity costs in, 91
  planned, 87
  scarcity in, 93
  in Southeast, p168, p169, 169–173, p170–171, p172
  in Southwest, p234, 235–239, p236–237, p238–239
  supply and demand in, 89
  in West, p267, 267–273, m268–269, p270, p271, p272
Ecosystems, 76

Edge, John T., 179, q179
Edison, Thomas Alva, 47
Education
  research and, 173
  school desegregation and, 157, p157, 180, p180
Elections
  of 1860, 41
  of 1932, 54
Elevation, m77
  effect of, on temperature, 85
Elevation maps, 77, m77, m85
Eliot, T. S., 214, p214, q214
Ellis Island, 124, p124, 147
Emancipation Proclamation, 43
Energy
  hydro-electric, 133, d133
  oil, 61, 170
  solar, 238
  wind, p60–61, 201
England. See also Great Britain
  exploration and settlement by, 178
English colonies, 20
  Great Britain and, 25
  Native Americans and, 20, p20
  purchase of New Netherlands, 21
Enslaved people, 40, p40–41
Entrepreneurs, 88
Equator, 85
Erie Canal, 36, p36–37
Erosion, 72
Everglades National Park, 159, p159
Executive branch
  in federal government, 110, p110
  in state government, 102, p102
Expedition, 34
Extreme weather, 90–91

Fallen Timbers, battle of, 33
Fall lines, 132
Farming, 76. See also Agriculture
  dairy, 137, 204
  by Eastern Woodlands people, 10–11
  in Midwest, 73, 201, 205, p205
  in Southeast, 72
Federal government, 109
Federal Reserve System, 98
Fermilab, 207, p207

Fertile, 194
Fertile soil, 194, 210
Fifteenth Amendment, p45
Finger Lakes, 129
Fishing industry, 269, p269
Flamingoes, 159, p159
Florida, space research in, 173
Ford, Henry, 51, 206
Founding fathers, 2, p2
Four Corners, 226
France
    American Revolution and, 30
    French and Indian War and, p22, 22-23, 24
    sale of Louisiana and, 34
Franklin, Aretha, 183
Free enterprise system, p86, 87
French
    Native Americans and, 19
    in North America, p18, 18-19
    settlement of, in Southeast, 178-179, p178-179
    settlement of Midwest, 210
French and Indian War (1754-1763), p22, 22-23
    costs of, 24
Frontier, 38
Fuel, 130
Fulton, Robert, 36
Fur trade, 19, 210

Ganondagan State Historic Site, 124, p124
Gateway Arch, 69, p69
Geographic region, 79
Geography, facts of, c71
Gettysburg, battle of, 3, p3, 42-43
Geyser, 261
Glaciers, 129, 193, 196
    melting of, 194
Global Connections
    International Trade, 272, p272
    Kansas Wheat, 205, p205
    United Nations, 112, p112
Global grid, m107
Gold, discovery of, in California, 39, p39, 253, p253, 267
Golden Gate Bridge, 278
Government, 101
    federal, 109
    local, p100, 101, c101, p104, 104-105

municipal, 104
national, 109-111
state, 101, c101, 102
tribal, 113
Governor, 102, p102
Grand Canyon, 221, p221, 223, p223, 228-229, p228-229
Grand Canyon National Park, 221
Graphs, 99, 167
    bar, 199, p199
    circle, 167, g167
    line, 99, g99,199, p199
Grave Creek Burial Mound, p209
Great Basin, 74, 76
Great Britain. See also England
    American Revolution and, 26-27, p26-27
    French and Indian War and, p22, 22-23, 24
    Parliament of, 25
    surrender of, in American Revolution, 30
    taxes on colonies, 24, 25
    victory in French and Indian War, 23
Great Depression (1929-1941), 52-53, p52-53
    end of, 55
Great Lakes, 73, 189, p189, 193, 196, 198, 201
Great Migration, 211
Great Plains, 12, 74, 269, p269
Great Salt Lake, p256, 259, p259
Green Mountains, 132
Grids, 106
Gulf Coastal Plain, 225
Gulf of Mexico, 90, 91, 164, 225, 228, 239
Gullah, 179, p179
Gumbo, 179, p179

Haiti, 210
Handu, Seema, q277
Handy, W. C., 182
Harbors, 130
Harlem, New York, 125, p125
Harney Peak, 196
Hartwig, Bill, 189, p189
Hawaii, 75, p75, 257, 261, 268, p268, 271
    climate of, 263
Hiawatha, 11
Hispanics
    in Northeast, 147, p147

in West, 246-247, p247
History, reasons for studying, 4-5
Hitler, Adolf, 55
Holland, Michigan, 212, p213
Hollywood, California, 270, 278
Homeland Security, U.S. Department of, 60
Hopi, 241, 246
    reservation for, 113
    Tribal Council of, 113, p113
Hot springs, 261
House, Donna, 66, p66
House of Representatives, U.S., 111
Houston, Sam, 38
Human resources, c95
Hunter-gatherers, 10-11, p10-11
Huron, 11
Hurricane Katrina, 61, p90, 91, p165, 166
Hurricanes, 90, p90, 91, 165, p165
    damage from, 166
Hydro-electric power plant, p133

Ice Age, 8
Iditarod, 278, p278
Illinois, 207
    immigrants in, 211
    service industries in, 207
Immigrants, 46, 47, 124, p124
    in Midwest, 211, p211
    in Northeast, 144, p146, 146-147, p147
    in Southeast, 178-179, p178-179
    in Southwest, 144-145
    in West, 276-277, p277
Independence Hall, 2, p2, 26, p26
Indianapolis 500, 191, p191
Indianapolis Motor Speedway, 215, p215
Indigo, 169
Industry, 139
    computer, 238
    fishing, 269, p269
    movie, 270
    oil, p223, 235
    textile, 138-139, p139-140, 172
Interdependent, 82
Interest, 96
International trade, 272
Interstate highway, 264

Inuits, 275
Inventions, 47, 203, 244
Iowa
    farming in, 194, 204
    service industries in, 207
Iron, mining for, in Midwest, 202, p202
Iroquois, 11, 30, 124, p124, 145
Iroquois Confederacy, 30
Iroquois League, 11
Irrigation, agriculture and, 236
Islands in Southeast, 163, p163

J

James I, King of England, 20
Jamestown, 20
    settlement of, 178
Jazz music, 182, 214
Jefferson, Thomas, 34, 115, q115
Jim Crow laws, 44
Johnson, Andrew, Reconstruction plan of, 44
Johnson, Lyndon Baines, p180, q180, 181
Johnson Space Center, 239, p239
Jones, Addison, 221, p221
Joplin, Scott, 51, p51
Judicial branch
    in federal government, 111
    in local government, 105,
    in state government, 102,
Jury, 115
Justice, 118
Jackrabbits, 76

K

Kansas, farming in, 204, 205, p205
Kerosene, 235
Kilauea, 253, p253, 260
Kind, Ron, 81
King, Coretta Scott, p119
King, Martin Luther, Jr., 2, p2, 58-59, p58-59, p116, p119, p180, 180-181
King Center, 2
Korea, war in, 57
Krauss, Alison, 214

L

Labor unions, 49
Lake Champlain, p150-151
Lake effect, 88, p88, 198
Lake Erie, 129, 193
Lake Huron, 193
Lake Michigan, 193
Lake Ontario, 88, 129, 193

Lake Superior, 88, 193
Lakotas, 12, 46, 209, 275
Land breeze, 164, p164
Landforms, p70, 71, m73, 80
  in Midwest, 196-197,
  in Northeast, 130-133
  in Southeast, 162-163
  in Southwest, 224, 225,
    226-227, 228-229,
  in West, 71, 74-75, 257,
    258-259
Lange, Dorothea, 276, p276
Larcom, Lucy, 139
Large-scale maps, 135
Latitude, 106
  climate and, 262-263
  lines of, 106, p106
Lava, 261
Laws, 118
  bill becoming, c103
  enforcement of, 104
Leaders, choosing, 109
Lee, Robert E., 42
Legislative branch
  in executive branch, 111,
    p111
  process of bill becoming
    law, c103
  in state government, 102,
    p102
Lenape, 11, 145
Levees, 166, p166
Levittown, New York, p56-57
Lewis, Meriwether, 34-35,
  p34-35
Lexington, Battle of, 27
Lighthouses, 134, p134
Liliukalani, Queen, 75, p75
Lincoln, Abraham, 43, p43,
  189, p189, 211
  assassination of, 43
  in election of 1860, 41
  Emancipation Proclamation
    of, 43
Lincoln Memorial, 2
Lincoln National Historic Site,
  189, p189
Line graphs, 99, g99, 199, p199
Little Bighorn, 46
Lizards, 76
Local governments, p100, 101,
  c101, 104-105
  services provided by, 104,
    p104
  sharing of power and, 101,
    c101
  taxes of, 105
Logging, p267
Longitude, 106
  lines of, 106, p106

Louisiana Creole, 179
Louisiana Purchase (1803), 34
Louisiana Territory, 34
Louis XIV, King of France, 19
Love, Nat, 221, p221, 237
Lowell, Francis, 138, p138
Lowell Factory, p139

Madison, James, 30, p30
Magma, 258
Magnolia, 158, p158
Maine, p117, 127, p130
Makah people, 14
Manhattan Island, 21
Manufacturing, new methods
  of, 206, d206, p206
Map and Globe Skills
  Comparing Maps at
    Different Scales, 135, m135
  Understanding Latitude and
    Longitude, 106-107, m106,
    m107
  Using Elevation Maps, 77,
    m77
  Using Road Maps, 264-265
  Using Special Purpose Maps,
    232-233, m233
Maple syrup, production of, in
  Northeast, p131, 145
Map scale, 135, m135
Marquette, Jacques, 188, p188
Marsalis, Wynton, 156, p156
Mass production, 206
McDonald, Alvin, q196, p196
Megalopolis, 143, p143
Meridians, 106
Mesas, 227, p227
Metropolitan areas, 143
Mexican dancers, 220, p220
Mexican War (1846-48), 38-39
Michigan
  farming in, 204
  service industries in, 207
Micmac, 11
Midwest, p187, 188-215, p190-
  191, m190-191, p192
  agriculture in, 201, p204,
    204-205, p205
  animals in, p190, p192, 193,
    p193
  art in, p214
  climate of, 198, p198
  economy of, p200, m201,
    201-204, p202, p203,
    p204
  festivals in, 212-213, p212-
    213, 214
  geography of, p189, p192,

  193-197, p194-195,
    p196-197
  immigrants in, 211, p211
  industry in, 206, d206, p206
  landforms of, 196-197,
    p196-197
  literature in, 195, 114
  mining in, 202, p202
  music in, 214
  Native Americans in, 209,
    p209
  natural resources of, 201,
    m201
  people in, p208, 209-211,
    p211
  plants in, 192, p192, 193,
    p193
  service industry in, 207
  settlement of, p210, 210-
    211, p211
  tourism and leisure in,
    p188-191, 196-197, p196-197,
    p212-213, 212-215, p214, p215
Minerals, 71
  as natural resource, 76
  in Southwest, 235, c235,
    267, p267
Mining
  coal, 72, 82, p83, 170, p170,
    171
  copper, 235, c235, p267
  gold, 39, p39, 253, p253, 267
  iron, 202, p202
  silver, p267
Minnesota
  immigrants in, 211, 212
  lakes in, 193
  manufacturing in, 206
Minuit, Peter, 21
Missions, 18
Mississipians, 9
Mississippi River, 73, 74, p80,
  81, 158, p158, 161,
  194-195, 201
  levees along, p166
Missouri, immigrants in, 211
Missouri River, 34, 195, 201,
  259
Money, 96-97
Monitor (ship), 42, p42
Monument Valley, 226, p226
Moose, p76
Motown, 183
Mound builders, 8-9, 9, p9,
  209, p209
Mountain men, 252, 276
Mount Elbert, 258
Mount Hood, 68, p68, p84, 85
  elevation of, m85
Mount McKinley, c71

Mount Mitchell, 163
Mount Rushmore, p65, 190,
  p190
Mount St. Helens, 260,
  d260-261
Movie industry, 270, p270
Muir, John, q262
  Wilderness Area, p262
Municipal governments, 104
Music
  African Americans and,
    p182, 182-183, p183
  country, 158
  jazz, 182, 214
  ragtime, 51
  rock and roll, 57, 182, p183
  soul, 183, 214
  in Southeast, 182-183,
    p182-183

Nashville, Tennessee, 158
National Aquarium (Baltimore,
  Maryland), 150, p151
National Cowboys of Color
  Museum and Hall of Fame
  (Fort Worth, Texas), 221, p221
National government, 109-111
National Historic Trail, 157
National Mississippi River
  Museum and Aquarium, 188
National Museum of American
  History, 67
National parks, 159, p159, 197,
  p197, 221, 254, p254, 261, 273,
  p273
National Wildlife Refuge
  System, 189
Native Americans, 113, 119, 146.
  See also specific group
  in American Revolution, 29
  conflicts with colonists and,
    20, p20, 22, p22
  Eastern Woodland, 10-11,
    p10-11
  forceful resettlement of, 211
  French and, 19
  in French and Indian War,
    22-23, p22-23, 24
  in Midwest, 209, p209
  mound builders, 8-9, p8-9
  in Northeast, 144, 145, p145
  powwows of, 246, p246
  reservations for, 113, 241
  in Southeast, 156, p156,
    177, p177, 178
  in Southwest, 12-13, p12-
    13, 241, p241, 246, p246
  use of resources, 130

in West, 14–15, *p14–15*, 274, 275, *p275*
Western settlement and, 33
Natural resources, 71, 80. See *also* Minerals; Mining
in linking regions, 82–83, *c95*
in Midwest, 201, *m201*
in Northeast, 128, 133, 137, *m137*
in Southeast, 170–171, *p170–171*
in Southwest, 235, *p235*
in West, 71, 267–268, *m268–269*, 270
Navajo, *p236*, 241, *p241*
Nebraska, immigrants in, 211
Needle-leaf trees, 131, *p131*
Needs, 93
Netherlands, immigrants from, 146
Nevada, 271
New Amsterdam, *p20–21*
New Deal, 54
New France, 19, 188, *p188*
New Mexico, 242
Albuquerque, 246, *p246*, 247
computer industry in, 238
New Netherlands, *p20–21*, 21
New Orleans, *p90*, 91, *p176*
hurricane damage in, 166
New Spain, settlement of, 242–243, *p242–243*
New York City
growth of, 130
Statue of Liberty in, 49, *p49*
Nez Perce, 15
Niagara Falls, *p117*, 127, *p132*
Nonrenewable resources, 172
Nor'easters, 134
North America
English in, 20, *p20*, 21, 25, 178
French in, *p18*, 18–19
New Netherlands in, *p20–21*, 21
Spanish in, *p18*, 18–19, 178, 220, *p220*, 241, 242–243, *p242–243*, *p276*
Northeast, *p123*, 126–127, *m126–127*, *p126–127*, 126–151
African Americans in, 146, *p147*
animals of, 129, *p129*
cities and suburbs in, *m142*, 142–143, *p143*
climate of, 129, 134, *p134*
economy in, 137–141
environment in, 151
festivals in, 144, 148, *p148*,

149
factories in, 138–139, *p138–139*
forests in, 130–131, *p131*
geography of, *p128*, *p129*, 129–133, *p130–131*, *p132*, *p133*
glaciers in formation of, 129
Hispanics in, 147, *p147*
immigrants in, 144, *p146*, 146–147, *p147*
industry in, *p131*, 139, *p139*
mountains in, 132–133
Native Americans in, 144, 145, *p145*
natural resources in, 128, 133, 137, *m137*
people in, 144, 145, *p145*, *p146*, 146–147, *p147*
plants of, 129, *p129*
services in, 140–141, *p140–141*
tourism and leisure in, *p123*, *p124–127*, 150–151, *p150–151*
water resources in, 130, *p132*, 132–133, *p133*
working in, *p136*, 137–141
North Pole, 85, 262
Northwest Passage, 19
Northwest Territory, 32–33, *p32–33*

Oconaluftee Village, 177
Ogallala Aquifer, 231
Oglala National Grassland of Nebraska, 197
Ohio
fertility of soil in, 194
immigrants in, 211
settlement in, *p32–33*
Ohio River, 195, 201
Oil, 61, 223
Alaskan, 267
Oil derricks, 223, *p223*
Oil industry, *p223*, 235
Oil refineries, 171
Oil spill cleanup, 271, *p271*
Ojibwa people, 209
O'Keeffe, Georgia, *p244*
Okefenokee Swamp, 161, *p161*
Okies, 52, *p52*
Oklahoma
computer industry in, 238
grasslands of, 230
Old Faithful, 261, *p261*
Olympic Peninsula, 263, *p263*
Open-pit mining, 202, *p202*

Ore, 202
Oregon, 268, *p269*
Ozette, 14

Pacific Ocean, 71, 74, 75
Painted Desert, 227, *p227*
Parallels, 106
Parks, Rosa, *p180*, 180–181
Parliament, 25
Patriotism, 117, *p117*
Patriots, 30
Peace Corps, 117
Pearl Harbor, Japanese surprise attack on, 54–55, *p55*
Peninsula, 162
Pennsylvania, 126, *p126*
mountains of, 72
Petroleum, 170, 235
Philadelphia, Independence Hall in, 2, *p2*, 26, *p26*
Phoenix, Arizona, 244
population in, *m245*
Pickett, Bill, 221, *p221*, 237
Piedmont, 162
Pilgrims, 20, *p20*
Pioneers, 211
Plains people, 12, 209
Plains War, 46
Planned economy, 87
Plants
in Midwest, 192, *p192*, 193, *p193*
in Northeast, 129, *p129*
in Southeast, *p158*, 161, *p161*
in Southwest, 224, *p224*, *p225*, *p231*
in West, *p256*, 257, *p257*, *p263*
Plateau, 74, 226
Pledge of Allegiance, 117
Plymouth, 20, *p20*
Pocahontas, 21, *p21*
Polar bears, 255, *p255*
Pollution, 80, 171
Pony Penning, 157, *p157*
Population density, 232, *m233*
Population distribution, 232, *m233*
Population growth in Southwest, *p244*, 244–245, *m245*, *g245*
Population maps, 232–233, *m233*
Pottawatomie, 11
Powell, John Wesley, 221, *p221*
Powwows, 246, *p246*

Prairies, 196
Precipitation, 86, *p86*, 263
Prehistory, 8
Presidents, 101, 110
Presley, Elvis, 57, *p57*, 182, *p183*
Prime meridians, 106
Printz, Johan, 146, *p146*, *q146*
Producers, *p86*, 94
Puebla, battle of (1862), 247
Pueblo, *p12*, 241
Pueblo people, 13, 241
Puerto Rico, 163, *p163*

Ragtime music, 51
Railroads, 37, *p37*, *p46*, 46–47, *p46–47*, 276
Rainfall, mountains and, *p86*, 87
Rain shadow, 87, 263
Reconstruction, 44
Redcoats, 27, *p27*
Red Cross, 116
Red Star, Kevin, *p275*
Regions, 79
resources in linking, 82–83
Renewable resources, 170
Reservations, Native American, 113, 241
Resources, 71. See *also* Natural resources
capital, *c95*, 96
human, *c95*
in linking regions, 82–83
mineral, 76
nonrenewable, 171
renewable, 170
Revere, Paul, 27
Revolution, 25
Rhode Island, textile industry in, 138–139
Rice, 169, 236
Richardson, Bill, 238
Rio Grande, 229, 259
Rivers
mouth of, 161
source of, 161
tributaries of, 73
Road maps, 264
Rock and Roll Hall of Fame, 214, *p214–215*
Rock and roll music, 57, 182, *p183*
Rockefeller, John D., 48, 49, 90
Rock 'n roll, 57
Rocky Mountains, 15, *p70*, *p74*, 229, 252, *p252*, 257, *p258*, 258–259, 262, 263
Rodeo, 279, *p279*

Roosevelt, Franklin Delano, 54, *p54*
Roosevelt, Theodore, 229, *q229*, *p229*
Roosevelt, Theodore, National Park, 197
Route 66, 255, *p255*
Rule of law, 118

Sable, Jean Baptiste Pointe du, 210
Sacagawea, 34, *p34*, 35
Safety elevators, *p203*
St. Augustine, 178
St. Francis de Assisi Church, 220, *p220*
Saint Patrick's Day, 148
Sales taxes, 105
Sampson, Deborah, 28, *p28*
Savings accounts, *p96*
    link to automated teller machines (ATMs), 97
    reasons for opening, 97
Scarcity, 93
School desegregation, 157, *p157*
Sea breeze, 164, *p164*
Sea level, 77
Sears Tower, *p203*
Seattle, Washington, 278
Seattle World's Fair, 254, *p254*
Segregation, 180
Senate, 108, *p102*, 111
September 11, 2001, terrorist attacks, 60
Sequoia National Park, 254, *p254*
Sequoias, 254, *p254*
Sequoyah, 156, *p156*, 177, *p177*
Sequoyah Birthplace Museum (Vonore, Tennessee), 156, *p156*
Services
    in Midwest, 207
    in Northeast, 140–141, *p140–141*
    provision of, by local government, 104, *p104*
    in Southeast, *p174*, 175, *p175*
    in West, *p243*, 273
Sheperd, Alan B., 172
Sierra Nevada, 75
Silicon, 238
Silicon Valley, 270
Silver, discovery of, 267
Sit-ins, 181
Skiing, 255, *p255*
Skyscrapers, 47, *p203*

Slater, Samuel, 138
Slavery, 43, 44, 146, 180
Small-scale maps, 135
Smith, Jedediah, 252, *p252*
Smithsonian Institution, 66
Snake Dance, 246
Social Security, 54
Solar energy, 238
Sonoran Desert (Arizona), 230
Soul music, 183, 214
South Dakota, service industries in, 207
Southeast, 79, *p155*, 156–183, *p158–159*, *m158–159*
    African Americans in, 178
    agriculture in, *p168*, 169, *m169*
    animals in, 159, *p159*, *p160*, 161, *p161*, *p165*
    climate of, *d164*, 164–165
    coal mining in, *p82–83*, *p170*
    economy of, *p168*, *p169*, 169–173, *p170–171*, *p172*
    festivals in, *p156*, 181, *p181*
    French settlers in, 178–179, *p178–179*
    geography of, *p157*, *p158*, *p161*, 161–163, *p162–163*
    immigrants in, 178–179, *p178–179*
    industry in, 172, *p172*, 172–173
    islands in, 163, *p163*
    jobs in, *g173*
    landforms in, *p162*, 162–163
    music in, 182–183, *p182–183*
    Native Americans in, 156, *p156*, 177, *p177*, 178
    natural resources in, 170–171, *p170–171*
    people of, *p83*, *p176*, *p177*, 177–179, *p178*, *p179*
    plants in, *p158*, 161, *p161*
    protecting cities in, 166, *p166*
    rivers and wetlands in, 161, *p161*
    services in, *p174*, 175, *p175*
    technology in, *p172*, 173
    tourism and leisure in, *p155*, *p156–159*, *p174–175*, 175, 177, *p177*, *p178*
South Pole, 85, 262
Southwest, 12, 79, *p219*, 221–247, *p222–223*, *m222–223*
    agriculture in, *p234*, 236–237, *p236–237*
    animals in, 223, *p223*, *p224*,

225, *p225*
    building styles in, *p78*, 243, *p243*
    cattle in, 237, *p237*
    climate of, 222, 224, 230, *p231*, 244
    culture of, *p79*, *p220*, *p246*, 246–247, *p247*
    economy of, *p234*, 235–239, *p236–237*, *p238–239*
    festivals in, 220, *p220*, *p246*, 246–247, *p247*
    geography of, *p224*, *p225*, 225–231, *p226–227*, *p228–229*, *p230–231*
    immigrants in, 244
    industry in, 235, 238
    landforms in, 224, 225, 226–227, *p226–227*, 228–229, *p228–229*
    mines in, 235, *c235*
    Native Americans of, 12–13, *p12–13*, *p240*, 241, *p241*, 246, *p246*
    natural resources in, 235, *p235*
    people of, *p240*, 241–245
    plants in, *p224*, 225, *p225*, *p231*
    population growth in, *p244*, 244–245, *m245*, *g245*
    Spanish exploration and settlements in, 220, *p220*, 241, 242–243, *p242–243*
    technology in, 230, *p230*, *p234*, 238–239, *p238–239*
    tourism and leisure in, *p219*, *p220–223*, 226–227, *p226–227*, *p246*, 246–247, *p247*
    underground water in, 230–231
Sovereign, 113
Soviet Union, communism in, 57
Soybeans, 204
Space exploration, Armstrong, Neil, in, 3, *p3*
Space Needle, 254, *p254*, 278
Space research, 59, *p59*, 172, *p172*, 173, 239, *p239*
Spain, American Revolution and, 30
Spanish
    exploration and settlement by, *p18*, 18–19, 178, 220, *p220*, 241, 242–243, *p242–243*, *p276*
    missions of, 18, *p243*
    Pueblo and, 13
Specialization, 88

Stamp Act, 25
    State governments, 101, *c101*, 102
    executive branch in, 102, *p102*
    judicial branch in, 102, *p102*
    legislative branch in, 102, *p102*
    sharing of power and, 101, *c101*
    taxes of, 105
Statt, Isaac, *q277*
Statute of Liberty, *p49*, *p114*, *p117*, 127
Steamboats, 36, *p36*, 158, *p158*
Steam engines, *p37*
Steel, 202–203
Stock market crash, 52
Storms, climate and, 91
Stowe, Harriet Beecher, 41, *p41*
Submarine Force Museum (Groton, Connecticut), 150
Suffrage, women's, 50, *p50–51*
Supreme Court, U.S., 111, *p111*
Sutter's Mill, 253, *p253*
Sweden, settlement of, 146

Taxes, 24, 105
Technology, 13
    education and, 173
    explosion in, 60, *p60*
    impact of, 47
    in Midwest, 207
    in Southeast, 172, *p172*, 173
    in Southwest, 230, *p230*, *p234*, 238–239, *p238–239*
    space, 59, *p59*, 172, *p172*, 173, 239, *p239*
    in West, 270, 271, *p271*
Tecumseh, 33, *p33*
Teepees, 12, *p12*
Telecommunications, 270
Telephones, 47
Temperature, 85
    average January, *g89*, *m89*
    effect of elevation on, 85
Terrorism, 60
Texas
    computer industry in, 238
    grasslands of, 230
    Houston, 239
    settlement of, 38–39
Texas Independence Day, 247
Textile industry, 172
    in Northeast, *p138*, 138–139, *p139–140*
    in Southeast, 172

Thanksgiving, 20, p20
Timberline, 262, p262
Time lines, reading, 6, p6-7
Tlingit dancers, p274
Tlingit people, 14, 15, p15
Toadstool Geologic Park, 197
Toledo, Ohio, manufacturing in, 206
Tornado Alley, 90
Tornadoes, 90, p91, 198, p198
Totem pole, p15
Tourism, 134, 273
Trade
  agricultural products in, 205, p205
  fur, 19, 210
  international, 272
Traditions, 213
Trail of Tears, 177
Travel
  airplanes in, 276
  automobiles in, 276
  canals in, 36, p36-37
  dogsleds in, p266
  railroads in, p37, p46, 46-47, p46-47, 276
  steamboats in, 36, p36, 158, p158
Treasury, U.S. Department of, 98
Tribal government, 113
Tributaries, 73
Truth, 118
Twain, Mark. See also Clemens, Samuel, 195, p195

U

Uncle Tom's Cabin (Stowe), 41
Underground Railroad, 211, p211
United Nations, 112, p112
  Korean War and, 57
United Nations Children's Fund (UNICEF), 112
United States
  average January temperatures in, m89, g89
  elevation of, m77
  landforms of, m73
  regions of, m81
U.S. Capitol Building, 69, p69, p108
U.S. Grand Prix, 215
U.S. Mint, 67, p67
U.S. Space and Rocket Center, Huntsville, AL, 3, p3
Upper Mississippi River Wildlife Refuge, p81
Uranium, 267

Urban, 142
Utah, 271

V

Valley Forge, 29, p29
Valley Forge National Historic Park, 29, p29
Vanderbilt, Cornelius, 48
Vietnam War (1965-1975), 59
Virginia, 20
Virginia (ship), 42, p42
Volcanoes, p260, 260-261
  in Hawaii, 75
Volcanologists, 253, p253
Volunteering, 116, 117, p117, 271
Voting rights, 67, p67, p109, 115
  for African Americans, 181
  for women, 50, p50-51
Voting Rights Act (1965), 181

W

Wagon trains, p38-39, 276
Walker, C. J., 66, p66
Walker Building, 66, p66
Wants, 93
Washington, George
  in French and Indian War, 23, p23
  at Valley Forge, 29, p29
Washington D.C., 110
  Lincoln Memorial in, 2
  U.S. Capitol Building in, 69, p69, p108
Washington, 268, p269
Water power, 133, p133
Water resources in Northeast, p132, 132-133, p133
Weather. See also Climate
  defined, 85
  extreme, 90-91
  patterns of, 89
West, p68, 68-69, m68-69, 74-75, p74-75, 254-255, m254-255, p254-255, 257-263
  agriculture in, p268, 268-269
  animals of, p256, 257, p257, 259, p259
  climate in, p256, 262-263
  earthquakes in, 260, p260
  economy of, p267, 267-273, m268-269, p270, p271, p272
  festivals in, 278-279, p278-279
  geography in, c71, p256, 257-261
  growth of, 277, p277

immigrants in, p276, 276-277
industries in, p266, p267, 268-269, 270, p270
landforms in, 71, 74-75, 257, 258-259, p258-259
mountains in, 258, p258
Native Americans in, 14-15, p14-15, p274, 275, p275
natural resources in, 71, 267-268, m268-269, 270
people of, p274, 275-277
plants of, p256, 257, p257, p263
rivers and lakes in, 258-259, p258-259
service jobs in, 273, p273
settlement of, 276, p276
technology and, 270, 271, p271
tourism and leisure in, p251, p252-255, p260, 260-261, p266, 273, p273, 278-279, p278-279
volcanoes in, p260, 260-261
West Virginia, mountains of, 72
Wetlands in Southeast, 161, p161
Wheat, 204, 236 farming of, in Kansas, 205, p205
White House, p110
Wilder, Laura Ingalls, 188, p188, 214
Wilder's log cabin, 188, p188
Wind Cave National Park, 196, 197, p197
Wind energy, p60-61, 201
Wisconsin
  farming in, 204
  immigrants in, 211
Women
  in American Revolution, 28, p28
  voting rights for, 50, p50-51
  in World War II, 55, p55
Workers, labor unions for, 49
Works Progress Administration (WPA), 53, p53
World War I, 50, p50
  women in, 50
World War II
  African Americans in, 58
  Allies in, 55, 57
  Axis in, 55
  Japanese attack on Pearl Harbor, 54-55, p55
  women in, 55, p55

Y

Yellowstone National Park, 261
Yo Yo Ma, 151

Z

Ziolkowski, Korczak, 214, p214
Zuni people, 241
Zydeco, 182

Index

Chico